Jerusalem Bound

Jerusalem Bound

How to Be a Pilgrim in the Holy Land

Rodney Aist

CASCADE *Books* · Eugene, Oregon

JERUSALEM BOUND
How to be a Pilgrim in the Holy Land

Cascade Books
An Imprint of Wipf and Stock Publishers
199 W. 8th Ave., Suite 3
Eugene, OR 97401

www.wipfandstock.com

PAPERBACK ISBN: 978-1-7252-5526-5
HARDCOVER ISBN: 978-1-7252-5527-2
EBOOK ISBN: 978-1-7252-5528-9

Cataloguing-in-Publication data:

Names: Aist, Rodney, author.

Title: Jerusalem bound : how to be a pilgrim in the Holy Land / by Rodney Aist.

Description: Eugene, OR: Cascade Books, 2020 | Includes bibliographical refer-
ences.

Identifiers: ISBN 978-1-7252-5526-5 (paperback) | ISBN 978-1-7252-5527-2
(hardcover) | ISBN 978-1-7252-5528-9 (ebook)

Subjects: LCSH: Christian pilgrims and pilgrimages—Israel—Guidebooks |
Christian shrines—Israel | Israel—Description and travel | Christian pilgrims
and pilgrimage | Sacred space

Classification: DS107.4 A47 2020 (print) | DS107.4 (ebook)

Manufactured in the U.S.A.   08/27/20

To Janet

Contents

Preface

Integrating historical sources, on-the-ground experience, and the voices of global pilgrims, *Jerusalem Bound* resources Holy Land travel through the lens of Christian pilgrimage. The book's genesis lies in an opening lecture on Holy Land pilgrimage that I gave at St George's College, Jerusalem for short-term courses on the footsteps of Jesus. Though merely scratching the surface, the lecture discussed the history of Holy Land pilgrimage, questions of pilgrim identity, and some tenets of pilgrim spirituality. While the course itself focused upon the landscapes and narratives of the Bible, participants generally felt that a pilgrim identity turned Holy Land travel into a transformational experience. It is not unusual to hear pilgrim-talk in the Holy Land. For the most part, however, the language is superficial, and applications are tentative. *How* to be a pilgrim in the Holy Land—its history, motives, identities, traditions, practices, and challenges—has been largely ignored.

Though programs vary, the Holy Land is the unrivalled destination of Christian travel. The region is indispensable to biblical studies. The Living Stones, the Palestinian church, and the Israeli-Palestinian conflict cast attention to contemporary issues. Jerusalem offers a unique setting for interfaith dialogue, and as the gathering place for global Christianity, it is the undisputed center of historical Christianity, offering rich possibilities for ecumenical engagement. By contrast, the image of pilgrimage as the pious, personal pursuit of the holy places can be seen as the more popular but less laudable form of Holy Land travel: a weaker cousin to more commendable endeavors.

There are better ways than others to visit the Holy Land. However, when its breadth, depth, and applications are properly understood, the lens of pilgrimage not only transforms traditional expressions of Holy Land pilgrimage, it strengthens other forms of Jerusalem travel as well. Pilgrimage relates to the way we see, discern, and shape the world. It is an exercise in transformation. When the investigation of Scripture seeks contemporary application, we have moved into the realm of pilgrimage. While pilgrimage is personal, first-hand experience, it is not a self-centered endeavor. Pilgrimage takes us beyond ourselves. It crosses boundaries and borders and traverses unknown landscapes. Pilgrimage is rooted in the image of the stranger, and pilgrims engage the Other. Pilgrimage provides a template for compassion ministry, social justice, mediation, and reconciliation.

Pilgrimage is broad, pliant, and applicable. It provides language, themes, and resources for a holistic approach to the Christian life. The modern resurgence of pilgrimage—as good as it is—has largely focused upon certain expressions, and, overall, our notion of pilgrimage still appeals to the individual, spiritual journey. We need to stretch the tent pegs. Pilgrimage is not merely an experience that takes us on an inner journey—it is the inner reflection upon experience that takes us beyond ourselves. The object of pilgrimage is the union of God, self, and the Other. Its character is autobiographical and corporate, incarnational and metaphorical.

The Holy Land provides a unique, layered landscape for the application of pilgrim spirituality. Before jumping into the Holy Land material, however, *Jerusalem Bound* presents, in summary form, an original methodology for pilgrimage, or a pilgrim-themed spirituality, addressing questions of definition, identity, and biblical expression. To frame the Holy Land experience—and to move pilgrimage forward as a whole—we need a definitional methodology. A good methodology turns theory into praxis, and pilgrimage, above all, is practical theology. The formulation of my model has benefitted from conversations with Michael McGhee and Bingham Powell.

Having framed the subject, the heart of the book is the Holy Land material, which integrates historical sources with the contemporary Holy Land experience. Unique among Holy Land resources, *Jerusalem Bound* addresses subjects that are seldom addressed or sufficiently detailed on a Holy Land journey: the motives of Holy Land pilgrimage, the history of the Christian Holy Land, understanding the holy sites, pilgrim practices, material objects, and the challenges of Holy Land travel. How should one prepare? What happens in the aftermath?

Life experience is highly transferable, and journeys outside of Jerusalem have shaped the book. Voices, insights, and perspectives from an around-the-world pilgrimage and experiences on the Camino de Santiago apply to Holy Land travel. My experience in camping and retreat ministry, particularly as the director of a one-week family camp, has informed my work with pilgrim groups. I am grateful to Bill Jones for allowing me to serve twenty-five summers at Camp Lake Hubert in northern Minnesota. I went to the University of Wales to study Christian pilgrimage. My advisor, Thomas O'Loughlin, directed me towards Jerusalem. The book pays tribute to Tom.

My specific knowledge of the Christian holy sites and the dynamics of Holy Land pilgrimage stems from on-the-ground experience in Jerusalem, and I am especially grateful to two institutions. My PhD research on pre-Crusader pilgrim texts was supported by residential fellowships at the W. F. Albright Institute for Archaeological Research. As the course director at St. George's College, I led, taught, and guided short-term pilgrim courses. Holy Land pilgrimage is a non-stop conversation and listening to pilgrims debrief the sites and their impressions of the journey was a highlight of the job. Reading student journals as part of joint courses with Virginia Theological Seminary allowed me to observe consistent themes in people's experience of the holy sites, their quest for spiritual connections, and the challenge of group travel. While I have been influenced by countless, one-off conversations with friends, colleagues, and fellow travelers, I have benefitted from hearing certain people speak about the Holy Land on repeated occasions, including Graham Smith, Michael Billingsley, Mary June Nestler, Andrew Mayes, Rivkah Fishman, Mustafa Abu Sway, Bishop Hosam Naoum, Bishop Richard Cheetham, and Archbishop Suheil Dawani. To integrate the voices of others is to make them your own, which risks the possibilities of errors and distortions. While I am solely responsible for the views of the book, its pages are a tribute to an untold number of people who have influenced my journey.

Abbreviations

Biblical Texts

Gen	Genesis	Rom	Romans
Exod	Exodus	1 Cor	1 Corinthians
Deut	Deuteronomy	Eph	Ephesians
Josh	Joshua	Phil	Philippians
1 Sam	1 Samuel	Col	Colossians
1 Kgs	1 Kings	1 Thess	1 Thessalonians
2 Chr	2 Chronicles	1 Tim	1 Timothy
Ps	Psalms	Heb	Hebrews
Isa	Isaiah	1 Pet	1 Peter
Ezek	Ezekiel	Rev	Revelation
Matt	Matthew		

Bibliographical Citations

PPTS	*Palestine Pilgrims' Text Society*
NPNF	*Nicene and Post-Nicene Fathers*

1

Introduction

"Many visitors leave Palestine disappointed, but I am sure
the fault is not in Palestine.

The traveler has not known how to make the trip or
has been inwardly unfitted to make it."

—Henry Emerson Fosdick, *A Pilgrimage to Palestine*, 1927.[1]

Holy Land pilgrimage is a journey from the manger to the cross. Full
of movements, stations, and mini-journeys, it enables pilgrims to reenact the story of Jesus' life. From the empty tomb, the resurrection ripples
from Jerusalem to the ends of the world, and pilgrims return home replicating the gospel. The Holy Land experience is an investigation of scripture, an
encounter with Christ on native soil, a return to the roots of the Christian
faith. Holy Land travelers can either assume or ignore a pilgrim identity, but
what does it mean to be a pilgrim in the first place? What are the biblical
images, historical expressions, and contemporary experiences of pilgrimage, and how can they enhance the Holy Land journey? *Jerusalem Bound*
explores the motives, practices, and challenges of Holy Land pilgrimage.
Applying historical sources and present-day perspectives, *How to be a
Pilgrim in the Holy Land* offers practical ideas and spiritual insights from
pre-trip planning to post-trip reflections. Responding to Fosdick's lament
that travelers come and go without knowing how to make the trip, *Jerusalem
Bound* lays the ground for a successful journey.

---

1. Fosdick, *A Pilgrimage to Palestine*, 23.

A Unique Resource for Holy Land Travel

Encouraging participants to tackle the challenge for themselves, a rope course instructor refrains from telling climbers exactly what to do. It is up to the individual to test possibilities, to make decisions, and to execute the required maneuvers. Experience is more meaningful when it reflects our own decisions. *Jerusalem Bound* takes a similar approach. Avoiding checklists and step-by-step instructions, the book suggests possibilities without telling pilgrims where to put their feet. Setting the course for Jerusalem pilgrims, the book surveys past and present traditions, challenging Holy Land pilgrims to think beyond their theological baselines, to engage in creative practices, and to focus upon the Other as much as themselves. By recognizing the normative dynamics of the Holy Land experience, such as pilgrim fatigue, the book reassures travelers who wonder whether their journey has gone astray. By espousing a spirituality that emphasizes God's presence in the actuality of lived experience, the book encourages pilgrims to derive meaning in both the highs and lows of Holy Land travel.

Jerusalem Bound is unique among Holy Land resources. While traditional travel books and archaeological guides detail the sites, providing travel tips from opening hours to coffee shops, *Jerusalem Bound* equips Christian travelers with a reflective apparatus rooted in biblical, historical, and contemporary images of the pilgrim life. The book discusses a number of questions that are seldom, if ever, addressed. How should we think about the holy sites, and what language and concepts can we use to describe them? What are the common practices, past and present, of Holy Land pilgrims, and what is the role of religious souvenirs? What are the particular challenges of Jerusalem travel, and how should pilgrims respond? Attentive to the transformational nature of pilgrimage, *Jerusalem Bound* is ultimately interested in Christian formation and the aftermath of the Holy Land journey.

About the Author

The approach of *Jerusalem Bound* reflects my background as a Jerusalem scholar, pilgrim practitioner, and Protestant minister. As a young clergy, I went on a one-year, around-the-world pilgrimage, visiting Christian communities and historical sites in twenty countries, ending with a forty-day hermitage experience in the Ozark Mountains. I spoke about place and journey with Christians around the world and produced a memoir of my pilgrim travels.[2] I

---

2. See Aist, *Voices in the Wind* and *Journey of Faith*.

have walked over seven hundred miles of the Camino de Santiago, reflecting upon the pilgrim life and listening to the stories of fellow travelers.

Personal experience has led to scholarly pursuits. While obtaining a masters degree in Celtic Christianity, a subject rich in themes of place and journey, my scholarship has focused on Jerusalem pilgrimage before the Crusades.[3] I have been a research fellow at the W. F. Albright Institute for Archaeological Research in Jerusalem, which, in turn, led me to St. George's College, Jerusalem, where, as course director, I guided short-term pilgrim courses for laity and clergy from around the world. Along with an expertise in the holy sites, I have a specialty in short-term Christian community. I am familiar with the dynamics of group travel and strategies for enhancing the pilgrim experience. I know, firsthand, that Jerusalem pilgrimage is ultimately an exercise in Christian formation—that empirical knowledge of the biblical landscapes, an intimate understanding of scripture, and the embodied experience of religious travel transform the Jerusalem pilgrim in life-changing ways.

Like anyone who has spent time in the region, I have friends and colleagues from various religious and ethnic backgrounds. Navigating Israel–Palestine is difficult, especially since the centrifugal forces of the conflict resist a common, middle ground. Even so, *Jerusalem Bound* seeks the radical center. Pilgrims are instruments of reconciliation, raising attention to injustices, praying for peace, and embodying Christ's vision of the kingdom of God. The words, actions, thoughts, and prayers of Christians should not divide people; instead, they should beckon people to the table. That does not mean that we lack positions: the book supports the local, Palestinian church and the end of the military occupation. Incorporating a wide range of voices, the views of *Jerusalem Bound* are based upon my on-the-ground experience and ultimately upon the perspectives of local Christians.

My interest in pilgrimage came about in a curious way. Upon finishing a three-year pastorate in northern Arkansas, I received a calling to go on pilgrimage. Having lived abroad thrice in my twenties and interested in furthering my global experience, I was granted "permission" to go on an around-the-world journey, which God qualified by saying "but it has to be a pilgrimage," a concept that seemed to come out of the blue—more likely, it was an echo from the past. While I had not had any recent exposure to pilgrimage, almost ten years earlier I had taken a college course entitled, "Medieval Images: Pilgrimage." I absolutely loved the class, but I

---

3. See Aist, *The Christian Topography* and *From Topography to Text*. On Celtic pilgrimage, see Aist, "Pilgrim Traditions."

interpreted my affinity as an interest in medieval history. Pilgrimage did not stick at the time; it struck a decade later.

In short, I came to pilgrimage as a calling grounded in personal experience while serving as a young Methodist minister in rural America. Pilgrimage has been fundamental to my life ever since. I have done so fully Protestant, unapologetically, and without threat to my Methodist identity. Protestant writings—even those that affirm the practice—often contain an underlying apologetic. Pilgrimage "has been enduringly contentious,"[4] but it has also been unduly eschewed. Generally uneasy with physical expressions of the pilgrim life, Protestants have embraced its metaphorical target: that pilgrimage is really about the inward, spiritual journey. There is no inner journey, however, apart from embodied existence, and casting pilgrimage merely as metaphor stifles its transformational impact. Pilgrimage is a spirituality of the senses, and God is present in the details of lived experience. Pilgrimage embraces the physicality of the earthly journey and the interplay between the spiritual and material world. Focused on Christ, the Word-made-flesh in time and place, pilgrimage is an incarnational celebration that has a natural affinity with the Protestant spirit.

The Protestant relationship to pilgrimage has often been driven by an anti-Catholic identity. Yet, Protestants owe it to themselves to rethink pilgrimage, especially in light of its biblical imagery and its significant, if largely untapped, potential for spiritual formation. In short, I approach pilgrimage as a normative, Protestant-friendly expression of the Christian faith. My work focuses upon its positive aspects, giving limited attention to traditional critiques while recognizing Catholic and Orthodox contributions to pilgrim spirituality.[5]

Pilgrim Readers

Jerusalem Bound invites Christian travelers into a conversation on pilgrimage and the Holy Land experience. Espousing an ecumenical vision of the pilgrim life, the book offers a pilgrim spirituality for Protestants but not a Protestant spirituality per se. *Jerusalem Bound* resources Christians of various backgrounds while challenging readers to encounter traditions other than

---

4. Wynn, *Faith and Place*, 138.

5. Pilgrimage critiques include the practice of indulgences, superstitious piety, the tendency of emotion to subvert rational judgment, the moral behavior of pilgrims, and the omnipresence of God. For a summary of common objections to pilgrimage, see Brown, *God and Enchantment*, 154–63 and Inge, *A Christian Theology*, 98–101. Also see Wynn, *Faith and Place*, 139.

their own. Although the discussion often assumes a Western perspective, the material speaks to Christians around the world.

The book's attention to group experience reflects the fact that organized programs—either as trips originating from home or as courses run through Holy Land institutions—are the dominant form of Jerusalem travel. The book likewise equips individuals, couples, and small groups who want their Holy Land experience to be a pilgrimage independent of an organized course.

Jerusalem Bound is a valuable resource for those giving pastoral care and spiritual guidance to pilgrims and for anyone working in the pilgrim industry, including guides, scholars, institutional staff, and tour operators. The material can be used for promoting a trip, recruiting participants, and helping would-be pilgrims discern a calling to "come and see" the Holy Land. Much of the book applies to Christian travel to other destinations.

Pilgrims should read *Jerusalem Bound* as part of their pre-trip preparations, familiarizing themselves with the concepts, themes, and images of the pilgrim life. Throughout the journey itself, Holy Land travelers can use the book to review knowledge-based information, consult concepts for spiritual reflection, and integrate practical ideas. The actual themes of the trip will emerge along the way, and what actually happens will determine which concepts best apply.

Holy Land Programs

While *Jerusalem Bound* is geared for traditional programs on the holy sites, pilgrimage is always contextual. Local context, living communities, and engaging the Other are pilgrim values. Christian pilgrims are encouraged to dedicate at least 20 percent of their time to interacting with the Living Stones, or the local residents of the Holy Land, with attention given to the Palestinian church and the Palestinian–Israeli conflict. Programs should include both Jewish and Muslim voices, while engaging traditions of the Orthodox church.

The book's themes are not meant to replace, diminish, or compete against the biblical, historical/archeological, and contemporary emphases of Holy Land programs. Rather, pilgrimage powerfully frames these subjects and fills in the gaps. Merging biblical story with personal narrative brings us directly into the realm of pilgrimage. Engaging the Other is pilgrimage by any other name. The pilgrim material supports biblical approaches, ecumenical encounters, and initiatives of peace and reconciliation.

Summary of Contents

Jerusalem Bound is implicitly divided into three parts. Chapters 2–4 focus upon the image of pilgrimage. Chapter 2 offers a fresh, definitional approach to pilgrimage. Chapter 3 explores biblical expressions of pilgrimage. Looking at the pilgrim–tourist dichotomy, chapter 4 addresses the question of pilgrim identity.

Chapters 5–10 focus on the Holy Land itself. Chapter 5 discusses the reasons, past and present, why Christians travel to Jerusalem. Chapter 6 surveys the history of the Christian Holy Land from the New Testament to the present day. Addressing a number of seldom-addressed questions, chapter 7 offers an original discussion on the holy sites. How do they function? How should we think about them, and what terms and concepts can we use to describe them? What tendencies should we be aware of? Are there alternative sites? Do places ever move? While exploring the concepts of commemoration, religious imagination, and commemorative credibility, the chapter presents the Holy Land as a unified, though expansive, landscape. Chapter 8 discusses pilgrim practices, or the ways in which pilgrims reenact biblical stories and engage the physical settings of the holy sites. The chapter looks at the Holy Land as an open-eyed encounter and explores concepts of pilgrim spirituality that pertain to observation, perception, discernment, and memory. Chapter 9 explores the blessings of pilgrimage, or the material takeaways of religious travel. Material objects—mementos and souvenirs—are physical reminders of spiritual experience, and Christians of all backgrounds desire a tangible connection to the Holy Land. Chapter 10 looks at the challenges of Holy Land travel, its risks, temptations, noise, and fatigue. Pilgrims respond by practicing perseverance, navigating emotions, managing expectations, and focusing on others.

The book concludes with the before and after of Holy Land travel. Chapter 11 discusses pre-trip preparations, including spiritual and educational resources. Taking the reader from home to the Holy Land, the chapter offers perspectives on departure, the outbound journey, and Holy Land arrival. Chapter 12 looks at the aftermath of Holy Land pilgrimage: one's final hours in the Holy Land, the homebound journey, and the celebration of return. The lessons of Emmaus remind us that the pilgrim's ultimate destination is not Jerusalem but the sacred landscapes of home, where, on familiar ground, one discerns God's call to Christian service. What happens in Jerusalem can't stay in Jerusalem, and the object of Holy Land travel is to translate the gospel back home.

Terminology

While the book covers a number of concepts (see appendix 1), a few terms should be explained from the start. Pilgrimage, pilgrim spirituality, pilgrim theology, and the pilgrim life, along with the Christian life and the Christian journey, are used interchangeably. Pilgrim instead of pilgrimage is commonly used to modify phrases, such as pilgrim spirituality (instead of pilgrimage spirituality). The Other, which denotes other people, particularly strangers and foreigners, God as mystery, and, more generally, the unknown, is capitalized. While the concept of a Christian Holy Land emerged during the Byzantine period, the term is used throughout the book, despite the occasional anachronism.[6] Unless the context is specified, Jerusalem and the Holy Land are used as synonymous terms, e.g., Jerusalem/Holy Land travel and Jerusalem/Holy Land pilgrimage. The Holy Sepulchre denotes the entire complex of buildings that covers the traditional sites of Jesus' death and resurrection. It is never used as a specific reference to the tomb of Christ. Calvary and Golgotha are used interchangeably for the place of Jesus' crucifixion. The spelling, Sion, which reflects the historical usage of the pilgrim sources, will be used throughout the book, except for biblical quotations, e.g., Mount Sion, Holy Sion (a church on Mount Sion), and Sion Gate. Biblical quotations are from the New Revised Standard Version.

---

6. On the historical development of the Christian Holy Land, see Wilken, *The Land Called Holy.*

2

Defining Pilgrimage

Jerusalem Bound enhances Holy Land travel through a broad approach to the pilgrim life. Equipped with an understanding of pilgrimage, Holy Land travelers can engage the experience in richer, life-changing ways. The book goes a step further. By viewing Holy Land pilgrimage as an exercise in spiritual formation, the book grounds the Christian traveler in a pilgrim-themed spirituality that speaks to the everyday journey back home. To set this in motion, we begin with a working definition of pilgrimage.

Defining Pilgrimage

Pilgrimage conjures up word pictures inspired by art, hymns, and literature, influenced by biblical, medieval, and contemporary practice, and informed by personal experience. Pilgrimage involves journeys, destinations, departures, and arrivals; it evokes images of temples, relics, and sacred tombs, Jerusalem, Rome, and the Celtic fringe. Pilgrims are long-distance travelers and restless wanderers, strangers and sojourners, migrants and second-place people. Pilgrims attend feasts and festivals and flee religious persecution. They are pious, patient, and penitent, gullible and godly, saints and sinners.

Pilgrimage is a crowded tent, and while we may instinctively know what it is, when we move from image to definition, it becomes more difficult to put our finger on it. What does Abraham's call to leave his homeland have in common with the magi's journey to Bethlehem? Do Dante and *Pilgrim's Progress* describe the same phenomenon? What are the parallels between the Camino de Santiago and the earthly journey? Is a pilgrim a religious traveler or simply a stranger? Pilgrimage is both physical and metaphorical; it is an individual journey and a corporate experience. It includes round trips, one-way journeys, and never leaving home. Time and memory are as important as place and journey. How can pilgrimage be captured in a simple definition?

My personal experience testifies to the multifaceted nature of pilgrimage; there are many kinds of pilgrims. On my around-the-world journey, Sister Giovanna, a pilgrim nun who walked the streets of Italy helping those in need, told me: "by being a pilgrim, my heart learns to hear the cries of those who have no choice but to be pilgrims." Pilgrimage embraces compassion ministry and social justice; it speaks to multicultural interactions, international partnerships, and relationships between dominant and non-dominant cultures.

Linguists point out the problem of deriving definitions from etymologies. Terms develop over time, and we are interested in what pilgrimage means today. Etymologies are still useful, though, offering insights that inform present-day applications. The English word, pilgrim, is ultimately derived from the Latin, *peregrinus*, meaning foreigner or traveler. The ideas are related insomuch as a foreigner has left home and has traveled elsewhere. Abraham is regarded as the first biblical pilgrim primarily due to his foreign status (Gen 12:1; Gen 23; Heb 11:8–19), and few themes have more application to a contemporary understanding of pilgrimage than engaging the Other.

One way to secure a definition is to look for a common denominator. Pilgrimage, however, conspicuously lacks one, a point that is not commonly recognized. Being a stranger in a strange land is different from a journey to a holy site; physical travel is not the same as spiritual metaphor. Journey is not always a defining feature: there are time-based expressions of the pilgrim life. To conceptualize pilgrimage, we turn to the family resemblance theory made popular by Ludwig Wittgenstein, which argues that "things which could be thought to be connected by one essential common feature may in fact be connected by a series of overlapping similarities, where no single feature is common to all of the things."[1] Pilgrimage is not a single entity but a category of religious expressions. No one concept or feature defines it. Certain themes, such as journey, stranger, and place, are generally present, but they may be absent or inconspicuous in a given expression.

In sum, we are looking for a definition that captures the breath of pilgrimage while retaining a sense of familiarity, one that considers biblical

---

1. The quote is a standard description of Wittgenstein's theory. See, for instance, Sussman, *Substance and Behavioral Addictions*, 29, 317. Wittgenstein himself indicates, "we see a complicated network of similarities overlapping and criss-crossing." Wittgenstein, *Philosophical Investigations*, paragraph 66. Also see paragraphs 65–67. The idea of applying the family resemblance theory to pilgrimage comes from Michael McGhee, personal communication.

and historical expressions yet reflects contemporary practice. The definition will suggest a series of overlapping themes rather than a single subject.
To facilitate Christian formation, the definition must be robust enough to
examine the religious life, providing a framework for spiritual reflection
and personal application:

> Pilgrimage is the experience of God, self, and the Other through
> the dimensions of time, place, journey, and people and the
> thoughts, images, and reflections thereof.

The definition is based upon biblical and historical sources, contemporary practice, personal experience, and reasoned interpretation. It is familiar
enough to meet expectations, broad enough to be inclusive, distinct enough
to give clarity, conventional enough to engage tradition, and permissive
enough to encourage innovation. The definition provides a framework for
lived experience, spiritual reflection, and Christian formation.

Our working definition is but one element of a methodological approach to Christian pilgrimage, or a pilgrim-themed spirituality. The chapter will qualify the statement; it will also develop it, defining the character of
pilgrimage as incarnational, metaphorical, autobiographical, and corporate.
We will also break pilgrimage down into its component parts, which include
themes, templates, elements, images, virtues and values, lived experience,
and adages and aphorisms.

The above definition is not the only one in play. Our approach in-
corporates alternative definitions, such as those that differentiate between
pilgrims and tourists and pilgrimage as time set aside for a particular purpose. It is important to understand how the definitions differ. Dictionary
definitions generally describe pilgrimage as a journey to a sacred place or
any long journey with a quest or purpose. They are seldom comprehensive
statements; rather, they describe specific expressions, or templates, which is
part of our critique. As opposed to textbook terms, pilgrim praxis utilizes a
host of aphoristic definitions, often couched as "pilgrimage is" statements,
which, though ultimately incomplete, are particularly useful. Pilgrimage is
an intentional journey. Pilgrimage is life intensified. Pilgrimage confronts
life's most important questions. Aphoristic definitions, or the adages and
axioms of the pilgrim life (see below), encapsulate the spirit of the religious
journey. As subjective definitions that people claim as their own, they help
determine when one is "on pilgrimage" and function as invaluable tools for
guiding, probing, and exploring lived experience.

Richard R. Niebuhr describes pilgrims as "persons in motion passing
through territories not their own, seeking something we might call completion, or perhaps the word clarity will do as well, a goal to which only the

spirit's compass points the way."[2] It is an evocative definition, incorporating images of journey, stranger, and arrival, but it is merely a snapshot of the pilgrim life. We need something more comprehensive, something that addresses pilgrimage as a whole, something that holds on to individual experience while developing social applications. We need to resource the pilgrim life with a richer breadth of images, to understand pilgrimage in a broader context, in more creative ways. A comprehensive methodology fuels the transformative potential of pilgrim experience.

In the meantime, all definitions remain in play. They are likewise open to critique, including my own, which some may consider to be too broad. Definitional tensions will always be a part of pilgrimage. To begin with, pilgrimage refers to specific life experiences as well as to life as a whole. How do we differentiate in meaningful ways between particular, circumscribed expressions and lived experience more generally, especially since any experience—at home or in the Holy Land—can be considered pilgrim material? Secondly, pilgrim definitions include both objective and subjective statements, and we need to maintain both types. A primary function of a comprehensive definition, such as the one presented here, is its ability to recognize the potentials and possibilities—the depth and breadth—of pilgrim expressions, which, in turn, fuel, inspire, and enhance the engagement of lived experience, or the discernment of when one is "on pilgrimage". In other words, a broad approach resources subjective definitions, like pilgrimage as an intentional journey.

The Object of the Pilgrim Life

The pilgrim's quest is the search for God in whom "we live and move and have our being" (Acts 17:28) yet whose thoughts and ways are not our own (Isa 55:8). God is our journey and destination, our guide and companion, our essence and agency. Pilgrimage, more generally, is about life itself. Life experience, particularly travel, teaches us about ourselves, and self-identity is shaped by moving beyond our familiarities. When we do so, we discover our passions and dependencies, our strengths and limitations, our dreams and anxieties. Pilgrimage is often perceived as an exercise in self-actualization, personal fulfillment, and the inward spiritual journey. However, God inhabits the Other, and social relations are at the heart of the pilgrim life. Pilgrimage is a comprehensive spirituality with social and ethical dimensions, and the union of God, self, and Other is the quintessential object of the pilgrim life.

2. Niebuhr, "Pilgrims and Pioneers," 7.

Qualifying the Sacred

It is worth noting that the sacred is not a definitional qualifier: our experiences of God, self, and the Other are not limited to the holy. Pilgrimage traverses the profane as well as the sacred, marking the good, the bad, and the ugly. Reaching beyond the sacred does not weaken or de-spiritualize pilgrimage; rather, it expands the spiritual landscape, allowing us to explore lived experience with a more thorough regard for the human condition. The pilgrim life is more richly layered when sacred places are understood as only one way of encountering God spatially. God is found in all types of places, high and low, far and near. The same holds true for time: pilgrims perceive God through periods of perseverance, in the ordinary moments of everyday life, and in the singularity of sacred occasions. Pilgrim theology does not seek to make all things sacred but to discover God in the undulations of the earthly journey.

The Dimensions of Pilgrimage

Cursory reflections on the fourfold dimensions of time, place, journey, and people reveal the rich and varied contexts in which pilgrimage is pursued.

Time

Time is linear and circular, sacred and ordinary. Pilgrimage embraces the past, present, and future, often simultaneously. Pilgrims acknowledge God's past actions, live faithfully in the present moment, and anticipate God's future promises. Pilgrimage is an exercise in personal and collective memory, and virtues—like hope, patience, and perseverance—have temporal qualities. Circular time is recurring: pilgrims feast and fast; they celebrate the seasons. A sojourn is a stational pause within a journey, while pilgrimage is the bracketing of time for a particular purpose.

Place

Place speaks to physical, spiritual, and emotional location. One can be in place or out of place, lost or found, at home or displaced, here or elsewhere. A place may be a paradise or a wilderness, a sanctuary, refuge, or hiding place. A space may be special or commonplace; spaces change and stay the same.

Journey

Journeys are marked by departures and arrivals. To depart denotes the beginning of something and the end of something else. Arrivals likewise involve beginnings and endings. A process is finished; a goal is completed; an experience is over. Then something else begins. Graduation is a commencement, the start of something new. The journey itself consists of movements and transitions, opportunities and dead ends, progress and change. Pathways have straights and intersections; they diverge, turn, and merge. Journeys have detours and delays, breaks and pauses. We wander, get lost, and persevere. Things come and go. Journeys fail; we lose things along the way. There are one-way trips and return journeys. We travel forward into the unknown. We come full circle, returning to the point of departure.

People

Pilgrimage is a call to companionship. Disconnected from others, the individual pilgrim is a diminished figure. The pilgrim life is a shared experience, involving guides, hosts, and fellow travelers. Pilgrims are dependent upon strangers. They receive succor, encouragement, and inspiration from others. Hospitality and generosity, gratitude and thanksgiving, compassion and clemency are the currencies of exchange. Pilgrims hear the cries of those who have no choice but to be pilgrims: refugees, migrants, and asylum seekers, the homeless, the weak, and the weary. Pilgrimage is occasionally a pathway to a sacred place but is always the streets of everyday life where we attend to those in need.

The Character of Pilgrimage

Pilgrimage is incarnational, metaphorical, autobiographical, and corporate. It is a comprehensive expression of the Christian faith.

Pilgrimage is Incarnational

Christian pilgrimage is patterned upon the incarnation. God blessed creation and inhabited human flesh in time and place. God was embodied; Word became flesh; the immaterial took material form. Christ assumed human attributes and was subject to mortal suffering. Salvation played out upon a landscape of blood, sweat, and tears. Christ was made impotent upon a tree before rising from the dead.

Pilgrimage is an embodied spirituality, engaging the senses and embracing the physicality of religious experience. It is a sensuous theology full of sights, sounds, and smells. Christ taught spiritual truths using material examples as simple as seeds and salt and set aside common, ordinary objects, such as bread and wine, for spiritual consumption. The incarnation is a divine declaration that matter matters. We experience God through the everyday events of our earthly lives, and pilgrimage is the reckoning of the facts in which we find ourselves. God is present in the actualities of life, experienced through actual events, real people, and specific locations.

Tracing the footsteps of Jesus, the Holy Land experience is an incarnational journey. According to Ernest Renan (d. 1892), the land reveals Jesus as a living figure.[3] It does so as a sensuous encounter. Cyril of Jerusalem told his fourth-century catechumens that "others merely hear, we see and touch," while Paulinus of Nola (d. 431) noted that "no other sentiment draws people to Jerusalem than the desire to see and touch the places where Christ was physically present."[4] Contemporary travelers are captured by the sensuous nature of the Holy Land—its sights, sounds, tastes, and smells—while the incarnational emphasis on embodied spirituality prepares pilgrims to encounter God through the actualities of the journey: its surprises, insights, and revelations as well as its challenges, questions, and difficulties. As physical witnesses of the gospel story, Christian pilgrims commemorate the incarnation in time and place as they sojourn through the Holy Land.

Pilgrimage is Metaphorical

While pilgrimage thrives on a spirituality grounded in the physicality of everyday life, its incarnational emphasis is complemented by a metaphorical perspective. Metaphor, in many ways, has been poorly understood. Its core function is neither to explain difficult concepts in simpler terms nor to tell us what we already know. Rather, a metaphor is a tool of exploration that allows us to discover things that, otherwise, we would not be aware of.

A metaphor is "a figure of speech whereby we speak about one thing in terms which are seen to be suggestive of another."[5] It pretends that "this" is "that." It takes something we know (a source) to explore a less familiar target. That, of course, is how we learn: using the familiar to explore the unknown, finding similarities between dissimilar entities. Yet, herein lies

---

3. On Renan's idea that the land of the Gospels reveals the person of Jesus, see chapter 5, "The Fifth Gospel."

4. Cyril of Jerusalem, *Catechesis*, 13.22; Paulinus of Nola, *Letter*, 49.14.

5. Soskice, *Metaphor and Religious Language*, 15.

the essence of metaphorical understanding: the interaction between source and target creates a new perspective whose meaning cannot be conveyed in any other way. To change the source alters the insight; thus, a given metaphor is irreplaceable and irreducible. The metaphor of life (target) as journey (source) uses what we know about travel and movement to explore the mysteries of our earthly existence. We can use other images—e.g., life is a box of chocolates—but the concept of journey renders insights into the earthly life that we cannot otherwise obtain.

Whenever we describe abstract concepts, we instinctively resort to metaphor. Since transcendent realities, such as God, cannot be directly known, religious language requires indirection. God is a shepherd; Jesus is a vine. Using one thing to describe another, metaphor employs indirect and non-literal thinking. Jesus is not literally a vine; God is not literally a shepherd, but metaphorical imagery allow us to explore the nature of God in effective ways. The fallacy of literalist thinking is equating the source with the target.

When Protestants say that the inner journey is what really matters, they are instinctively appealing to the abstract targets of metaphor. We should be careful, though, not to put the physical and spiritual dimensions of the Christian life at odds. Our focus on incarnational theology places a premium on embodied experience and cautions against an overly spiritualized approach to pilgrimage. Metaphor is based on non-literal thinking, but it is not opposed to concrete, empirical realities. Abstract targets are funded by less abstract sources; metaphor uses one to explore the other. In order to probe the spiritual world, metaphor has a foot in both concrete and abstract thought, and it is overly simplistic to equate metaphorical theology with a spiritualized approach to the pilgrim life. If anything, our pursuit of metaphorically produced insights calls us to engage physical expressions of pilgrimage in greater depth and detail. The effectiveness of the life-as-journey metaphor is dependent upon our knowledge of actual, physical journeys. Despite appeals to the metaphorical journey, Christian pilgrimage—and Christian formation more generally—has yet to fully employ the utility of metaphorical exploration. Complementing an incarnational approach, metaphorical theology draws upon the interplay between physical realities (source) and spiritual insights (target).

Life-as-journey is just one of countless pilgrim-related metaphors. We use metaphorical language to speak about time and place. Our God-talk is a metaphorical discourse. We encounter the unknown, the stranger, and the Other with metaphorical thinking that seeks connections between the unknown and the familiar.

Metaphor is an unexamined aspect of the Holy Land experience. Pilgrims enjoy a firsthand, empirical encounter with the land as they investigate scripture, history, and archaeology. But metaphor is never far away. We engage foreign places by using what we know to examine what we don't. As soon as we explore the meaning of Jerusalem or make connections between the holy places, pilgrim travel, and our earthly lives, we are delving into metaphor, thinking of something in terms of something else. Holy Land travelers should engage metaphorical thinking as a tool of spiritual exploration, employing metaphorical language in their reflections of God and the pilgrim journey, including their descriptions of places, events, and emotions.

Pilgrimage Is Autobiographical

Pilgrimage is first-person experience, viewed through a first-person perspective. Pilgrimage emphasizes the context and narratives of our individual lives: each unique, distinct, and sacred. Our earthly existence is conditioned by age, gender, health, personality, family, culture, and ethnicity. We have our own thoughts and emotions, passions and preferences, gifts, skills, and talents. Our life stories differ is striking ways, shaped by events and circumstances, incidents and accidents, choices and decisions, obligations and responsibilities. We are on individual journeys of goals, adventures, and plateaus, repentance and return, healing and wholeness. Pilgrimage is personal narrative, and every Holy Land venture is a unique, irreplicable experience.

Pilgrimage is Corporate

While pilgrimage assumes a first-person perspective, it is not a self-centered journey. The pilgrim life is a shared experience that takes us beyond ourselves into the company of others. Pilgrims are called to journey as a sacred people: living well together, committed to a corporate experience of God. Pilgrimage is an exercise in collective memory and public commemoration, marked by monuments, rituals, and festivals. Using the holy sites to commemorate the life of Christ, Holy Land pilgrimage is a public act of Christian memory enacted through the context of a short-term Christian community.

A Comprehensive Expression of the Christian Faith

Pilgrimage is life intensified, a microcosm of life itself. Pilgrimage must move beyond narrow perceptions of personal spirituality to a holistic approach that values the Other. The pilgrim life speaks to all areas of Christian practice from prayer and worship to acts of mercy and compassion—from the sanctuary to the street. The Holy Land journey is a crash course in the comprehensive claims of the gospel story.

The Component Parts of Pilgrimage

Themes

Themes are unifying ideas, prominent motifs, and reoccurring subjects. Along with the quest for God, self, and the Other, pilgrimage coalesces around two primary sets of themes—(a) time, place, and journey and (b) the stranger, the foreign, and the unknown. The themes are not unrelated— insomuch as a stranger may be one who travels—yet they stand on their own. Pilgrimage contains secondary motifs as well: quest, discovery, and personal challenge; identity, narrative, and autobiography; commemoration, collective memory, and sacred topography; monuments and shrines; feasts and festivals; rituals and embodied prayer. While the Holy Land experience focuses upon biblical landscapes and narratives, history and archaeology, ecumenical and interfaith issues, and peace and reconciliation, every journey has its own personal and incidental themes.

Templates

Templates are the common types, or patterns, of pilgrim expression, which are formed by various criteria and degrees of specificity. Pilgrim templates are neither fixed nor finite but are logically and flexibly construed. A given pilgrim expression may be associated with more than one template, while distinct templates may share common features. There are round-trip templates and one-way journeys. A journey to a holy place is a particular pattern, while liturgical processions and prayer walks are another. Some templates focus on people rather than places—some on personal issues, others on the Other. There are local pilgrimages, global travels, secular adventures, and physical challenges. Short-term mission trips and pilgrimage as "the street" embrace evangelism, compassion ministry, and social justice as forms of the pilgrim life. The modern popularity of pilgrimage has focused upon a few specific templates, such as long-distance walking and alternative tourism, while other expressions have received less attention.

By appreciating the spectrum of pilgrim expressions, we can apply various templates and their corresponding themes to the Holy Land experience. The Abraham story reminds us that pilgrimage is about following God in a foreign land. People-focused templates turn our attention to the Living Stones. Pilgrimage as reconciliation positions us as peacemakers in a land of conflict. Long-distance walking models the virtue of perseverance for tired pilgrims. The template of the earthly life envisions New Jerusalem as our spiritual destination, creating a reflective juxtaposition with the present-day city.

Elements

Elements are the parts of pilgrimage that, on their own, do not comprise a complete expression of the pilgrim life, such as departure and arrival, home and holy places, prayer and journaling, baggage and souvenirs. Elements include almost anything associated with an act of pilgrimage: God, self, and the Other; time, place, and journey; logistical details, local context, and pilgrim companions.

Images

Images, like elements, refer to virtually any aspect of pilgrimage with one imposed distinction: images may be independent of actual expressions. A case in point are scriptural images, such as Jesus as the alpha and the omega, that relate to time, place, and journey. Jesus is the way, the gate, and the good shepherd. He is the light of the world, the bread from heaven, and the water of life. Christological images offer pilgrims standalone content that can resource religious travel in significant ways.

Virtues and Values

Virtues are the principles that guide pilgrim behavior. They are the "what" that pilgrims always do. While pilgrims pursue the fruits of the Spirit (Gal 5:22–23; Col 3:12; 1 Tim 6:11), pilgrimage has particular associations with certain virtues, such as hope, patience, and perseverance; hospitality is its constant companion. Pilgrim theology claims the virtues of compassion, respect, self-awareness, and personal responsibility. Pilgrimage also espouses a number of secondary or relative values that are not operative in every situation. Pilgrims navigate between intentionality and spontaneity, austerity and extravagance, confidence and humility, boldness and caution, which underscores the importance of context, discernment, and decision-making in pilgrim spirituality.

Lived Experience

Lived experience is the currency of pilgrimage. It is the actual content of the journey, the events, emotions, and episodes that we interpret and reflect upon. Pilgrimage is embodied, first-person experience, or the actuality of lived experience in time and place.

Adages and Aphorisms

Pilgrims are constantly translating lived experience into short interpretative phrases that express the wisdom of religious travel. They are the quotable quotes and shareable sayings concerning life and faith that emerge throughout a pilgrimage, which we will collectively refer to as adages and aphorisms.[6] God is in the facts; life is a journey of losing things along the way; the journey is never over. Forged from experience or borrowed from others, they are concentrated verbal tools for perceiving, exploring, and interpreting the pilgrim life. They are the lessons of the road, rules to live by, which help us size up situations and readjust our thoughts and behavior. They remind us of who we are, where we are, what to do, and where to go, charting the course we need to take and projecting the ideals we seek to obtain. They incite and inspire.

While conveying insight and wisdom, adages are not necessarily—or always—true. They are assertive statements that are perspectival in function, emphasizing points of view that may not pertain to every situation. "The journey is more important than the destination" offers a valuable perspective; it is, at best, a half-truth. But that's the point: adages are not truth claims per se but verbal tools for probing reality and focusing our attention. The Holy Land pilgrim is alert to the quotable sayings, group mantras, and personal mottos that emerge throughout the experience,

---

6. The pilgrim life is full of short, quotable sayings that go by a number of names, including axioms, adages, aphorisms, bromides, dictums, epigrams, maxims, mottoes, parables, platitudes, precepts, proverbs, quips, quotations, slogans, truisms, and witticisms (the list is courtesy of Geary, *The World in a Phrase*, 8). While the terms may differ slightly—and a statement about God may function differently from one about life in general—we will refer to the concise sayings of pilgrim wisdom as adages and aphorisms.

noting how accumulated wisdom and short interpretive sayings frame the ongoing journey.

Moving Forward

The aim of the book is to enhance Holy Land travel through a comprehensive approach to the pilgrim life that offers pilgrims a spectrum of ideas and perspectives for exploring the Jerusalem experience. Holy Land pilgrimage is more than walking in the footsteps of Jesus, visiting the holy places, and following the traditions of ancient travelers. It is being a stranger in a strange land, following God in a foreign country, and receiving hospitality from others. It is an exercise in engaging the Other, listening to voices that are not our own, valuing ecumenical and interreligious relations, sharing in the hopes and struggles of the Living Stones, and promoting peace and reconciliation. Holy Land travel is an incarnational journey in time and place. It is about personal narrative, collective memory, and shared experience. The Jerusalem pilgrim embraces the mystery of life: walking into the unknown, receiving revelation as the journey unfolds, and celebrating the sanctity of the present moment.

Focusing on God, self, and the Other through time, place, journey, and people gives purpose, direction, and structure to the Holy Land experience. The Jerusalem-bound traveler uses the experience as an exercise in Christian formation, which forms the basis for a pilgrim-themed spirituality back home. With an eye towards the future, Holy Land pilgrims seek long-term transformation. They return from the Holy Land shaped by the lessons of the journey and with new understandings of scripture, the life of Christ, and the kingdom of God. Seeds take root upon return, resourcing a lifelong journey of faith. Whether at home or in the Holy Land, the object of the pilgrim life remains the same: the union of God, self, and the Other.

3

Biblical Expressions

T he following chapter resources Holy Land travelers through a survey of
biblical images that speak to our experience of God, self, and the Other
through time, place, journey, and people. Scripture departs from Eden,
traverses Calvary, and arrives in New Jerusalem. Exile and return are central themes of the Old Testament: Egypt to the promised land, Babylon to
Jerusalem. The New Testament also contains a collection of journeys: the arrival of the magi, the flight to Egypt, the prodigal son, the road to Emmaus.
Jesus' journey to Jerusalem provides the climax to the Synoptic Gospels,
while missionary journeys spread news of the risen Christ. Pilgrimage is
about place as much as journey, and the scriptures are set upon a religious
topography of centers, points, and edges, pathways and intersections,
boundaries and borders, profane and sacred locations. Biblical places, like
Golgotha, Mount Sion, and the Jordan River, assume spiritual meanings
that transcend their physical dimensions. The Bible contains perspectives
on time, hope, and memory, on compassion and hospitality, on the Other
and the earthly life. When its themes are collectively considered, pilgrimage
is one of the dominant images of the Bible.

How does the Bible resource the modern-day pilgrim? While the Bible
contains recognized expressions of the pilgrim life, pilgrimage is never
defined.[1] There is neither a Greek nor a Hebrew word that specifically or
consistently means pilgrimage, and the word "pilgrimage" only occasionally
appears in English translations of the Bible.[2] Instead of focusing upon specific terms, our interest is in biblical content that contains pilgrim themes.

---

1. Scholars likewise point out that neither the kingdom of God nor the church are
defined in the Bible. Biblical expressions require interpretation.

2. The word "pilgrimage" occurs three times in the King James Version (Gen 47:9;
Exod 6:4; Ps 119:54), twice in the New International Version (Gen 47:9; Ps 84:5), and
five times in the New Jerusalem Bible (Ps 84:5; Isa 30:29; Amos 8:14; Acts 8:27; 24:11). It
is not found in the New Revised Standard Version. The Old Testament references utilize

The Biblical Prototype

Christian pilgrimage is implicitly governed by a biblical prototype, or metatemplate, that envisions the Christian life as a journey to New Jerusalem. The prototype is an amalgamation of biblical images, stories, concepts, and teachings that depict our relationship with God as a movement from sin to salvation, or, in pilgrim language, from being lost to being found, from being out of place to spiritual arrival, from alienation to union with God. The spiritual life is one of change, transition, and progress; destination represents wholeness, completion, and fulfillment. The prototype presents the human condition as being lost, depicts a pathway to God full of assistance, choices, and challenges, and conveys destinational images of banqueting tables, the kingdom of God, and New Jerusalem. To repent is to change direction, to make a u-turn, to find the right path. Grace is the strength to act in the first place and includes times of being carried. The metatemplate is also informed by the Mosaic narrative: wilderness wandering, the Jordan River crossing, and arrival in the promised land. The prototype is not a concrete blueprint of the Christian life; rather, it governs as a composite ideal. While the prototype contains a number of indelible images, it has a kaleidoscopic quality that is open to interpretation, as evidenced by the spectrum of Christian traditions.

Even so, the prototype has a fundamental influence on our understanding of the Christian life. To begin with, it depicts the Christian faith as a journey to God—Paul describes it as a race. Secondly, Christian pilgrimage is not about *any* or *every* journey but those that appeal in some way to the prototype, which distinguishes *Christian* pilgrimage from non-Christian expressions. Third, the character of pilgrimage as incarnational, metaphorical, autobiographical, and corporate, and pilgrim virtues, such as patience and perseverance, are grounded in the prototype. Fourth, providing an unparalleled context for examining the pilgrim's relationship with God, Holy Land travel metaphorically patterns the New Jerusalem destination of the Christian prototype.

---

various Hebrew words. *Magurim*, the plural form of *magor*, which appears in Gen 47:9, Exod 6:4, and Ps 119:54, means sojourn. *Mesillah*, better translated as highway (see Isa 40:3), occurs in Ps 84:5. *Derek*, used in Amos 8:14, is the common word for road. *Hag*, which denotes a festival, is used in Isa 30:29. The examples underscore the diversity of pilgrim concepts: Acts 8:27 refers to Jerusalem worship, while Gen 47:9 concerns the earthly sojourn. Thanks to Andrew Davis for help with the Old Testament terms.

The Journey of the Magi

We begin our survey of the biblical material with a favorite Christmas story: the magi's journey to Bethlehem (Matt 2). The magi left their country, traveled a long distance, worshipped the Christ Child, and returned home. The story provides a narrative template for Holy Land pilgrims, who likewise leave home on a long-distance journey to see the places of Christ. Focusing on the key elements of the story, the narrative lends itself to a series of reflective questions.

> The Star: What are the signs and indications that you should go to the Holy Land? What is calling you, and how will you be guided along the way?

> Herod: What are possible obstacles, dangers, and fears? What could compromise your purpose, deceive you along the way, or threaten the well-being of others?

> The Dreams of the Magi: Similar to the role of the star, how will God communicate with you throughout the journey to direct your thoughts and actions? What will warn and guide you? What will be the source of revelation and insight?

> The Christ Child: What does it mean to search for the Christ Child in the Holy Land? How and where will you locate him, and what may surprise you when you do? How will you worship Christ on the journey?

> Gifts: What does it mean to bear gifts to the Holy Land? What gifts are you taking, and how will you use them? Are there good and not-so-good gifts to offer? What are the gifts and contributions of other foreign pilgrims?

> Home by Another Way: How will you return home differently? How will your Holy Land encounter change your life back home?

The magi's journey to Bethlehem offers a surprisingly robust narrative for ordering the Holy Land experience.

Remembering Abraham

Abrahamic applications have largely escaped the attention of Holy Land pilgrims. God called Abraham to go to the land that God would show him (Gen 12:1). Abraham obeyed, leaving his country, his kindred, and his father's house, and followed God to the land of Canaan, which was subsequently promised to Abraham's offspring (Gen 17:8). Throughout his years in Canaan, Abraham's faith was frequently tested, most poignantly in the divine command to sacrifice his son, Isaac, the heir of God's promise. Abraham is often regarded as the first biblical pilgrim, and the trials of the earthly life, a popular image of pilgrimage, is exemplified in the patriarch's story.

What makes Abraham the quintessential pilgrim, however, is his foreign identity. The Bible describes Abraham and his descendents as aliens (Gen 15:13; 17:8; 21:23). Upon the death of Sarah, Abraham told the Hittites at Hebron: "I am a stranger and an alien residing among you" (Gen 23:4), and Abraham's descendents would remain "resident aliens in a country belonging to others" (Acts 7:6). Abraham's foreign status is emphasized in Hebrews: "by faith Abraham obeyed when he was called to set out for a place that he was to receive as an inheritance; and he set out, not knowing where he was going. By faith he stayed for a time in the land he had been promised, as in a foreign land, living in tents" (Heb 11:8–9). To be a pilgrim in the mold of Abraham is to experience God in a foreign place.

To reiterate the point, personal trials, obeying God, and life as a journey of faith are important aspects of Abraham's legacy. So, too, is the virtue of hospitality. We lose key applications of the story, however, if we overlook the literal nature of Abraham's foreign status. Abrahamic pilgrimage is about being away from home, living in a place that is not our own, and following God as strangers in a foreign land.

Holy Land pilgrims identify with the Abraham story. Called beyond the familiarity of home, the Holy Land traveler experiences foreign cultures, currencies, and languages. They feel the disorientation, confusion, and anxiety of being aliens in a distant land and are dependent upon the hospitality of strangers. Holy Land pilgrims are called to follow God in a strange land, to overcome trials and challenges, and to live faithfully out of place. To be a Holy Land pilgrim is to walk in Abraham's footsteps.[3]

Entering the Promised Land

Commingling confusion and rebellion with God's guidance and protection, the Israelite wilderness experience was a journey from bondage and slavery to the brink of the promised land, which culminated in the crossing of the Jordan River. The river was a physical and symbolic boundary, a limen, or

---

3. While our focus here is upon his foreign status, as a regional figure common to Christians, Jews, and Muslims, Abraham is an important starting point for interreligious dialogue. See Levenson, *Inheriting Abraham*, which details how the patriarch is distinctively viewed by Judaism, Christianity, and Islam.

threshold, from the old to the new, from journey to arrival, from promise to attainment. Crossing the Jordan River was an act of transformation: to cross was to change. Life was different on the other side.

The narrative reminds us that we arrive in the Holy Land with a personal, social, and religious past, sometimes after years of wandering. God has been faithfully present, but we have wandered in circles. We arrive at the banks of the Jordan—or stand before the gates of Jerusalem—with mixed histories and personal baggage. To enter the Holy Land is to consider how we leave the wilderness behind in permanent, life-changing ways. What is the meaning of the promised land? How does Holy Land arrival represent a new beginning? How is the Jordan River a threshold of transformation? Where, on the journey, are the points of personal change? Engaging the metaphorical qualities of the Holy Land, Christian pilgrims are in step with the Israelite experience.

Erecting Memorials

The Old Testament records the practice of erecting monuments to remember important events. Abraham built an altar in Shechem after God pledged the land of Canaan to his offspring (Gen 12:6–7). Jacob set up a pillar at Bethel after dreaming about God's promise of descendents, land, and blessings (Gen 28:10–22), and the Israelites created a twelve-stone memorial in Gilgal after crossing the Jordan River so their children would remember the benevolence of God (Josh 4:19–22). Holy places are expressions of religious memory, markers of our spiritual past, which continue the centuries-old practice of the Gilgal stones. The Christian Holy Land works on the same principal: an original event, like an episode in the life of Christ, the erection of a church or a commemorative marker at or near the site, and subsequent visitation to remember the event. The Christian shrines continue the biblically sanctioned practice of marking places of spiritual importance.

The Jewish Pilgrim Festivals

Appearing before God at a place of God's choosing, the people of Israel were required to attend three annual festivals: the festival of Unleavened Bread (Passover), the festival of Weeks (Shavuot, or Pentecost), and the festival of Booths (Sukkot, or Tabernacles).[4] Offering a biblical parallel to Christian pilgrimage, the Jewish festivals include elements of divine calling, sacred time, place, and people, and the reenactment of sacred stories.

4. See Deut 16:16–17; Exod 23:14–17; 34:18–23.

Called by God

Although pilgrimage has never been a Christian mandate, God is constantly calling Christians to the Holy Land. Receiving a calling to go on pilgrimage comes with a number of obligations, including prayer and journaling, sharing the experience with others, and a renewed commitment to Christian service. What is often overlooked, however, is that a calling lowers the weight of undue expectations. Having received a calling to take a one-year, around-the-world journey, I was released from the pressures of a perfect trip. It was *God's* business and that made all the difference. Bolstered by a sense of calling, I was able to make purposeful decisions, was satisfied skipping certain attractions, and remained content when I was sick or tired. Times of sadness, loneliness, and disappointment were felt with meaning, and weather simply framed the experience. Whatever happened, God was in the facts; what actually occurred was infused with divine presence.

The same holds true for the Holy Land: being called to Jerusalem reduces the pressure of a perfect journey. That is comforting because aspects of the Holy Land can be unnerving. As with any trip, there are irritants and unpleasantries. Not everything goes as planned. When the Holy Land is approached as a once-in-a-lifetime event, there is an insidious pressure to relish the experience. But pilgrimage can be a rainy-day parade. By approaching one's appearance in the Holy Land as a divine summons, as an act of faith left in the hands of God, success is not measured by the enjoyment of the trip. When God calls you, it becomes God's business, and that makes all the difference. A calling equips us to confront the challenges of the journey and to perceive God's presence amidst frustrations and unexpected detours. Plans may go awry; parts of the trip may be difficult and disappointing. But that's okay. God is imbued in the actualities of life, rain or shine. Pilgrims hope for pleasant conditions and enjoyable experiences, but their primary calling is to journey faithfully, to live holy in the Holy Land, and to carefully attend to what God reveals along the way.

A Sacred People

Just as Jerusalem pilgrimage shaped Israelite identity as a sacred people formed by God, the Holy Land experience fosters a particular expression of corporate holiness: the short-term Christian community. To be a sacred people on pilgrimage is to engage the holy as a corporate experience. Pilgrims participate in a common life, sharing together in worship, meals, travel, site visits, and presentations. While the group experience is a meaningful part of the journey, short-term community has its own set of struggles. Common life requires a commitment to patience, respect, and mutual cooperation. The difficulty of living well together is accentuated by the challenges of the journey from exhaustion to the encounter of foreign cultures. The tardiness of others, the idiosyncratic behavior of fellow pilgrims, and the pursuit of personal interests are additional challenges of group travel. Short-term Christian communities live faithfully together through a covenantal arrangement that honors God, respects the individual, and fosters the group experience while recognizing personal needs and cultural differences. Seeking a balance between intentional community and facilitating community formation in natural, unforced ways, pilgrims live out their calling as a sacred people.

Holy Land pilgrimage raises the larger question of what it means to be a Christian in today's world. Jerusalem is unrivaled as a place of ecumenical and interreligious gathering, offering pilgrims a unique opportunity to explore issues of Christian identity: what are the defining beliefs and behaviors of the Christian faith, and how is Christian identity shaped by one's cultural context? Along with the global influx of Christian pilgrims, there are thirteen historical denominations in Jerusalem, primarily of eastern origins. The Holy Land is an encounter with Judaism, past and present, while, to many people's surprise, the region is a model of Muslim–Christian coexistence. Examining the question of Christian identity, Jerusalem pilgrimage explores our relationship with the religious Other.

Sacred Places

The Jewish festivals occurred at the place of God's choosing, a concept that likewise appears in the call of Abraham (Gen 12:1) and the binding of Isaac (Gen 22:2). A place is holy by virtue of the fact that we have been called by God to go there, summoned to see something that God will reveal, an act that is both intimate and mysterious. For Jerusalem pilgrims, the Holy Land is sacred for the same reason: it is a divinely determined destination, a place of contemporary revelation.

The Jerusalem temple was ultimately chosen as the festival venue and was considered holy for a number of reasons. The temple was recognized as the dwelling place of God, epitomized by Jesus' boyhood reference to "my father's house" (Luke 2:41–49). The image of the house of God evokes the question of divine presence, which is at the heart of pilgrim spirituality: where is God? Is God more present in some places than others? Is God somehow confined or, at least, located by human constructions of holy sites?

What is the meaning of a consecrated place? Emphasizing Christ's presence in the gathered community, the New Testament church largely transcended the idea of sacred places. The Holy Spirit is ubiquitous; God inhabits the world. A temple religion became a table religion, and Christ was recognized in the breaking of the bread (Luke 24:30–35). Yet, the idea of a holy site as a dwelling place of God still appeals to Christian experience, and "God is everywhere"/"there are holy places" is a theological tension that fuels the pilgrim quest. Pilgrims seek God's presence in special places, and personal experience is sometimes at odds with our own theology.[5]

The temple's holiness was enhanced by the idea that a significant event had previously occurred there, namely, the binding of Isaac (Gen 22:2). Following God's instructions, Abraham was about to sacrifice his son, Isaac, before the angel of God intervened, providing him with a sacrificial ram. Identified as Mount Moriah (2 Chr 3:1), the temple site had Abrahamic associations of sacrificial worship. Recalling the previous discussion on monuments, the idea of a sacred place as the setting of a past event is fundamental to the Christian Holy Land: places are holy because special events in the life of Jesus happened there. Moreover, given the divine nature of the incarnation, the holy sites have theophanic connotations: they are meeting points between heaven and earth. Like the temple, certain Christian sites are enhanced by primal narratives. Christians place the tomb of Adam and the binding of Isaac at Calvary. Jesus' baptism site draws upon the Israelite crossing of the Jordan River and the ministry of Elijah.

Beyond consideration of past events, Judaism views the temple site as a place that is inherently sacred—it was created holy. The temple was the navel of the world, the cosmic center that gave life to all creation, and Judaism envisions the created world as a set of concentric circles of decreasing holiness emanating outwards from the temple: the holy of holies, the temple precincts, the city of Jerusalem, the land of Israel, and the rest of the world. Christians have likewise viewed the places of Christ's passion in cosmological terms—as places created for a divine purpose—and have associated the Holy Sepulchre with the center of the world. Yet, the tradition is relatively minor: the Christian sites appeal to sacred history rather than divine cosmology.[6]

5. In light of the doctrine of God's omnipresence, can we claim the existence of differentiated spaces? While pilgrim theology holds the tension in place, pilgrimage becomes significantly less interesting if physical space is completely undifferentiated. See Wynn, *Faith and Place*, which explores the question.

6. Whereas Jewish tradition conceives the world as a series of concentric circles of decreasing holiness, Islam recognizes the elevated sanctity of three locations: the Great Mosque in Mecca, the Mosque of the Prophet in Medina, and the Al-Aqsa Mosque in Jerusalem. By comparison, Christianity has never promulgated a similar view of inherently distinct sacred space.

The concept of the center of the world introduces a spirituality of power and proximity. The existence of centers implies edges, the elsewhere, and everything in-between. The idea speaks to physical, social, and spiritual location and our accessibility to the holy; it likewise applies to the imbalance of power that characterizes our world. How do we define centers in spiritual, political, and economic terms? Are your religious, cultural, and racial identities defined by their proximity to recognized spheres of power or by distance and separation? Do you live near centers of influence, or are you on the outside looking in? The contemporary Holy Land is a complicated demographical landscape full of centers, borders, and boundaries, while the majority of global Christians lack the means to make a visit. The holy places give pause for reflection upon proximity, distance, access, and isolation. What does Holy Land pilgrimage tell us about power, resources, and authority?

In sum, the temple introduces several concepts of sacred place:

- A place is holy because one has been called by God to go there.
- A holy site is a dwelling place of God.
- A holy place is a venue of ritual worship.
- A sacred place is where something significant took place; it is a place of special memory.
- Some places are inherently sacred; they were created holy.

Pilgrims perceive the world as containing spiritual thresholds, tissue-thin landscapes, and meeting points between heaven and earth, and personal experience can turn any location into a holy place. While Holy Land pilgrimage is not reliant upon a particular idea of sacred space, religious travelers explore how spatial location influences their experience of God, self, and the Other.

Sacred Time

Just as scripture mandated the time and length of the Jewish festivals, Holy Land pilgrimage is a divinely appointed event. Pilgrims travel in God's time. While the Jewish festivals were seasonal, Christians travel to the Holy Land twelve months a year. The specific dates of group travel are determined by a number of factors that are generally out of the control of the individual pilgrim, but that is precisely the nature of sacred time: it chooses us. Regardless of when we go, to embark on a Holy Land journey is to enter sacred time, leaving ordinary time behind. Pilgrimage is time set aside for a particular purpose; it is a time-based endeavor.

Linked to the agricultural cycles, the Jewish festivals were times of thanksgiving for God's material blessings and providential care. Jerusalem pilgrimage continues to be a celebration of God's creation. Modern pilgrims are struck by the flowers, fruits, and fragrances of the land, from almond blossoms to pomegranates. What agricultural seasons, both home and in the Holy Land, correspond with your travels, and how will you mark thanksgiving in the land of the Holy One? What Christian seasons and holy days will occur while you are there? Will visiting certain holy sites have additional meaning due to the liturgical season? Will you or others in your group celebrate a special occasion or mourn a difficult anniversary? What events will occur back home while you are away?

Reenacting Sacred Stories

Commemorating the Hebrews' flight from Egypt, the Jewish Passover expresses a basic practice of Holy Land pilgrimage: the reenactment of sacred stories (Deut 16:3, 6; see Exod 12:1–28). The Christian holy sites are stations of biblical storytelling, and pilgrimage is the practice of remembering stories of faith. Pilgrims enter the sacred narratives by reading scriptures, observing the sites' natural features and religious imagery, and engaging in informal practices. As a journey of religious imagination, pilgrims assume the role of various biblical figures. One follows Mary to the house of Elizabeth to hear the Virgin pronounce the Magnificat. Pilgrims imaginatively don the guise of the shepherds and adorn the mantle of the magi in Bethlehem. Pilgrims are immersed in the Jordan River with Jesus, drink from Jacob's well, sail on the Sea of Galilee, and enter Jerusalem with palm fronds in hand. Pilgrims witness prayer, betrayal, and arrest in Gethsemane, overhear accusations and denials at the house of Caiaphas, follow Christ to Calvary, and enter an empty tomb. Holy Land pilgrims reenact the stories of Christian salvation.

The Psalms of Ascent

The Jewish festivals were replete with psalms and singing, such as the Psalms of Ascent (Pss 120–34), which refer to both the physical elevation of Jerusalem and the spiritual status of the temple. Galilean pilgrims generally approached Jerusalem by the steep ascent of the Jericho Road, while the vast majority of pilgrims entered the temple precincts by its stepped southern entrance, many coming up from the lowest point of the city, the pool of Siloam, a place of ritual purification. Pilgrims voiced these psalms as they drew near to the holy mountain: "who shall ascend the hill of the LORD? And who shall stand in his holy place?" (Ps 24:3).

> How lovely is your dwelling place, O LORD of hosts! My soul longs, indeed it faints for the courts of the LORD. . . . Happy are those who live in your house, ever singing your praise. Happy are those whose strength is in you, in whose heart are the highways to Zion. . . . For a day in your courts is better than a thousand elsewhere. I would rather be a doorkeeper in the house of my God than live in the tents of wickedness (Ps 84).

Christian pilgrims read the festival psalms in appropriate locations: on the bus as they ascend the Jericho highway towards the Holy City and, most poignantly, on the southern steps of the Temple Mount.

The Babylonian Exile

A central motif of Hebrew scripture, the Babylonian exile is the most formative event in early Judaism. An expression of coerced pilgrimage, the exile is a testament to remaining faithful in trying circumstances and highlights how one can be strengthened through difficult experiences. The exile speaks in profound ways to time, place, and journey, while its culminating theme, the Jerusalem homecoming, is about returning home as transformed people. Although Holy Land pilgrimage is a privileged experience, it is not without its challenges. Pilgrimage is about being faithful in all circumstances, allowing experience to strengthen us, being transformed yet remaining the same. While Jerusalem arrival may evoke a sense of homecoming—the Holy City has the tensional quality of being immediately familiar and forever foreign—the goal of Holy Land pilgrimage is to sojourn faithfully, returning home as transformed people.

Jesus as Pilgrim

The Imitation of Christ

Pilgrimage is the emulation others; above all, it is the imitation of Christ. To be a Holy Land pilgrim is to walk in the footsteps of Jesus: "for to this you have been called, because Christ also suffered for you, leaving you an example, so that you should follow in his steps" (1 Pet 2:21). Christians share the mind of Christ, who "did not regard equality with God as something to be exploited, but emptied himself, taking the form of a slave, being born in human likeness" (Phil 2:5–7). The Christian life is one of service and humility, and just as Christians imitate Christ in their everyday lives, the Jerusalem pilgrim lives holy in the Holy Land.

The Flight to Egypt

To imitate Christ is to remember that Jesus himself was a pilgrim. After the magi returned home, Herod unleashed his jealous fury, killing the infant males in the region. Warned in a dream, the Holy Family took flight to Egypt. Seeking safety through distance, they sought the succor of strangers. As a political refugee, the infant Jesus patterns the physical, emotional, and spirituality vulnerability of the pilgrim life. How might the flight to Egypt apply to today's Holy Land experience?

Jesus in the Wilderness

Jesus' wilderness experience embodies pilgrimage as time set aside for a special purpose. Jesus spent forty days in prayer and fasting discerning his identity, purpose, and calling: confronting temptation, persevering in faith. We find the same concept in the visitation. Mary spent the first three months of her pregnancy at the home of Elizabeth, her older cousin, who was likewise pregnant with John the Baptist. They presumably spent the time focused on self-care, shared experience, and interpersonal relations. While pilgrimage as bracketed time may—or may not—include an extended physical journey, a distinct location, and the suspension of one's regular day-to-day routine, Holy Land travel is commonly used as a time set aside for learning, prayer, discernment, and healing.

Jesus as Wayfaring Messiah

As an itinerant prophet with no place to lay his head, Jesus led a peripatetic life (Matt 8:19–22; Luke 9:58–62). Jesus did not have a home nor did he linger for long in any one place. The relentless urgency of Jesus' ministry is emphasized in Mark's Gospel, which contains the Greek word *eutheos*, meaning "immediately" or "straight away," over forty times. Jesus' ministry was marked by the imperative of the present moment and the immediacy of the kingdom of God. He told a potential disciple who wanted to bury his father to "let the dead bury their own dead; but as for you, go and proclaim the kingdom of God" (Luke 9:59–60). To another who wanted to say farewell to his family, Jesus replied, "no one who puts a hand to the plow and looks back is fit for the kingdom of God" (Luke 9:62).

Following Jesus meant leaving the past behind, traveling without bodily comforts, and never staying too long in the same place. He was a wayfaring messiah, constantly on the road, always on the go, at home in other people's houses. Pilgrims likewise live in the urgency of the present moment, proclaiming the good news of God, called to locations where people have no place to lay their heads. Jesus' disciples are travelers on the road, servants of the street, guests along the way.

Holy Land pilgrimage is a whirlwind of non-stop movement. Reflecting upon the wayfaring Messiah turns privileged travel into an exercise of Christian formation, focusing our attention on the movements of Jesus' ministry, the urgency of the present moment, and the image of the kingdom of God. Walking in the footsteps of Jesus is a peripatetic journey, which causes us to reconsider our attachments to the earthly life.

Jesus as Jerusalem Pilgrim

Jesus, above all, was a Jerusalem pilgrim, who followed Jewish practices and frequented the temple festivals. Forty days after his birth, Jesus was dedicated in the temple (Luke 2:23–24). As a twelve-year-old boy, Jesus attended Passover with his family (Luke 2:41–50), and the Gospel of John places him at the Jerusalem festivals throughout his ministry. Jesus was attending Passover when he overturned the tables of the money changers and discussed eternal life with Nicodemus (John 2:13–25; 3:1–21). The healing of the paralytic at the pool of Bethesda occurred during an unnamed festival (John 5:1–18). John 7–10 concerns conversations during the autumn festival of Sukkot, while John 10:22–39 records Jesus' presence at the festival of Dedication, or Hanukkah. All four Gospels set the final week of Jesus' life during the Passover festival: he was a daily visitor to the temple and shared the Passover meal with his disciples. Notwithstanding Jesus' critique of temple practice and his prediction of its impending destruction, Jerusalem pilgrimage was fundamental to Jesus' life and ministry, and his relationship to the temple escapes easy characterization. While reflecting upon his Jewish background, Holy Land travelers assume Jesus' identity as a Jerusalem pilgrim.

Pilgrimage as Mission

Having commissioned his disciples for a mission journey, Jesus sent them out to proclaim the good news of God, giving them authority over unclean spirits and power to cure disease and illness (Matt 10:1, 7–8). Pilgrimage is the proclamation of the kingdom of heaven. Pilgrims are missionaries—just as missionaries are pilgrims—actively engaged in Christian service, constantly witnessing to the love and power of God. What does it mean for pilgrims to practice the gift of healing, to possess authority over unclean spirits, and to proclaim the kingdom of God?

It important to understand that proselytizing, or the attempt to convert someone to another religion, is illegal in Israel, with significant implications for individuals, groups, and institutions that engage in the practice. Christians used to the religious freedoms of Western societies are often troubled to learn this. The prohibition, which offers protections as well as restrictions, is imperative for peaceful co-existence. Religious identity functions very differently in the Middle East than it does in the West, where individuals are free to choose and change their religion and may claim multiple religious identities or none at all. Religious identity in the Middle East is determined by the family into which one is born and is fundamental to one's personal, social, and legal standing. While it is legal to voluntarily convert to another religion, people seldom do so, which would likely threaten the status and security of their family. To proselytize in the Holy Land puts you, your group, and your host institution at risk.

Instead, Holy Land churches are engaged in public ministry in the form of educational, vocational, and healthcare institutions. Given the population disparity between Muslims and Christians, church institutions predominantly serve Muslim communities, offering both jobs and services. Pilgrim groups are encouraged to make institutional visits, and volunteer opportunities can be arranged, especially for individuals. Called to imitate Christ in their service to others, Christian pilgrims learn from the missional witness of the Palestinian church.

The Ascetic Pilgrim

When Jesus commissioned the Twelve, he told them to "take no gold, or silver, or copper in your belts, no bag for your journey, or two tunics, or sandals, or a staff" (Matt 10:9–10). Jesus told his disciples to travel light. What should pilgrims take on their journey? What supplies are needful, and which ones should be left at home? The questions raise the issues of material possessions, dependency on God, and the degree to which life in Christ is one of asceticism and self-denial. While the harsher words of Christ champion a life of self-renunciation, Jesus was ambivalent about the ascetic life, especially in contrast to John the Baptist. Jesus was criticized for not fasting like other religious leaders, and viewing his presence on earth in terms of a bridegroom at a wedding feast, Jesus said: "the wedding guests cannot mourn as long as the bridegroom is with them" but will fast "when the bridegroom is taken away from them" (Matt 9:14–15).

The question is not whether Christians should engage in ascetic practices, such as fasting and self-denial, but when, where, and how often. Should Holy Land pilgrims view the entirety of their Jerusalem sojourn as time celebrated in the presence of Christ—as an Easter experience? Or, it is more meaningful to recognize both common and sacred time, both restraint and celebration, depending upon the liturgical season, the scriptural themes of the daily sites, and one's situational context?

Life as Pilgrimage

The life-as-journey metaphor probes our life from the cradle to the grave with attention given to the temptations and struggles of our earthly existence. The Bible often views the world as a foreign landscape: Christians are in pursuit of a spiritual homeland, couched in terms of a heavenly Jerusalem. Christians are "strangers and foreigners on the earth . . . seeking a homeland . . . a better country, that is, a heavenly one" (Heb 11:13–19). We are resident aliens who are in the world but not of the world (John 17:14–15). Holy Land pilgrimage is a metaphorical reenactment of the biblical prototype: the salvific journey to New Jerusalem. At the same time, it is a significant event in a pilgrim's earthly life.

Christological Images

As previously discussed, the Bible contains standalone images that directly appeal to the pilgrim life. Replete with pilgrim language, Psalms provided the contemplative texts for my walk on the Camino de Santiago: "you have delivered my soul from death, and my feet from falling, so that I may walk before God in the light of life" (Ps 56:13); "make me to know your ways, O LORD, teach me your path" (Ps 25:4); "for your steadfast love is before my eyes, and I walk in faithfulness to you" (Ps 26:3). God leads us along the pathway, securing our steps as we go. Even though we walk through the darkest valley, God is with us; though we stumble, we will not fall (Pss 23:3–4; 37:23–24). The heavenly shepherd leads his sheep to green pastures and still waters. He provides, comforts, guides, and protects: "you are a hiding place for me; you preserve me from trouble; you surround me with glad cries of deliverance" (Ps 32:7). God is our shelter and sanctuary.

Christological images likewise contain pilgrim themes. Jesus is our spiritual guide. He is the way, the light of the world in a land full of darkness (John 8:12). Providing spiritual nourishment, he is the bread from heaven and the water of life. As protector, he is the shepherd as well as the sheep gate (John 10:9, 2–4). As the sum of our lives, Christ is the alpha and the omega, the A and the Z, the beginning and the end—or, the beginning *through* to the end. Christ is our departure, our destination, and every step in-between. We encounter Christ in the middle and in the meantime. He is our past, present, and never-ending future: "on the road the pilgrim learns that searching for God is already to have found him and that direction is much more important than destination, because God is not just an end, nor a beginning, but for us he is always a beginning without end."[7] Likewise, in the words of Boethius:

> To see Thee is the end and the beginning.
>
> Thou carriest us, and Thou dost go before,
>
> Thou art the journey and the journey's end.[8]

Christological images fuel the pilgrim experience.

Conclusion

Scripture speaks in plentiful ways to our experience of God, self, and the Other through time, place, journey, and people, and we can easily cite more examples. Pilgrimage confronts life's most important questions: Job and Ecclesiastes provide the manuals. The book of Ruth is about a foreigner who becomes the matriarchal Other in Jesus' bloodline. Prophetic voices challenge the quest for power, the love of money, and the oppression of the poor, reminding us that pilgrimage should be an exercise in virtue, compassion, and mercy rather than an empty form of religious ritual. God favors justice and righteousness over solemn assemblies (Amos 5:18–24).

This raises two related points: scripture critiques certain aspects of pilgrimage, and the Bible records the evolution of ideas and attitudes, like those toward holy places. In light of Christ's resurrection and the temple's destruction, the New Testament church sought God in the gathered community rather than in designated places and replaced temple theology by emphasizing the presence of Christ in the breaking of the bread. Yet, we must still contend with Old Testament scriptures that sanction practices counter to Christian sensibilities, while pilgrim-related concepts, such as a theology of the land, diatribes against foreigners, and a covenantal understanding of a chosen people, raise questions regarding their present-day applications. Having surveyed scriptural images for Holy Land pilgrims, the chapter encourages further conversation on how the Bible informs contemporary expressions of the pilgrim life.

---

7. Hughes, *In Search of a Way*, 50.

8. Quoted in Appleton, *The Oxford Book of Prayer*, 7.

4

Pilgrim Identity

Pilgrims and Tourists

The Authentic Pilgrim

How does one become a pilgrim? Who authenticates the pilgrim life? The following scene played out before me on the Camino de Santiago. Three middle-aged Norwegian women were walking the Camino. One of them was fit; the other two struggled, alternating between walking and taking a bus. One afternoon, as a number of us were waiting in a café for the pilgrim hostel to open, the slower two women arrived by bus and placed their packs in the queue next to the hostel door. At once, another pilgrim removed their bags and escorted the women to get a nearby hotel. If you take a bus, you forfeit your right to a free bed: so goes the rules of the road.

That night, six of us, including the Norwegian women, went out to eat. Assembled around the table was a collection of pilgrims with various levels of physical strength and emotional well-being—common people with dissimilar views and experience. Sometime after the first course, the conversation turned to the question of who is a real pilgrim and what is the correct way to do the Camino. A Dutch man who had started from his doorstep in the Netherlands and had been on the trail for a hundred days asserted narrow opinions in a loud, edgy voice. The mood turned tense.

"No, you're wrong," someone replied. "That's ridiculous. There's no right way to do the Camino." The Norwegian women sat listening in silence, nursing physical ailments, and licking wounds of rejection, struggling with their self-confidence, and dealing with issues back home. One of them left the room in tears.

Rules have been established on the Camino de Santiago to give official sanction to the modern-day experience, to regulate behavior, and to create a pilgrim culture. Pilgrims must carry a special passport, walk, bike, or ride a horse to get a bed in a pilgrim hostel, and do the same for the last hundred kilometers to receive an official certificate. The rules, however, do not determine who is a genuine pilgrim. People decide that for themselves.

A Finnish journalist split time between walking with pilgrims and preparing a documentary. The Norwegian women occasionally took a bus. Who is to say that they aren't pilgrims or that their experiences of God, self, and the Other are of less value? Does a working holiday or a walk full of tears preclude a pilgrim identity? The spiritual journey is not defined by others nor is the Holy Spirit deterred by the rules of the road.

Pilgrim identity is *self*-determined. It is a person's prerogative, and assessing the pilgrim nature of another is fundamentally misdirected. At the same time, pilgrimage is a voluntary, non-requisite endeavor, a take-it-or-leave-it spirituality. There is nothing incumbent about it. People decide for themselves when, where, and for how long they will assume a pilgrim identity. Pilgrims value intentionality over misguided notions of authenticity.

We should be cautious of using standards to valorize the pilgrim life. Pilgrimage fails as an exclusive spirituality, and an inflated self-purpose that dismisses the intentions, efforts, and experiences of others is antithetical to the pilgrim spirit. Pilgrimage is an uncornerable market: we are individual experts on the pilgrim life.

Pilgrims and Tourists

Mark Twain famously wrote: "travel is fatal to prejudice, bigotry, and narrow-mindedness."[1] While critiques abound, there is nothing inherently frivolous about being a tourist, and we miss the point if we simply promote pilgrimage as a superior form of travel.[2] I love vacations, and I enjoy being a tourist. I have traveled extensively, but I only consider certain experiences to have been pilgrimages in the fullest sense. There is a time to be a tourist and a time to be a pilgrim—but the categories can overlap. Vacations are meaningful; pilgrimage has touristic elements. I know colleagues who do not allow the words "tour" or "tourist" to be used on a Holy Land pilgrimage. Their position recognizes the power of words in shaping thought and experience. However, tourist-like activities are part of the pilgrim life, and there is nothing wrong with naming them. Holy Land pilgrimage has moments of diversion, relaxation, and entertainment.

1. Mark Twain, *Innocents Abroad*, chapter 61.

2. While our focus here is on tourists and pilgrims, secular commentators contrast tourists and travelers in similar ways. Tourists are vulgar, docile, superficial, and one of a herd, while travelers comport themselves with vision, understanding, and sophistication. The distinctions, of course, are tenuous. See Todd, *The Thing Itself*, chapter 2.1, "Touring."

Pilgrims take tours of museums and archeological parks and float in the Dead Sea. Our intent should not be to discard tourist categories but to realize the transformational possibilities of pilgrimage. Likewise, we are not interested in labeling the traveler but in using the respective concepts as lenses for navigating experience in meaningful ways. While pilgrim spirituality invites us to engage the world as pilgrims even when we are not "on pilgrimage," by reflecting upon the image of pilgrims and tourists, we can discern when an experience is a personal pilgrimage, even retrospectively. In short, the pilgrim–tourist dichotomy provides reflective fodder for religious travel. How does a pilgrim think and behave differently than a tourist? How does pilgrimage differ from a holiday?

Etymologies

Sauntering though the Sainte-Terre

In his 1862 essay, *Walking*, Henry David Thoreau (1817–62) explores the etymology of the word "saunter," which he believes is from the French, *Sainte-Terre*, or Holy Land. According to Thoreau, it purportedly refers to "'idle people who roved about the country, in the Middle Ages, and asked charity, under pretense of going à la Sainte Terre,' to the Holy Land, till the children exclaimed, 'There goes a Sainte-Terrer,' a Saunterer, a Holy-Lander." Thoreau admits another possibility—that saunter could come from *sans terre*, or "without land or a home, which, therefore, in the good sense, will mean having no particular home but equally at home everywhere," which touches upon other pilgrim themes. He then applies sauntering to the art of walking. For Thoreau, "true walking is not directionless wandering about the countryside, nor is it physical exercise." Slipping into Christian exceptionalism, he envisions every walk as "a sort of crusade." The walking to which Thoreau aspires demands that walkers leave their life behind in the "spirit of undying adventure, never to return." One is "to go forth and reconquer this Holy Land from the hands of the Infidels . . . [and] so we saunter toward the Holy Land." *Walking* exemplifies how the Holy Land has been used as an image for everyday pursuits.

Saunter, however, stems from neither *Sainte Terre* nor *sans terre*; its derivation is unknown. Yet, false etymologies can still be useful tools. Evoking Thoreau, to saunter has been used to exhort Holy Land pilgrims to slow down on their journey, despite the fact that its contemporary meaning—to walk in a slow, relaxed manner or a leisurely stroll—seems to misdescribe the pilgrim disposition. It feels a bit frivolous to saunter through the Holy Land, let alone the Stations of the Cross. The Jerusalem experience is ideally a slow-paced, reflective journey. This is seldom the case, however, as Holy Land programs have notoriously packed schedules, and one has little control over the pace of the journey. Rather, the art of group pilgrimage is making effective use of the brief intervals that open up throughout the day, including bus time, meal breaks, and waits and delays, when one can slow down, engage in conversation, or find some reflective solitude. One can saunter in spurts.

Thoreau, however, is not talking about slowing down or taking leisurely strolls. For him, sauntering is about purpose and perseverance, adventure, imagination, and thoughtful deliberation: "you must walk like a camel, which is said to be the only beast which ruminates when walking." The concept is more akin to the late Middle English sense of saunter—to muse or wonder—which captures elements of surprise, mystery, meditation, and astonishment. Saunter, in the end, speaks to the pilgrim spirit.

Towers and Tourists

The most secure derivation of "tourist"—or "to tour"—is the Old English *turian* (Old French, *toner*), which comes from the Latin *tornare*, meaning to turn on a lathe or a tool for turning, thus, describing a circle. A tourist is one who turns, one who goes around in a circuit, one who travels and returns back home. Applied to pilgrimage, it raises the distinction between round-trip journeys and one-way templates that never return to the point of departure. How does the pilgrim journey return us to where we first began, and how are we changed in the process? How, on the other hand, is pilgrimage a phenomenon of never returning home, the experience of constantly arriving at a new destination? Another idea is that tour comes from the French word for tower, which implies a place of observation. A tourist, therefore, is one who observes, often from a safe, isolated distance, and the image of the static tourist has been contrasted to pilgrimage as *per* + *ager*, or "through the field." While tourists observe from afar, pilgrims traverse social and physical landscapes, crossing boundaries and engaging the Other.

Life's Most Important Questions

On vacation, one goes to get away from life;
On pilgrimage, one confronts life's most important questions.

Irrespective of what one does or where one goes, the aim of a vacation is temporary detachment, or the momentary suspension of commitments and responsibilities. We go to the beach to get away, to escape the demands of everyday life. We seek distance from our daily stress, breaks from our everyday routines. Vacations allow freedom of movement, participation in novel activities, and interaction with other people. Whether vacations are restful or adventurous, they are meant to clear our minds.[3] A successful vacation is not easy to achieve. Stress is hard to leave at home, and the concerns of life infringe upon us. One contemplates the pressures of work. Thoughts about health, family, and finances naturally arise.

Whereas vacations are times for getting away, a pilgrimage addresses life's most important questions. Pilgrims reflect upon matters of faith, vocational calling, and personal relationships. Pilgrimage may be a response to personal transitions, such as divorce or the death of a loved one. To be on pilgrimage is to confront life's most pressing issues.

A sixth-century pilgrim from Piacenza, Italy recalls his visit to Cana of Galilee where Jesus attended a wedding with his mother (John 2). The church purportedly contained the original wedding couch, and the pilgrim confesses that "on it, undeserving though I am, I wrote the names of my parents."[4] The reference to holy graffiti at the Cana church is both humorous and touching. The pilgrim is following the practice of blessing couples—in this case, his own parents—where Jesus had blessed a wedding. The Holy Land is a time of remembering the meaningful, a journey of thanksgiving and intercessory prayer, a prayerful recognition of life's most treasured blessings.

Change and Transformation

Tourists change their environment;
Pilgrims let the environment change them.

The adage implies that tourists manipulate their environment for the sake of comfort and familiarity, while pilgrims adapt to their physical surroundings. A related cliché—tourists walk through the land, while pilgrims let the land walk through them—expresses the same sentiment. The assertions address the degree to which travelers adhere to the norms of unfamiliar places or change their surroundings to suit their tastes. In short, how do pilgrims act when they are in a foreign context like the Holy Land? To what degree do they adapt to local customs, and when and to what extent do they

---

3. There are, of course, meaningful aspects to vacations and holidays, including time spent with family. A vacation may broaden our mind, foster self-confidence, and facilitate personal growth.

4. Piacenza Pilgrim, *Travels*, 4.

take respite in culturally familiar amenities? Christian travelers navigate between the unknown and the familiar, between accepting their surroundings and altering their environment.

Leaving Home Behind

In *One Fine Day in the Middle of the Night*, a 1999 Scottish crime novel by Christopher Brookmyre, a decommissioned North Sea oil rig off the coast of Scotland has been kitted out with all the trappings of British recreational culture—hotels, swimming pools, bowling alleys, discos, pubs, and fish and chip shops. The "floating holiday experience" was to be located off the North African coast where it would provide a haven for British tourists who wanted a vacation in the sun without the hassle of actually interacting with a foreign culture. A week of sunshine could be enjoyed, complete with British amenities, without otherwise leaving home. Two special events were planned on the rig while it was still in Scotland: a gathering for the investors and, prior to that, the project developer's high school reunion. Needless to say, the terrorists arrive on the wrong weekend. *One Fine Day* plays off the idea that tourists desire to control their environment or, in this case, to literally take it with them.

One Fine Day is a foil for the pilgrim life, challenging those who want to encounter the land of Jesus without engaging local culture. Pilgrimage is always contextual, and Holy Land travel is a journey to foreign climes. Abraham was called to experience God out of place, and pilgrims seek God in foreign places far from home. Being out of place exposes our cultural dependencies and personal affinities, our weaknesses and vulnerabilities. Pilgrimage makes us more aware of our desires and limitations.

One Fine Day speaks to travel preferences, conveniences, and necessities. Even with baggage restrictions, people can take a surprising amount of their world with them. We take things for health and safety, for comfort and convenience, for pleasure and enjoyment, and for educational and devotional purposes. What are the necessities of Holy Land travel? To what extent is accessibility to cultural amenities, such as food, music, news, and sports, important for maintaining our equilibrium, which, in turn, allows us to better engage the Holy Land content, and to what extent do they diminish the pilgrim experience? On the other hand, what is the value of foregoing convenience? Does it enhance or hinder our focus? Is there spiritual benefit in doing so, even on a temporary basis? The Abraham narrative can guide our approach. Holy Land travelers experience the blessings of pilgrimage on foreign soil; they do so by leaving most of home behind.

The Submissive Pilgrim

The idea that pilgrims let their environment change them suggests a posture of submission. Having limited control over their schedule, pilgrims assume the rhythms of a life that is not their own. They are guided by others, dependent upon the services of strangers. Pilgrims follow; they don't lead. They forfeit initiative; they yield to others. They are passive and compliant; they adjust and adapt. Pilgrims defer to outward forces, and, as a result, they are inwardly transformed. They do not change their environment; their environment changes them.

Pilgrimage has goals, risks, and difficulties that we would not generally accept on a vacation, but to what degree should pilgrims put up with sub-standard situations? What are the terms and conditions of pilgrimage? Is it an exercise in accepting things as they are? Do pilgrims forfeit the right to complain? The Holy Land is not cheap; yet, amenities are not always up to Western standards. Pilgrims occasionally encounter cold rooms, uncomfortable beds, a lack of hot water, uninspiring food, and poor internet connections. They may feel ripped-off by a shopkeeper. Wait staff may be slow or unresponsive; a taxi driver may overcharge. To what extent should pilgrims complain? Shouldn't they "change their environment" when something is unacceptable, whether due to comfort, value, or safety? Should pilgrims tolerate situations that they would not endure on holiday or remain passive to poor service? In order to get the most out of the Holy Land experience, shouldn't personal comforts, such as a good night's sleep, be a priority? Or, is there an "as it should be" quality to the pilgrim life? Our situational reactions often depend upon our personalities and cultural norms, which is another reason why the question merits our attention: when should we assert ourselves, and when should we assume the role of the submissive pilgrim?

Simple Decisions

To change the environment is to shape the world into an image of home. Notwithstanding health and diet restrictions, few things are more representative of our relationship to the unfamiliar than food and drink, precisely because they pertain to necessary, frequent, and personal behaviors. With respect to foreign cuisine, do you prefer local options or familiar choices? While it has limited moral significance, something as common as a cup of coffee is latent with spiritual implications. Pilgrimage is an exercise in intentional decision-making, a litany of never-ending choices, a concentrated study in self-management. Our faith lives are forged by our daily decisions, and changing one's environment speaks to simple behaviors.

Global markets make it increasingly easy for pilgrims to satisfy their cravings. The Holy Land is replete with cappuccinos and Big Macs, which are constantly in the pilgrim's peripheral vision. One of the first rituals that many pilgrims go through on their first morning in the Holy Land is the pursuit of a good cup of coffee as the coffee in hotels and institutions can be hit or miss. Pilgrims want what they have back home or something agreeably better. While Italian and American-style coffee is easy to find, locals drink Arabic coffee, a strong, bitter drink containing cardamom. Some learn to like it; others drink it for the cultural experience or as a way of grounding themselves in time and place. While some never develop a taste for it, they drink it in deference to the cultural context. I have also seen the best of pilgrims go to great lengths to get a good cappuccino. Coffee locates us and mitigates—or accentuates—the sense of being out of place. Some will drink the local coffee (they will be changed by their environment), while others will drink a Western style that better suits their taste (they will change their environment).

What does the pursuit of coffee say about our preferences, dependencies, and desires? Why is it easy to adjust to some things yet significantly more difficult to adapt to others? The Holy Land serves up a nice mint tea. Do British pilgrims, renowned for their fastidious love of tea, bring their own bags from home, which they commonly do, or drink the local product? What does a cup of tea tell us about ourselves? How does savoring a good cup of tea in the Holy Land, regardless of its source, foster a sense of feasting, celebration, and spiritual blessing? In short, relatively innocuous items, such as coffee and tea, lie at the heart of pilgrim decision-making, revealing one's disposition, determining experience, and providing content for personal reflection.

The identical decision can be made for different reasons. Consequently, the same act can assume different meanings. Drinking cappuccinos in the Holy Land can be seen as a cultural dependency, as a way of taking home on the road, which lacks engagement with the local culture. Or, since the Holy Land journey is a time of celebration, drinking cappuccinos may be viewed as a positive, spiritual indulgence. Depending upon the meaning ascribed to it, the same cup of coffee can expose weakness, limit experience, and be swallowed with a tinge of guilt or express spiritual sagaciousness, savored gratitude, and a sense of festivity. Regarding simple, everyday decisions, the goal is not consistency. Rather, intention interprets the context, and choice fosters reflection. There is nothing wrong with eating a Big Mac in the Holy Land; it is a lost opportunity not to reflect upon the reasons for doing it.

Even giving in to a personal indulgence can be turned into a moment of spiritual self-awareness.

A Lenten Approach to the Holy Land

The Christian practice of Lent, which uses personal choices about relatively insignificant things to foster self-examination and to enrich the Easter celebration, offers an added dimension to pilgrim decision-making by appealing to concepts of sacred time. The Lenten disciplines are not about giving up bad habits precisely because the observance of Lent is as much about breaking the fast on Easter as it is about giving something up in the first place. We give up simple, innocuous items, like meat, soft drinks, ice cream, and chocolate, not because they are harmful, but precisely because we enjoy them.

Jesus likens himself to a bridegroom at a wedding feast (Mark 2:19). Guests fast when the groom is away but not in his presence. Lent positions us as anticipants of the bridegroom. Persevering in his absence, the wait ends with the Easter resurrection, and, with it, our time of fasting. Those who have given something up for Lent mark Easter by breaking their fast, thus, eating a bar of chocolate on Easter becomes a profoundly religious act, a savored indulgence full of spiritual meaning. Those who give up meat for Lent and celebrate Easter with a lamb dinner experience the feast more robustly than those who do not engage in a similar practice.

The Holy Land is the Easter of religious travel, and pilgrims may view their entire sojourn in terms of a wedding feast, reckoned as sacred time in the presence of the bridegroom, an Easter-type celebration given to indulging the senses and sampling its delicacies. Pilgrims who do so grab coffee and ice cream—or dates and pomegranate juice—at frequent junctures in the journey. In the land of the Holy One, personal disciplines give way to a celebration of the risen Christ.

At the same time, foreign travel leaves people feeling out of place, preventing an unfettered sense of Easter. We feel the foreignness of travel most acutely in the basics of food, drink, and the ordinary comforts of home. Separated from personal affinities, pilgrims may find themselves in a state of longing similar to Lent. Just as Lent enhances our spiritual lives through temporary periods of self-denial, the Holy Land journey can be approached in a similar way—by interpreting the absence of cultural amenities in terms of a Lenten fast. By associating the Jerusalem experience with the season of Lent, we give a familiar, meaningful structure to our status as foreign travelers.[5]

5. Whether the Holy Land sojourn is regarded as a time of feasting or fasting may

Just as Lent anticipates Easter, breaking a cultural fast becomes a time of celebration. Eating at McDonald's—or a much nicer Western meal—at the end of a Holy Land sojourn becomes a spiritual blessing rather than a surrender to a personal craving. Serial moments of cultural re-entry, which occur during the homebound journey and upon arriving back home, are normative aspects of foreign travel, which, through the lens of Lent, can be experienced with an enhanced sense of meaning. The same applies to Holy Land Sundays. By restraining weekday behavior, pilgrims can add special meaning to a resurrection day spent in Jerusalem by partaking in a personal indulgence. Rather than resorting to a Western treat, a plate of Middle East sweets nicely does the trick.

The Legacy of Holy Land Travel

Finally, as the shadow of the Western Crusader remains on the land, especially in the collective memory of Muslims, Jews, and Eastern Christians, modern-day pilgrims continue the legacy of foreign travelers to Jerusalem. Today, as the Palestinian church suffers moribund decline, some Christians are supporting the indigenous church, while others hold theologies that undermine it. While some advocate for peace and reconciliation, others back policies that are destabilizing the region. The Holy Land is a transformational experience, but the who, what, and how are open questions. How pilgrims are changing the Holy Land and how the Holy Land changes pilgrims remain matters of utmost importance.

also be influenced by pilgrim solidarity with the Living Stones.

5

Pilgrim Motives

Destination Jerusalem

W hat are the common reasons and motivating factors for Christian travel to the Holy Land? Prayer and the investigation of scripture have long been the primary motives. People also make the journey for personal discernment, on behalf of others, and as a witness for peace and justice. Some arrive reluctantly or with no agenda at all, while others are unable to go or choose to stay away. By understanding the range of pilgrim motives, Jerusalem-bound travelers can explore goals, clarify their calling, and find connections with other pilgrims, past and present.

The First Christian Travelers to the Holy Land

What do we know about the first Christian travelers to the Holy Land? Melito of Sardis (d. 180) traveled to "the place where these things were preached and done [in order to learn] accurately the books of the Old Testament."[1] Alexander of Cappadocia (d. 251) went to Jerusalem "in order to worship there and to examine the historical sites," while the third-century scholar Origen (d. 254) went "in search of the traces of Jesus, his disciples, and the prophets."[2] In short, the earliest Christian travelers went to the Holy Land for two main reasons: (1) for the investigation of scripture and the biblical events associated with the land and (2) for prayer and Christian devotion. The testimonies of present-day pilgrims reflect the same intentions: to know the Bible better and to deepen one's commitment to God. Christians go to the Holy Land to learn and pray.

1. Eusebius, *Church History*, 4.26.13–14.

2. Eusebius, *Church History*, 6.11.2; Origen, *Commentary on John*, 6.40.40. See Hunt, *Holy Land Pilgrimage*, 4, 92.

The Investigation of Scripture

Christians speak of returning to the roots of the faith and going to see where it all began. The sentiment expresses the desire to explore firsthand the origins of the Christian faith, to stand in the epicenter of Christianity. Holy Land pilgrims engage history, topography, and archaeology in order to elucidate scripture. They go to understand the Bible better. Jerome, who lived much of his life in Bethlehem, famously remarked: "Holy Scripture is studied with greater clarity by the [one] who has contemplated Judaea with his eyes and who knows the memorials of the ancient cities and places, whether their names are still the same or have been changed."[3] Firsthand empirical knowledge of the biblical landscapes enriches the meaning of the text. Pilgrims attend to the physical topography, historical geography, and material culture of the biblical past. They encounter the flora and fauna of the Bible and experience the sights, sounds, and smells of the land. Pilgrims become familiar with the diverse and often dramatic terrain of the Holy Land, comprehending its size and dimensions. As biblical events become linked to the landscape, stories assume an unprecedented clarity, and Jesus' movements become more intelligible. One's scriptural imagination shifts from black and white to color, and pilgrims begin to engage in richly in-formed speculations on the biblical drama, such as the personalities and motivations of its central characters.

The dramatic landscapes of the Judean Wilderness and the Jordan River Valley recall scenes of the baptism and temptation of Jesus. Christ's ministry comes alive around the Sea of Galilee, and Jerusalem and the Mount of Ol-ives set the story of Jesus' passion. Place names, like Bethlehem, Nazareth, Capernaum, Bethsaida, and Bethany, become real locations, and the parable of the Good Samaritan is powerfully visualized as one travels between Jeru-salem and Jericho. Biblical details are communicated through the design, art, and imagery of the Holy Land churches. The ancient mosaic of the fish and loaves at Tabgha, the modern statue of Mary and Elizabeth at the Church of the Visitation, and the tile panels of the Lord's Prayer in over 140 languages at Pater Noster make indelible impressions upon the pilgrim imagination, permanently forging a personal connection with place and story. Scripture becomes intimate; the gospel appears as flesh and stone.

By focusing on place, pilgrims categorize familiar material in new ways, enhancing their grasp of the Gospels. What narratives occurred in and around Capernaum, and how are they informed by the borders, boundar-ies, and pathways of the first century? Which stories took place in Bethany,

3. Jerome, *Prologus in libro Paralipomenon*, quoted in O'Loughlin, *Adomnán and the Holy Places*, 13.

and what was its importance to Jesus' ministry? Holy Land pilgrimage reflects upon familiar stories from different perspectives, considering the meaning of place and reorganizing narrative material according to location, proximity, and sequence. The category of place provides a simple but often overlooked structure for Bible studies, age-level curriculum, and sermon series.

Holy Land travel proffers a life-long familiarity with Gospel places, and upon returning home, Christians read the Bible with a newfound attention to detail while grasping its central truths in clearer ways. Pilgrims continually revisit the Holy Land through scripture, sermons, and the liturgical seasons. Once one has journeyed to Bethlehem, Christmas is never the same. Having entered the Holy City, we are permanently grounded in the Easter story. While the church is faithfully served by Christian leaders who have never been to the Holy Land, the body of Christ is enhanced when its members have a personal knowledge of the places found in the Gospels.

Investigating scripture in the Holy Land is not without its challenges and difficulties. How certain can we be that we are reading the land and, thus, the texts accurately? How reliable are the insights we derive from personal impressions and scholarly interpretations? An initial caution relates to the identification of the holy places. While the settings of the sites are generally credible, precise locations are seldom certain. We should proceed with care, recognizing that our knowledge is incomplete.

L. P. Hartley's 1953 novel, *The Go-Between*, begins with the line: "the past is a foreign country: they do things differently there." Holy Land pilgrims must navigate the highly mutable dimensions of time and space. Accurately imagining the biblical past—or any historical period—is notoriously difficult; the textual and material sources are limited, incomplete, and open to interpretation. Seeing the past anachronistically is a perpetual trap for religious travelers. Pilgrims imagine biblical characters living in the Ottoman houses of Jerusalem's Old City. A fourteen-century Gothic room encloses the traditional site of the Lord's Supper. The Bible is a foreign country and envisioning its past is a difficult endeavor. Unpacking the complexities of first-century Palestine—its cultural, religious, and political contexts—requires good resource material, highly trained guides, and the input of critical scholarship. Pilgrims should seek a range of informed opinions, recognizing that definitive answers are few and far between.

An additional challenge to envisioning scripture is that many of the holy sites are enshrined with churches that suppress rather than preserve their natural settings. The biblical story is more difficult to imagine at some sites than others. Is it easy to perceive the birth of Christ at the Church of the Nativity or to envision the events of Jesus' passion and resurrection at the Holy Sepulchre?

Monumental structures, singular discoveries, and common artifacts have significantly impacted our understanding of scripture. Yet, the relationship between archaeology and written sources is complex, and despite the image of early biblical archaeologists with a Bible in one hand and a trowel in the other, archaeology is misappropriated when used to prove a text or to link a place with a historical figure without a clear reason for doing so. Archaeology seldom recovers evidence that identifies those who used the space.

Over the centuries, biblical sites have been lost, and their locations have had to be reestablished. The ruins at Capernaum had to be identified; the pool of Bethesda was fortuitously rediscovered. The excavations of Bethsaida are most likely the New Testament site, but we lack verifiable proof. The dating of structures, such as tombs, synagogues, and theatres, informs the debate on the life and culture of Jesus' day, but the field has its share of controversies and disagreements. Nonetheless, topography, archaeology, and material culture give visual form to our understanding of scripture, and even if we see the biblical past dimly, it becomes more fully known by walking the land.

The Fifth Gospel

If scripture is a window into Jesus' life, does Holy Land travel engender a clearer, more concrete portrait of Christ? Does familiarity with New Testament landscapes render an accurate image of the historical Jesus? The Frenchman Ernest Renan (1823–92) thought so. In his nineteenth-century best-seller, *The Life of Jesus*, Renan describes how, after a long struggle to conceptualize Christ, his familiarity with the Gospel places brought Jesus to life. The land made Jesus legible:

> Such are the rules which have been followed in the composition of this work. To the perusal of documentary evidences I have been able to add an important source of information—the sight of the places where the events occurred. The scientific mission, having for its object the exploration of ancient Phoenicia, which I directed in 1860 and 1861, led me to reside on the frontiers of Galilee, and to travel there frequently. I have traversed, in all directions, the country of the Gospels; I have visited Jerusalem, Hebron, and Samaria; scarcely any important locality of the history of Jesus has escaped me. All this history, which at a distance seems to float in the clouds of an unreal world, thus took a form, a solidity which astonished me. The striking agreement of the texts with the places, the marvelous harmony of the Gospel ideal with the country which

served it as a framework, were like a revelation to me. I had before my eyes a fifth Gospel, torn but still legible, and henceforward, through the recitals of Matthew and Mark, in place of an abstract being, whose existence might have been doubted, I saw living and moving an admirable human figure.[4]

Renan uses the term Fifth Gospel to denote the physical landscapes of Jesus' life. Jerome applied the term to the book of Isaiah, and modern scholars have used it to describe non-canonical texts, such as the Gospel of Thomas. For Renan, the Fifth Gospel was the *land* of the Bible, and the Bible could be read from the land. Experiencing the Gospel places brought Jesus alive as a living figure, making lucid the abstract image of Christ. The Fifth Gospel provides modern-day pilgrims with a meaningful term for describing their encounter with the land and the clarity that it provides for understanding scripture and "seeing Jesus." Holy Land pilgrims familiar with the phrase can be heard towards the end of their journey reflecting upon their experiences of the Fifth Gospel.

Yet, what do we know about Renan's Jesus? Who was this "admirable human figure" that Renan saw before his eyes? What revelation did he have that was so in harmony with the Gospel ideal? Renan's portrait of Jesus is problematic, to say the least. Besides stripping Jesus of his divine qualities, Renan claimed that Jesus was an Aryan who had purified himself of his native Galilean Judaism. Renan promoted theories of racial supremacy, infused theology with issues of race, and depicted Jesus and the Christianity that he founded shorn of any Jewish influence.[5] Despite championing a historical view, one that he claimed was grounded in the harmony of land and text, Renan's Jesus is a distorted figure.

So where does this leave us? Does Renan render obsolete his own concept of the Fifth Gospel and with it the idea that the land reveals the face of Jesus? There is no question that familiarity with the physical topography and material culture of the Holy Land adds immeasurably to our understanding of the biblical text. In using the land to construct a portrait of Christ, how can we best assure a historically accurate and spiritually sound approach to our application of the Fifth Gospel? To begin with, pilgrims should use their time in the Holy Land to explore questions of Jesus' Judaism. Like so many before and after him, Renan created Jesus in his own image. Christianity affirms the idea that Jesus is knowable. The problem occurs when our portrait of Christ is based upon our own likeness, when culturally informed bias and misguided views of race and culture shape our vision of the divine, and when we deny

4. Renan, *Life of Jesus*, 31.
5. See Heschel, *The Aryan Jesus*, 33–37.

the influence of the Other upon our image of Jesus. The Fifth Gospel remains a useful concept for Holy Land pilgrims as long as we recognize that the Jesus of history as well as the Christ of faith inhabits the Other. When our Holy Land journey becomes little more than the confirmation of our theological and cultural identities, we are likely on the wrong path.

More positively, encountering the Fifth Gospel facilitates an informed speculation on the outstanding questions of Jesus, including his self-identity, the type of Judaism that he practiced, his attitude towards the temple, his relationship with religious and political authorities, the motives behind his movements and actions, the historical reasons for his crucifixion, and his eschatological perspectives. Pilgrim conversations commonly piece together the gaps in the Gospel story based upon their daily encounters in the field. Rather than a concrete form of Jesus, the fruits of the Fifth Gospel are the speculations that flourish in the religious imagination of the Holy Land traveler.

Spiritual Connections

The second main reason for Holy Land travel is a spiritual connection with God. Whereas the investigation of scripture concerns the acquisition of knowledge, Christians also go for religious practice, such as prayer and worship, seeking experiences that deepen their faith and strengthen their relationship with Christ. Spiritual reflection in the Holy Land happens in constant, natural, and informal ways. Holy Land prayer is an open-eyed encounter with the Fifth Gospel, and Paul's admonition to pray without ceasing describes the disposition of the Jerusalem pilgrim (1 Thess 5:17). Pilgrims remain in prayerful discourse throughout the day, and long bus rides are conducive for meditation. Pilgrims journal and review the scriptures associated with the daily sites. Devotional gatherings at the beginning of the day set the focus for what lies ahead, while debriefing at day's end solidifies details, memories, and meanings. Pilgrims also make spiritual connections by worshipping outside of their exclusive group setting, especially in a language or tradition that is not their own.

At the Holy Sites

Pilgrims pray at the holy sites. A number of factors impact one's experience at a site, including the narratives, themes, and pilgrim practices associated with the place, its architecture, art, and remnant archaeology, whether the site is indoors or outdoors, weather conditions, and the presence of other pilgrims. Every site has many faces, and it is never certain which one you will encounter.

Certain places are particularly conducive for prayer and worship. Pilgrims renew their baptism in the Jordan River, spend time in the Judean Wilderness reflecting upon themes of calling, discernment, and self-identity, and experience lakeside worship at the Sea of Galilee. In Jerusalem, Pater Noster is dedicated to the Lord's Prayer; Gethsemane is a place of prayerful silence; the Via Dolorosa is a devotional reenactment of Jesus' journey to the cross, and the tomb of Christ is a place of Christian vigil.[6] Engaging place and story, pilgrims contemplate and meditate, confess and repent, entreat and intercede.

Most Holy Land churches have suitable places to sit or stand, and some have areas for lighting candles. When the churches are all but empty, they have a profound meditative silence, and many of the sites have beautiful gardens—and the occasional bench—offering quietude for pilgrim reflection. The shrines, though, are visited by the masses, and while the churches try to restrict the noise, pilgrim groups can be rather loud. The commemorative focal points of sites, such as the Nativity grotto and the tomb of Christ, can have long lines with time at "the very spot" often measured in seconds rather than minutes. One does well to touch the place, take a photo, and say a short prayer. To linger is a luxury.[7]

All said, the Holy Land churches are conducive to prayer, especially if one has time to wait out the crowds. On a group pilgrimage, however, one is seldom at a site longer than an hour, usually less. After reading scripture and hearing presentations from guides and leaders, free time is often limited—and there can be a lot to cover: further exploring the site, using the restroom, and visiting the gift shop. Opportunities for personal prayer may be reduced to a few minutes sitting in a church or on a garden bench, and a long-anticipated visit to a holy place can be over before you know it. As Holy Land pilgrimage becomes a series of circumscribed prayers, the art of Jerusalem travel is discerning how to make use of one's limited free time.[8]

---

6. To arrange an overnight vigil in the Holy Sepulchre, visit the Franciscan sacristy near the Chapel of the Apparition. Individuals only.

7. Pilgrims must navigate both crowds and closures. A number of the churches close over lunch, and certain areas of a church may be temporarily closed due to a monastic or pilgrim liturgy. For the opening hours of the holy sites, see the Christian Information Center website (www.cicts.org).

8. The amount of time needed at a site—as well as the optimum group/individual time split—varies from place to place, and church visits differ from tours of large archaeological parks. Personal free time at holy sites, nature reserves, and archaeological parks is at the discretion of guides and leaders and depends upon their methods for leading groups, the length of their presentations, group dynamics, and the specific

The Elusive Nature of the Holy Land

While prayer is fundamental to the pilgrim life, feeling a discernible spiritual connection with God at a particular holy site is far more elusive. The quest for God in the land of the Holy One is unpredictable, and expectations of spiritual experience can lead to disappointment and frustration. The Holy Land is full of noise and distractions. Sites are crowded, and the days are packed. Anticipated connections and special moments may fail to materialize.

Even the most stoic pilgrim can be prone to insidious expectations. If such-and-such happened here, the reasoning goes, shouldn't I be experiencing x, y, and z? Some pilgrims feel that they have not arrived in the Holy Land until they have sensed a connection with God, and they begin to judge the success of their journey on the basis of their spiritual affect, a sort of spiritual litmus test that they fear to be failing. Christian sentimentality heightens in anticipation of Bethlehem, the Jordan River, and the Sea of Galilee. The tomb of Christ is the fount of the resurrection, the epicenter of the Christian faith. Divine miracles have taken place here, but I don't feel anything. If not in the Holy Land, then where?

For many, the spirituality of the land and the intimacy of walking in the footsteps of Christ are felt from the beginning. Others feel as if they are tugging on Superman's cape. One's initial encounter with the Holy Land may be full of empty nets, an emotionally uneven experience characterized by a series of mini-disappointments. The good news is that while disappointment is commonplace, more often than not, it quickly dissipates—partially because the journey keeps moving and attention turns to the next site, but also because the Holy Land ultimately delivers.[9] For every expectation that disappoints, pilgrims experience an unexpected surprise, and connections are made at places approached with little anticipation. Spiritual moments happen on pilgrimage when we least expect them, in big and small ways, at any juncture in the journey. God is profoundly present in the Holy Land, but its spiritual access points are often surprising.

While Jerusalem is a religious convention and a wide spectrum of religious life finds expression in its streets, encountering the holy is seldom a transcendental experience. Holy Land spirituality is physical, sensuous, and incarnational, and the Jerusalem pilgrim is transformed less by mystical

---

nature of each site. Time for prayer and exploration may not be possible at every site. Groups should discuss strategies and expectations together with their guides.

9. Since pilgrims generally visit around two dozen sites, they will be inevitably disappointed by some. There is no consensus on the individual sites. They are all beloved; they all, at times, disappoint.

moments than by the accumulation of visual, cognitive, and sensory content that embodies the gospel. That only makes sense. If God became human, assuming a blood, sweat, and tears existence in human history, then journeying to the land of the Word-made-flesh should reveal God's presence in similar ways. Spirit infuses the journey as pilgrims walk the sites, meet the people of the land, and experience God in time and place. A Fifth Gospel appears before our eyes, penetrating our religious imagination in mysterious and inexplicable ways, and we become indelibly linked to the land, connected by scripture, personal experience, and the footprints of Christ. While mystical experiences occur, pilgrims are more commonly transformed by the collective sum of the Holy Land journey.

Personal Reasons

While scripture, prayer, and spiritual connections are the primary motives for Holy Land travel, Christians journey to Jerusalem for other concurrent reasons. Holy Land pilgrimage provides Christians with a setting for self-reflection, personal discernment, and spiritual and emotional healing. Given its long, structured days and continuous movements, group pilgrimage does not permit stationary hours of personal reflection or controlled periods of silence.[10] The power of Holy Land pilgrimage lies in the convergence of place and story and in the layering of human life on Gospel soil. As the Bible speak to all aspects of the human condition, the Holy Land pilgrim encounters scriptural parallels to personal situations.

Personal Discernment

Pilgrimage is the bracketing of time for a specific purpose, and a Holy Land journey often functions as a time and place for important decisions. Whether a personal crossroads was a conscious reason for making the pilgrimage in the first place or only surfaced upon arrival, pilgrims use the Holy Land sojourn as a period of discernment, often related to vocational or relational issues. Vocational calling can emerge as a central theme of pilgrimage, and settings, such as Jesus' baptism site, the Judean wilderness, and the Galilean lakeshore, speak directly to Christian vocation. Should you take a certain job, recommit to your ongoing work, or leave your current employment? Are you being called to study or to pursue professional training? Are you considering taking on additional responsibilities or ending

10. While group pilgrimage offers few opportunities for extended prayer, the Holy Land is a good setting for individual retreats.

certain obligations? People use the Holy Land sojourn to reflect upon their life and work, including their volunteer commitments.

Pilgrims also reflect upon relationships, including family, friendships, and marriage. A conversation that I had years ago with an American pilgrim in Taizé could easily have taken place in Jerusalem:

> [This experience] has grounded me in God. I am at a transitional time in my life: getting married, a new job, having to move. I ask myself, "Is this the person for me? What do I want to do with my life?" and a hundred other questions. I often think too much, but I am reminded that God is in control. I won't leave here with many answers, but I feel that I have the faith resources to face whatever the future brings.

Her words beautifully express the function of pilgrimage as time set aside for reflecting upon imminent decisions while renewing one's faith in the face of an unknown future. Rather than distinct answers, the fruit of discernment is often the faith to move forward.

Along with vocation and relationships, pilgrims reflect upon life transitions. What does life look like once the kids have left home? How does one faithfully embrace retirement? While grief and healing are discussed below, Holy Land pilgrimage provides a platform for divorcees, widow(er)s, and former caretakers, among others, to discern a new sense of direction in their lives. A trip to the Holy Land fits well before or after a course of studies or before taking a new job. A cousin spent his last summer prior to medical school in the Holy Land. The Holy Land provides a setting for thought and reflection, and pilgrims seek ideas and inspiration as much as answers to specific questions. Times of transition call people on pilgrimage.

Personal Healing

Some pilgrims arrive in the Holy Land with a broken spirit, in need of spiritual and emotional healing.

> Blessed are the poor in spirit,
> for theirs is the kingdom of heaven.
>
> Blessed are those who mourn,
> for they will be comforted.
> (Matt 5:3–4).

Pilgrims deal with the death of loved ones, grieve over broken relationships, and struggle through the pain of divorce. Pilgrims carry the baggage of past disappointments and unfulfilled dreams, the weight of frustrations and bitterness, and the burden of stress and anxiety. The promise of abundant life has morphed into years of meaningless routine. Some arrive with emotional trauma, others with chronic or terminal illness. As the setting of past miracles, the Holy Land is a place of present-day wonders, and despite the region's contemporary wounds, narratives of healing and reconciliation pervade the land. Holy sites commemorate the healing ministry of Jesus. Crowned by Calvary and the tomb of Christ, the land of the Holy One is the story of God's reconciliation with humankind. Calvary is a call to repentance; Jesus' passion elicits contrition. Healing, forgiveness, and reconciliation interface and overlap. Restored in the image of God, the Holy Land pilgrim becomes a new creation in Christ.

While some pilgrims arrive well aware of their broken spirit, others require the journey to expose the pain. The Holy Land brings us face-to-face with failure and brokenness. Pilgrimage—and spiritual retreat in general—can become a time of personal struggle as unattended problems rise to the surface, exposing undesired truths and unresolved issues. On retreat on Iona, I became acquainted with Peter and Fiona, who had met each other years before on the Scottish island when Fiona was divorced and Peter was at the end of his marriage. Places like Iona and Jerusalem are double-edged swords. They are places of healing; they are also places of raw discovery, mirrors into the brokenness of our lives. "On a vacation, you go to get away. On a pilgrimage, you face your life. There is nothing to hide. On Iona, I came face-to-face with the problems of my life and marriage," reflected Peter, before adding: "but I was able to receive spiritual healing and self-affirmation. I discovered gifts and qualities about myself that I liked. I met people who affirmed who I was." After courting for a couple of years, they were married on Iona: the island that exposed their respective brokenness became a place of blessing. The Holy Land teaches us that we are healed through scars and reconciled through the resurrection. If painful realities unexpectedly surface, Jerusalem provides an appropriate setting for living vulnerably in the moment as the healing begins.

On Behalf of Others

Remaining spiritually connected with life back home, Jerusalem pilgrims journey on behalf of others. Holy Land pilgrimage is a venture in petitionary prayer. It is not unusual for pilgrims to receive prayer requests before they leave home—"pray for me in the Holy Land"—and compiling a prayer list is a requisite part of the journey. Pilgrims should consider packing small prayer objects, such as photos, crosses, and handwritten notes, that represent a person, group, or prayer need, which may be carried as physical prayers and blessed at the holy sites. Some pilgrims dedicate their trip to a person or prayer need.

Illnesses and accidents can occur at any moment, and given the time involved in planning a Holy Land trip, a situation regarding a friend or loved one may develop prior to departure. Is someone in personal, spiritual, or legal difficulties? Are you due to be away during a major surgery of a friend or family member? Will someone dear to you possibly die while you are gone? Should you go ahead with your plans or cancel your trip? If something happens while you are away, should you remain in the Holy Land or return home early? These are difficult decisions, and people respond faithfully in different ways. Being on pilgrimage while a loved one is in trouble can be an unsettling experience. It may also be a well-timed blessing: what could be better than offerings prayers from the Holy Land?

Those who are not able to make the trip themselves—perhaps due to age or illness, family responsibilities, work obligations, or financial reasons—often desire to be virtual pilgrims. Many parish groups employ some form of the practice, posting daily reports for those back home. Church groups can also share their journey with mission partners.[11] Recording experiences in real time has become increasingly easy, and vicarious travel, or pilgrimage by proxy, will become more common as the internet connects Jerusalem with pilgrims around the world.[12]

The Living Stones

Pilgrims go to the Holy Land to connect with local Christians and to support initiatives of peace and justice. One critique of Holy Land pilgrimage is that some groups go to Jerusalem solely interested in the what and where of the biblical past, looking for a sanitized Jesus reminiscent of their Sunday School childhood, and they do not want anything, such as the contemporary realities of Israel–Palestine, to stain their experience. Some come with political and theological leanings formed by media images and modern theories of the Last Days that ignore Jesus' message of loving others. Some ways of visiting the Holy Land are better than others.

---

11. Jerusalem offers a dynamic, neutral ground for the gathering of global partnerships. Church groups should consider inviting a mission partner to join their journey.

12. Real-time blogs should not replace the importance of post-trip presentations, which offer a more reflective, comprehensive perspective.

Understanding the Israeli–Palestinian conflict is difficult. What appears on the surface is just the tip of the iceberg, and one needs to become familiar with multiple perspectives to appreciate its intractable complexity. It is often said that those who go to the Holy Land for two weeks can write a book on the conflict, those who visit for two months a chapter, and those who stay for two years nothing at all. To be sure, the more time one spends in the region the more one understands; yet, the saying underscores the confounding nature of the conflict and the need to put easy-fix answers aside.

Although the dynamics are complicated, the violence, oppression, and human rights abuses warrant a Christian response. First of all, Christian pilgrims should not let their prayers and actions further divide people; they should promote reconciliation and peacemaking rather than taking sides. While engaging a range of religious, ethnic, and political voices, pilgrims should seek the radical center. That does not mean that Christians do not hold positions on the conflict, like ending the Israeli occupation of Gaza and the West Bank.

Secondly, just as supporting local Christians should be a focus of Christian travel anywhere, Christians pilgrims should be in solidarity with Arab-speaking Christians, whose heritage goes back to Pentecost (Acts 2:11). Over the past several decades, the Palestinian church has seen the steady emigration of its members to other parts of the world, significantly diminishing its numbers and depleting its generational vitality. A century ago, the Christian population in the region was around 25 percent; today, the Christian presence in Israel–Palestine is under 2 percent and falling. The future of the Palestinian church is precarious, and void of an indigenous Christian presence, the Holy Land will be reduced to an open-air museum full of shrines for foreign Christians. In the meantime, Palestinian Christians are often undermined by Christian theologies that are inimical to their well-being, are ignored by Christians who come on their tours and leave without any contact, and are bypassed by well-meaning Christians who take up their cause without listening to their counsel or realizing the impact their actions have upon the daily lives of the Christians they are trying to help. This is admittedly complicated by the fact that Palestinian Christians have differing views on how to respond to the Israeli occupation; however, Western Christians should not act on their own. Pilgrim groups should meet with local Christians, acting in solidarity with Palestinian partners.

The difficulty of holding the radical center is that biblical studies, historical theology, and contemporary politics have become inseparably intertwined and the centrifugal dynamics of the conflict deny a middle ground. The conflict often demands either/or choices that place pilgrims, often quite literally, on one side or the other. Most Holy Land experiences inevitably have a dominant narrative—one that is either sympathetic to a pro-Israeli view, undergirded by relatively modern views on the End of Times, or to a indigenous Christian perspective that highlights the plight of the Palestinians and issues of peace and justice.

Consequently, there are important choices to make in organizing or selecting a program. The first choice concerns the religious background of the primary guide. While Jewish perspectives should supplement the program and are especially important at certain sites, Christian pilgrims should generally have a Christian guide. Secondly, the program should have direct engagement with local Christians. It has been suggested by Christian partners working in the region that pilgrim groups should spend at least 20 percent of their time in relationship with indigenous Christian communities, which includes the use of guides and speakers, Sunday worship, and institutional visits. The next decision concerns the choice of accommodations in the Jerusalem area. Will you be staying in the Old City, East Jerusalem, West Jerusalem, or Bethlehem? Is it a Christian guesthouse, an Israeli-owned hotel, or a Palestinian business? There is strong correlation between the location of overnight accommodations and the narrative emphasis of the trip. Who owns the hotel, and who is benefitting from your presence in the Holy Land? Solidarity with the indigenous church includes patronizing the institutions, hotels, restaurants, and gift shops owned and operated by Palestinian Christians.

In sum, the Living Stones motivate Christians to travel to the Holy Land, and pilgrims on traditional programs often become engrossed in contemporary issues once they arrive. Listening to the stories of the Living Stones, observing the conditions of the Palestinians, and encountering physical manifestations of the conflict, like the Israel–Palestine Separation Barrier, turn a biblical journey into a gospel response to our present-day world. While Holy Land programs differ widely on how to address contemporary issues, a balanced approach engages the Palestinian church, listens to Muslim and Jewish voices, and looks at the Israeli–Palestinian conflict from multiple perspectives.

An Open Agenda

While pilgrims come for numerous reasons, many Christians find themselves in the Holy Land without a clear idea of why they are there. They are not disinterested in scripture, prayer, or contemporary issues; they are simply unable to identify a specific motive or overarching focus. While it can be disheartening to hear the impassioned goals of fellow travelers, those without an identifiable purpose are well-poised to marvel at the mysteries of the pilgrim life and to navigate the undulations of the Holy Land journey. It can be a blessing to arrive in Jerusalem without preconceived ideas, pressing expectations, or a fixed agenda, following where the journey leads and perceiving the Divine as the trip unfolds.

The agenda-less pilgrim has a broad profile. Some Christians have dreamed of Jerusalem all their lives; when they finally arrive, they are enthusiastically open to the experience ahead. Others appear by default; they have had little investment in the decision and have given limited thought to the journey. Some are accompanying family members or have been persuaded by fellow parishioners to join a church trip. Pilgrims who just months before never imagined being in the Holy Land arrive with a feeling of surprise and disbelief. The agenda-less traveler may also apply to returning pilgrims who are ready for a new adventure.

I had an open agenda when I walked the French Road of the Camino de Santiago. The first time I heard of the Camino was during an undergraduate course when my professor delivered a lecture dressed in the mantle of a Santiago pilgrim. A decade later, the Camino was meant to be a primary experience on my around-the-world journey. My itinerary, however, took me to Spain in late November, and I was ill-prepared for a cold-weather walk. During a day in Burgos, a city approximately 275 miles from Santiago, I caught my first glimpse of the yellow arrows and scallop shells that mark the Camino, and I was euphoric to be standing on the ancient pilgrim pathway. With mixed emotions of excitement and regret, I took the train to Santiago, spent a weekend exploring the city, and left determined to return by foot in the near future.

When I walked the Camino two years later, I was greatly anticipant of what lay ahead, but I did not have any particular expectations. I was spiritually prepared to absorb the experience, to consume its lessons, and to accept whatever transpired. There were no pressing questions of personal discernment. I was simply called to experience the blessings of pilgrimage. It was a profound journey, marked by reading psalms, offering intercessory prayers, and journaling. The walk was full of sunny pathways and pilgrim companionship; it also had its share of blisters and loneliness. There were no life-changing moments; yet, I returned home spiritually renewed with newfound insights into the Christian life and grateful for special memories shared with others. The same holds true for Jerusalem: it can be a blessing to arrive in the Holy Land shorn of goals and expectations yet open to the stirrings of the Spirit.

Two points are worth noting with respect to the agenda-less pilgrim. First of all, pilgrims who begin their trip with no expectations can incur the same pressure to make spiritual connections as the journey proceeds. The agenda-less pilgrim must still manage distractions and false expectations. Secondly, there is a fine line between engaging experiences without an agenda and being spiritually unprepared.

The Reluctant Pilgrim

Politics, safety concerns, and the dynamics of international group travel feed the ambivalence of Christian travelers, who, as reluctant pilgrims, enter the Holy Land on a daily basis. They may be convinced of the merits of the journey, but they are far from eager. My relationship with the Holy Land began as a reluctant pilgrim. When I received the calling to go on an around-the-world pilgrimage, I began drafting itineraries of my journey. I had a missionary friend in Costa Rica. I would spend a week respectively at the Iona Community in Scotland, Taizé in France, and the World Council of Churches graduate school in Switzerland. I wanted to see Santiago and spend time at a Methodist children's home near Naples. I planned to visit churches in Kenya and Africa University in Zimbabwe. I began securing Christian connections in Australia, New Zealand, Fiji, Korea, and Japan. While I took the planning very seriously, none on my initial itineraries included the Holy Land! I simply wasn't interested. I discussed my program with others, asking for their ideas and suggestions. Finally, a Baptist minister took me aside and told me that I had to go to the Holy Land. Having been there over a dozen times, he could not imagine that I would make an around-the-world Christian pilgrimage without visiting Jerusalem. He had a point. I reluctantly began looking for tours, and he once again dismissed my plans, telling me that I needed to go there on my own. In the end, I made a ten-day visit to Jerusalem, entering the Holy Land as a reluctant pilgrim.

I offer three insights for reluctant pilgrims. First of all, you are not alone. The reluctant pilgrim is a common phenomenon. Secondly, persevering through hesitations, ambivalence, and anxieties bears spiritual fruit; the reluctant pilgrim finds strength for the journey. Third, hesitations generally dissipate as pilgrims become familiar with their surroundings. As reluctant pilgrims become immersed in the Holy Land experience, they embrace the blessings of pilgrimage alongside their fellow travelers.

Staying Home

Holy Land travel is a privileged experience, and only a minority of Christians have ever entered the gates of Jerusalem. A countless number of global

Christians long to see the Holy Land, but lack the means or documents to get there. Many Western Christians cannot go, are disinterested in doing so, or have decided to stay away. Health reasons, family obligations, financial restrictions, and time restraints, along with politics and issues of safety, real or perceived, keep people at home. For some, the Holy Land has never captured their imagination. Others prefer the ideal of the Holy Land to its actuality. Gregory of Nyssa (335–94) affirms that "the grace of the Holy Spirit is not more abundant in Jerusalem than elsewhere," and many Christians find little reason to embark upon a distant journey in search for God when Christ is already present in their everyday lives.[13] The argument underscores the overall objective of pilgrimage. Whether at home or in the Holy Land, the principal motive of the pilgrim life is the union of God, self, and the Other.

13. Gregory of Nyssa, *On Pilgrimages*, 8–10.

6

A History of the Christian Holy Land

How did we get from the Bible to today's Holy Land? The Christian
Holy Land was developed in the Byzantine period (325–636), thanks
to local tradition, imperial patronage, burgeoning scholarship, monastic
support, pilgrim interest, and a reassessment of New Testament attitudes
towards holy places. It includes periods of stability and destruction under
non-Christian rulers, the Crusader rebuttressing of the commemorative
landscape, and the relative decline of the Christian sites in the centuries
leading up to the "rediscovery" of the Holy Land in the nineteenth century, which was characterized by the rise of biblical archaeology, the advent
of Protestant pilgrims, and the building of modern shrines. Focusing on
events that pertain to the holy places, the chapter presents a brief history of
the Christian Holy Land.

The New Testament Church

The New Testament rebuffs the idea that God resides in temples.[1] Paul tells
the Athenians that "the God who made the world and everything in it . . .
does not live in shrines made by human hands" (Acts 17:24). The idea of a
central temple, which was common to both Jews and Samaritans, is rejected
by Jesus in his conversation with the Samaritan woman:

> The hour is coming when you will worship the Father neither
> on this mountain [Mount Gerizim] nor in Jerusalem. . . . But the
> hour is coming, and is now here, when the true worshipers will
> worship the Father in spirit and truth. (John 4:21–23)

---

1. Ambivalence towards temples is also expressed in the Old Testament. See 1 Kgs
8:27–29.

The New Testament questioned holy places, defined Jerusalem as a spiritual concept, and proclaimed Christ as the temple's replacement. There was a shift in focus away from God being encountered in specific places to one in which God is encountered in Christ and in the gathered community.

Place names became metaphors of the Christian life. Paul tells the Galatians that "the Jerusalem above; she is free, and she is our mother" (Gal 4:26), while Hebrews bids the reader to "come to Mount Zion and to the city of the living God, the heavenly Jerusalem" (Heb 12:22). Jerusalem was no longer merely an earthly place in Judea; it was a spiritual realm, a heavenly city, a place not made by human hands (Mark 14:58; Heb 9:24). The imagery is most fully developed in Revelation 21, which depicts New Jerusalem as a place of divine presence, as God's home among mortals. The city, with streets of gold and pearly gates, is a place of eternal joy: death, crying, and pain are unknown. New Jerusalem is a templeless city. Christ stands in its stead as the great high priest whose sacrificial act made temple practice obsolete, once and for all (Heb 9:12, 26; 10:10).

While moving away from a physical emphasis on the temple, Christians continued to utilize its imagery, including its association as the house of God. Since Christ was the new temple, filled with God, and the Spirit inhabited people rather than place, the individual Christian was also a temple: "do you not know that you are God's temple and that God's Spirit dwells in you?" (1 Cor 3:16). The Jesus movement came to see itself as primarily a table religion rather than a temple religion, one more interested in the holiness of people than in the sanctity of place. The church was the body of Christ, embodied in the breaking of bread.

The Late Roman Period

The Late Roman period (70–325) covers the three centuries between the New Testament and the official Christianization of the Holy Land in the Byzantine era. The importance of the period lies in Christianity's nascent growth as an illicit movement, in the writing and dissemination of the Gospels, and in the extent to which the local church preserved knowledge of places associated with the life of Christ. It is less certain, however, which traditions go back to the New Testament period and which ones were established in the intervening years. In other words, to what degree are the Gospels' locational details derived from local traditions, and, conversely, to what extent did the Gospels incite Christians to locate events mentioned in the texts? The issue is complicated by the topographical discrepancies that occur between the Gospels, which relates to the

Evangelists' respective familiarity with first-century Palestine. John, for instance, knows the region better than Luke.

Aelia Capitolina

After the destruction of the temple in 70, the most significant event of the Late Roman period was Hadrian's refounding of Jerusalem as the Roman city, Aelia Capitolina, a combination of Hadrian's family name (Aelia) and the Capitoline Hill in Rome, which was associated with the Roman god Jupiter. While the relationship between the Bar Kokhba Revolt, or the Second Jewish Revolt (132–35), and the founding of Aelia Capitolina is a bit confused—whether cause or consequence—once the dust had settled, Jerusalem was a Roman city forbidden to Jews. Eusebius provides a list of Jerusalem bishops from James, the brother of Jesus, to Macarius, who attended the Council of Nicea in 325, which, barring two brief interruptions due to the destruction of the temple and the Bar Kokhba Revolt, attests to a continuous Christian presence in Jerusalem throughout the period.[2] The bishops prior to the revolt were Jewish, while those afterwards were Greek. Even if the list is somewhat contrived, by the end of the revolt, if not before, Christianity was primarily a non-Jewish movement.

Our main interest in Aelia Capitolina is topographical. The street grid of the Roman city is still evident today. Leading south from the Damascus Gate, two Roman arteries form the primary north-south pathways of the Old City. Aelia had a wide, colonnaded main street, or cardo maximus (today's Souk Khan el-Zeit), that ran along the Western Hill. To the east, a secondary cardo followed the Tyropoeon Valley (Al-Wad Street). Aelia had an eastern and a western forum, each with a monumental, free-standing gate. The remains of the eastern forum, previously thought to be Pilate's pavement (John 19:13), can be seen at Ecce Homo. The western forum was located in the present-day Muristan, immediately south of the Holy Sepulchre. A temple dedicated to Venus commanded the western forum, while a temple to Jupiter was placed on the Temple Mount.

Sources and Traditions

One of the oddities of the Holy Land is the absence of verifiable Christian archaeology prior to the fourth century. The Holy Land is full of archaeology from the time of Jesus, including remnants of the Temple Mount, and Jesus saw structures, walls, pools, and tombs that are still visible today. The

2. Eusebius, *Church History*, 4.5, 5.12.

Holy Land has substantial archaeology from the Late Roman period. What we do not have is material from the Late Roman period that is verifiably Christian. Archaeology seldom reveals the ethnicity or group identity of its users and occupants, and to identify archaeology as Christian, we need to find identifiable symbolism, Christian-specific objects, or clear evidence that a space was used for Christian ritual. The house of Peter at Capernaum presents the strongest case. While the textual sources provide glimpses of the Jerusalem church, the material evidence, if there is any, remains buried, undetected, or debated.

Written sources inform us that Late Roman Christians were interested in place and scripture. As mentioned in the previous chapter, Alexander of Cappadocia (d. 251) went to Jerusalem for "the investigation of the sites," while Origen (d. 254) traveled to Palestine "in search of the traces of Jesus."[3] A second-century text by Melito of Sardis (d. 180) places Jesus' crucifixion "in the middle of Jerusalem," an odd statement given the fact that it was known to have taken place outside the city (Heb 13:12).[4] The comment suggests that Christians thought Calvary was located in the area of Jerusalem that Agrippa I (d. 44) incorporated approximately a decade after Jesus' death. Eusebius' allusion to three mystic caves—Christ's tomb, the Nativity grotto in Bethlehem, and a site on the Mount of Olives where Jesus gave the Apocalyptic Discourse (Matt 24; Mark 13; Luke 21)—seems to refer to pre-Constantinian traditions of the Jerusalem church.[5]

One of the arguments for a pre-Constantinian core of holy sites is that the Romans tried to eliminate them by imposing pagan practices. Two second-century sources, *The Protoevangelium of James* and a text by Justin Martyr, refer to the site of Jesus' birth as a cave, an extra-biblical detail that accurately describes the Bethlehem site, suggesting that the location of Jesus' birth had already been established.[6] A century later, Origen states that "for the heathens, too, [Bethlehem] is a well known matter."[7] The pagan presence is most fully described by Jerome, who, writing several decades into the Byzantine period, claims that "Bethlehem, which now is ours, was overshadowed by the grove of Tammuz, that is, Adonis, and in the cave where once the infant Jesus whimpered, people bewailed the lover of Venus."[8]

3. Eusebius, *Church History*, 6.11.2; Origen, *Commentary on John*, 6.40.40. See Hunt, *Holy Land Pilgrimage*, 4, 92.

4. Melito of Sardis, *Paschal Homily*, 71–72, 93–94. See Hunt, *Holy Land Pilgrimage*, 4.

5. Eusebius, *In Praise of Constantine*, 9.16–17.

6. *The Protoevangelium*, 19–20; Justin Martyr, *Dialogue with Trypho*, 78.

7. Origen, *Contra Celsum*, 1.51.

8. Jerome, *Letter*, 58.3. Also see Paulinus of Nola, *Letter* 31.3.

The Roman Temple on Calvary

The argument of Roman suppression is fundamental to the credibility of the Holy Sepulchre, which is situated on the site of the former Venus temple. Fourth-century Christians, including Eusebius, believed that Hadrian had intentionally placed the temple over the tomb of Christ. By doing so, he preserved its location in the collective memory of the Jerusalem church, which allowed it to be rediscovered by Constantinian excavators in the fourth century. In other words, to link the fourth-century Holy Sepulchre with the New Testament site, the Jerusalem church had to remember the location of the tomb from the death of Jesus (c. 30) until the 130s. The area, which was an abandoned quarry, appears to have been publicly accessible, and Christians presumably went there to venerate the tomb. Once it was covered by the temple, the church preserved knowledge of the tomb's location for nearly two hundred years, or from c. 135–325. In short, the authenticity of the Holy Sepulchre depends upon Roman suppression and the continuity of Christian memory. The fact that the site contains first-century tombs and was outside the city at the time of Jesus enhances its credibility.[9]

A counterargument can also be made: Christians snuffed out the pagan sites, and the textual evidence is simply a Christian attempt to justify this. In other words, the location of the Holy Sepulchre was simply determined by the Roman temple. Reason suggests otherwise. The Constantinian workers went to tremendous efforts to eradicate a temple that could easily have been re-consecrated as a church. The massive Constantinian project requires a more compelling explanation—namely, fourth-century Christians really believed the site was the tomb of Christ.

The Byzantine Period

The Byzantine period (325–636) is the continuation of Roman rule centered in the East as a Christian empire and takes its name from Constantine's relocation of his capital from Rome to Byzantium, which he renamed Constantinople, now present-day Istanbul. Constantine took control of the western half of the empire in 312, issuing the Edict of Milan in 313, which removed legal restrictions to Christianity. Religious tolerance was realized in the East when Constantine assumed full reign of the empire in 324. The nature of Constantine's faith is disputed—he famously adopted Christian insignia

---

9. An abandoned quarry near the city walls would have been a suitable setting for public executions. John 19:42 states that the tomb was near the place where Jesus was crucified.

prior to the battle of the Milvian Bridge in 312 but was only baptized on his deathbed in 337—and Christianity did not become the official religion of the empire until 381, under Theodosius (347–95). These qualifiers are largely inconsequential to the Holy Land as Constantine Christianized Jerusalem, and—except for a short-lived effort by Julian the Apostate (331–63) to rebuild the Jewish temple—the development of the Christian Holy Land went unfettered for three centuries.

Helena and Constantine

Constantine and his mother, Helena (244–330), are indelibly associated with the Holy Land in both fact and fiction. Eusebius credits Constantine with four churches, one built on each of the three mystic caves—the Holy Sepulchre, the Church of the Nativity, and the Eleona—and one at Mamre near Hebron (Gen 18), a site brought to Constantine's attention by his mother-in-law, Eutropia, due to its pagan activities.[10] A fourth-century source states that Constantine gave permission to a certain Joseph of Tiberias to develop churches in the Galilee.[11] While Constantine likely commissioned more churches than the four mentioned by Eusebius, the Constantinian project is best understood as the treble footprint of Jerusalem, Bethlehem, and the Mount of Olives. Constantine initiated the tradition of imperial patronage of the Holy Land that has included the Byzantine figures of Justinian, Heraclius, and Constantine IX Monomachos, Western characters from Charlemagne to the Crusader kings, and modern leaders, such as Kaiser Wilhelm II and Mussolini.

Helena is the legendary darling of the Holy Land, which she visited in 326, linking local traditions with imperial possibilities. Although a number of churches and monasteries claim a dubious link to the empress, Eusebius associates her with only two sites: the Nativity church and the Eleona. His lengthy, contemporary account of the construction of the Holy Sepulchre is noteworthy in two respects. While focusing on the tomb of Christ, he makes no mention of Calvary, the cross, or the place of the crucifixion, and, secondly, he never refers to Helena. She was almost certainly involved in the Holy Sepulchre at some level; however, Eusebius associates the project exclusively with Constantine, conveying the underlying impression that the tomb of Christ—the place of Christian salvation—was the provenance of gods and emperors. The Holy Sepulchre was the pantheon of Christ and Constantine, the respective rulers of heaven and earth.

---

10. Eusebius, *Life of Constantine*, 3.51–53.

11. Epiphanius of Salamis, *Panarion*, 30.

Helena's legendary claim to the complex is her purported role in discovering the crucifixion crosses during the excavation of the Roman temple and her subsequent identification of the True Cross through a miraculous healing. Fourth-century sources refer to a relic of the Holy Cross, and noting the pilgrim practice of taking pieces as holy souvenirs, Cyril of Jerusalem (c. 313–86) remarks that "the whole earth is full of the relics of the Cross of Christ."[12] The earliest extant source that links Helena with the Holy Cross, however, is the funeral eulogy of Theodosius delivered by Ambrose of Milan in 395.[13] While Helena's association with the relic appears to be a later fourth-century development, the legend became a central fact of Holy Land pilgrimage.

A heroine in both life and legend, Helena was the first of a number of influential women who patronized the Holy Land in the Byzantine and Crusader periods. Others include Poimenia, the patroness of the Church of the Ascension, which was built before 392, the wealthy ascetics, Paula (d. 404) and Melania the Elder (d. 410), who respectively founded monasteries in Bethlehem and on the Mount of Olives, and the Empress Eudocia (d. 460), who rebuilt the city walls. Queen Melisende (d. 1161) is a key figure of the Crusader period.

The Holy Sepulchre

Based upon the belief that the temple of Venus had been built upon the tomb of Christ, the complex was excavated down to bedrock. Eusebius depicts the rediscovery of the tomb as nothing less than its own resurrection: "the venerable and most holy testimony (*martyrion*) of the Savior's resurrection (*anastasis*), beyond all our hopes, came into view; the holy of holies, the Cave, was, like our Savior, restored to life by its very existence, bearing clearer testimony to the resurrection of the Savior than any words."[14] Barring no expense, Constantine, who may have discussed potential ideas for developing the holy sites with Marcarius, the bishop of Jerusalem, at the Council of Nicea in 325, sent detailed instructions to the ecclesial leader for a complex of holy buildings that stretched from the tomb eastwards to the city's cardo maximus.[15]

---

12. Cyril of Jerusalem, *Catechesis*, 4.10, 10.19. See the colorful description of the True Cross in Egeria, *Egeria's Travels*, 37.1–3.

13. See Liebeschuetz, *Ambrose of Milan*, 174–203.

14. Eusebius, *The Life of Constantine*, 3.28.

15. Eusebius, *The Life of Constantine*, 3.25–40.

Contained within an abandoned quarry, the first-century site appears to have been an east-facing tomb that had been carved into a western-rising rock face. The Constantinian builders leveled the rock within a twenty meter radius of the tomb until all that remained was a rock shell that preserved the interior space of the burial chamber. The tomb's exterior was covered in marble and embellished with gold and silver, forming a little house, or aedicule. From west to east, the main features of the complex were: (1) a round domed building, approximately forty meters in diameter, known as the Anastasis (the Resurrection), or the Rotunda, that housed the tomb of Christ, (2) an inner courtyard, and (3) a large double-aisled basilica, known as the Martyrium, or the basilica of Constantine, which was oriented towards the west facing the tomb.[16] The place of the crucifixion, or the rock of Calvary, was associated with a fifteen-foot column of poor, unquarried rock and was accessed from the western end of the basilica's southern aisles. It could also be seen in the southeastern corner of the inner courtyard. East of the basilica, an outer courtyard and a monumental front entrance connected the complex to the cardo. Therefore, pilgrims entered the site from the east and encountered Calvary before reaching the tomb. The Constantinian complex, a veritable New Jerusalem, was dedicated on September 13, 335. Despite earthquakes, fires, riots, and looting, the complex remained essentially intact until its systematic destruction in 1009, which lead to partial restorations in the eleventh and twelfth centuries. To understand the present-day site, pilgrims should familiarize themselves with its original Constantinian layout.[17]

The Temple Mount

The image of New Jerusalem is important for understanding Byzantine attitudes towards the Temple Mount, an area of approximately thirty-six acres, which was left in ruins and never developed. As negative theological space that the Byzantines intentionally neglected, the temple ruins were a visible witness to the fulfillment of Jesus' prophecy. The temple had not only been destroyed, it had been replaced—by Christ, by the Christian believer, and

16. Some groups, preferring to emphasize Christ's resurrection over the image of an empty tomb, refer to the Holy Sepulchre as the Church of the Resurrection. Historically, the name, Anastasis (Resurrection), applied only to the Rotunda and not to the entire complex.

17. For a floor plan of the Holy Sepulchre prior to its destruction in 1009, see Gibson's plan in Aist, "The Monument," 48, a modified version of its original publication in Gibson and Taylor, *Beneath the Church*, 75, fig. 45. The northern wall of the complex has been removed.

now by the Holy Sepulchre. New Jerusalem had, in effect, descended from heaven. Byzantine Jerusalem was a templeless city centered upon the tomb-cum-throne of Christ (Rev 21:2, 10), and a later tradition claiming that the Holy Sepulchre did not cast a shadow on the summer solstice reflects the Revelator's reference to the city's perpetual light (Rev 21:22–24).[18] The Byzantine neglect of the Temple Mount was predicated on the prophesies of Jesus and the image of New Jerusalem.

To See and Touch

Notwithstanding a small core of sites associated with Jesus' life, as long as Christianity was an illicit movement within the Roman Empire defining itself against Judaism, it rejected the idea of sacred places, especially temples. Once the church received imperial backing, its attitudes towards place significantly changed. New Testament reticence gave way to a newfound affection for the settings of Christ. By the mid-fourth century, Cyril of Jerusalem could remind his catechumens that "others merely hear, we see and touch," while, a few decades later, Paulinus of Nola notes that "no other sentiment draws people to Jerusalem than the desire to see and touch the places where Christ was physically present, and to be able to say from their very own experience, 'We have gone into his tabernacle, and have worshipped in the places where his feet have stood.'"[19] Sentiments foreign to the New Testament writers, they reflect Christian desire to physically engage the places of Christ.

The Holy Land experienced three hundred years of continuous Christian development. As pilgrimage grew, so did the holy places, with sites, like the Nativity church in Bethlehem and the Lazarus church in Bethany, undergoing a second Byzantine expansion to facilitate the increasing demand of pilgrims. Christian enthusiasm for the holy places was not without its detractors. Gregory of Nyssa cautioned that "the grace of the Holy Spirit is not more abundant in Jerusalem than elsewhere," while Jerome affirmed that "access to the court of heaven is as easy from Britain as it is from Jerusalem."[20] There was nothing meritorious about walking in the footsteps of Jesus: "what is commendable is not to have been in Jerusalem but to have lived well in Jerusalem."[21] Despite Gregory's emphasis on the

---

18. See Adomnán, *On the Holy Places*, 1.11 and Nikulás of þverá, *Extract*, 80–87. Also see Aist, "The Monument," 42–47 and *The Christian Topography*, 89–90.

19. Cyril of Jerusalem, *Catechesis*, 13.22; Paulinus of Nola, *Letter*, 49.14.

20. Gregory of Nyssa, *On Pilgrimages*, 8–10; Jerome, *Letter*, 58.3.

21. Jerome, *Letter*, 58.2.

Holy Spirit and Jerome's appeal to the moral life, Christian interest in the holy sites continued to grow.

Palestinian Monasticism

Palestinian monks, largely of foreign origins, played a vital role as custodians of the holy sites, offering hospitality and serving as pilgrim guides. Although Christian monasticism began slightly earlier in Egypt, Palestinian monasticism was not far behind. It has its own history, saints, and sources and was renowned for its lauras, or monastic communities that combined the eremitical experience of living as a hermit with weekly communal gatherings for worship and meals.[22]

The Stational Liturgy

Holy Land pilgrims participated in the stational liturgy of the Jerusalem church, a unique liturgical system that utilized churches throughout the city. Known from ancient lectionaries and pilgrim texts, the daily, weekly, and annual services not only had assigned readings, they also had an assigned station, or church, where the worship took place. Moving from church to church through the streets of the Holy City, Jerusalem worship was public and processional.[23]

The Byzantine Sources

Our knowledge of the Byzantine holy sites comes from numerous sources. Scholars, namely, Eusebius and Jerome, compiled comprehensive gazetteers, or geographical dictionaries, on biblical place names, and information on the holy sites appears in church histories, sermons, lectionaries, letters, and biblical commentaries.[24] We also have a collection pilgrim texts, which either focus on an individual pilgrim or were written as short, impersonal guides. The texts describe the holy sites, refer to pilgrim practices, provide

22. The sixth-century *Lives of the Palestinian Monks* by Cyril of Scythopolis is the principal source. See Price, *Cyril of Scythopolis* and Chitty, *The Desert a City*. A number of monastic sites, such as Mar Saba, St. George in Choziba, St. Gerasimos, and the Holy Cross, are well worth a visit.

23. On the stational liturgy of Jerusalem, see Baldovin, *Liturgy in Ancient Jerusalem* and Smith, *To Take Place*. Also see the *Armenian Lectionary* in Wilkinson, *Egeria's Travels*, 181–92.

24. See Freeman-Grenville, *Palestine in the Fourth Century*. For a list of sources, see Wilkinson, *Jerusalem Pilgrims*, 395–406.

information on routes and pathways, and include the odd anecdote. The Bordeaux Pilgrim, who visited Jerusalem in 333, is our earliest source. The best-known account comes from Egeria, presumably from Spain, who traveled to the Holy Land in the 380s. The sixth-century report of the Piacenza Pilgrim (c. 570) is the most colorful text of the period.

The material remains of the Byzantine Holy Land are rather extensive, including continuous-use buildings, like the Church of the Nativity and portions of Mary's tomb and the Holy Sepulchre, archaeological sites of ecclesial ruins, such as Mamre and Kursi, and archaeological layers underlying many of the modern shrines. Artifacts, such as the Monza ampullae, reflect the material culture of pilgrimage, while mosaics, like the fish and loaves at Tabgha (the Church of the Multiplication) and the Armenian Bird Mosaic, 350 meters north of the Damascus Gate, represent the religious art of Byzantine Christians. Pilgrims should familiarize themselves with the Madaba Map (c. 600), a large floor mosaic of the Holy Land that was discovered in 1884 in the Jordanian village of Madaba. Its medallion of Jerusalem, containing walls, buildings, churches, and streets, is almost fully preserved. The Holy Sepulchre assumes the center of Jerusalem, which is placed at the precise center of the map. The Temple Mount is conspicuously absent. Combining biblical imagery, commemorative topography, and contemporary features, the map depicts the Holy Land at the zenith of its Christian development, offering an extraordinary window into the religious imagination of the Byzantine world.

The Early Islamic Period

Following the Persian Conquest of 614, which resulted in the sack of churches and the theft of the True Cross, the Jerusalem sites were mostly repaired, except for the Church of Holy Wisdom commemorating Jesus' trial before Pilate, which was permanently abandoned. A brief period of Byzantine restoration was marked by Heraclius' return of the True Cross in 629. However, Byzantine strength was spent in the region, and when the Arab armies appeared a few years later, the city was peacefully handed over to the caliph, Umar (584–644). While Sophronius, the Christian patriarch of Jerusalem, was showing the caliph around the Holy Sepulchre, Umar refused to pray at the appointed time, stating that if he did so his followers would turn the church into a mosque, an act that remains a standard for Muslim–Christian relations.[25]

25. Prior to 1009, there was a tradition of Muslim prayer in the outer front atrium of the Holy Sepulchre. The Umar (Omar) mosque, opposite the southern courtyard of the Holy Sepulchre, was built in 1193 after the church's entrance was moved to the south.

Instead, the Muslims developed the Temple Mount, renaming it the Haram esh-Sharif, or the Noble Sanctuary. The Dome of the Rock was built in 691, and the Al-Aqsa Mosque, the common name for the large prayer hall on the southern end of the esplanade, followed in 705. It is important to note, however, that when Muslims speak of Al-Aqsa, recognized as the third holiest place in Islam, they are not referring to a particular building but to the entire area of the Haram esh-Sharif, which, as an open mosque, includes both structures.

Throughout most of the Early Islamic period (636–1099), Christian pilgrimage was largely unchanged from late Byzantine patterns. As we know from pilgrims, such as Arculf (680s) and Willibald (720s), the commemorative fabric of the Holy Sepulchre remained the same, pilgrims followed the same pathways through the city, and places, like Jesus' baptism site on the Jordan River and the Ascension church on the Mount of Olives, profoundly captured their imagination. Despite the relatively benign co-existence of Muslims and Christians in the first few centuries of the Early Islamic period, the situation increasingly deteriorated, culminating in the destruction of the Holy Sepulchre in 1009 upon the orders of the Fatimid caliph, al-Hakim (985–1021). According to the chronicler Yahia, "only those things that were too difficult to demolish were spared."[26] The Holy Sepulchre was modestly restored in 1042 by the Byzantine Emperor Constantine IX Monomachos (d. 1055).

Why did al-Hakim target the Holy Sepulchre while leaving other sites alone? More specifically, how did the Nativity church in Bethlehem, one of the oldest churches of continuous use in the world, avoid being damaged by either the Persians or the Arabs? According to an argument put forth in favor of church images at the Jerusalem Synod of 836, the Persian invaders saw a mosaic on the Bethlehem church depicting the magi in Persian clothing and, subsequently, spared the building.

Why has the Bethlehem church withstood centuries of Muslim rule? Jesus is a venerated prophet in Islam, and his birth as well as his miraculous deeds are recognized by Muslims. They do not believe that Jesus was crucified and, therefore, reject his resurrection. They contend that someone else was crucified in his place and that Jesus ascended to heaven as a living person. Muslims have an affinity, though, for the Nativity church, including using its southern apse as a place of prayer.[27]

---

26. Quoted in Ousterhout, "Rebuilding the Temple," 69.
27. See Hawari et al., *Pilgrimage*, vii.1.b.

The Crusader Period

The Crusader period (1099–1187) is the second important phase in the development of the Christian Holy Land. While its legacy still reverberates throughout the region, in terms of the holy places, the Crusaders were interested in preserving recognized locations, albeit at the expense of other Christians. The Crusaders rebuilt the Byzantine sites; yet, here and there, where traditions were weak or unknown, the Crusaders established new ones and revised the narratives of existing places. The Crusaders refurbished holy places from Abraham's tomb in Hebron to their uncompleted project at the Annunciation church in Nazareth, leaving the Holy Land with a substantial material legacy. The Church of St. Anne in Jerusalem and the Emmaus church at Abu Ghosh are well-preserved Crusader churches, while Crusader art includes the frescoed mounting stone at Bethphage and the mosaic of Christ in Ascension on the ceiling of the Franciscan Chapel of Calvary. Crusader-era discontinuities include relocating Emmaus from Nicopolis to Abu Ghosh, shifting the pool of Bethesda, which had deteriorated due to siltation, to the nearby pool of Israel, and changing the commemoration of the Eleona from Jesus' Apocalyptic Discourse to the Lord's Prayer. Although the Crusaders brought new styles of architecture and changed the face of a number of holy sites, by rebuilding on location and recalibrating Christian memory of place and story, they were, for the most part, agents of commemorative continuity.

The Crusaders focused much of their attention on restoring the Holy Sepulchre. While the Rotunda retained its Constantinian footprint, the inner courtyard was roofed for the first time, becoming a central worship space and accounting for the building's second dome. A round ambulatory was built on the eastern end of the former courtyard further enclosing the space. The basilica was not rebuilt, but the space below it was excavated and turned into a crypt. The complex was now entered from the south, and the rock of Calvary was approached from the west instead of the east. The restored complex, which is essentially what we see today, was re-consecrated on July 15, 1149, the fiftieth anniversary of the Crusader conquest of Jerusalem.

Unlike their Byzantine counterparts, who left the Temple Mount in ruins, the Crusaders, captured by the mystique of King Solomon, occupied the space, referring to the Dome of the Rock as the Temple of the Lord and the Al-Aqsa Mosque as the Temple of Solomon. The Dome of the Rock was used as a church, while the latter functioned as a royal palace before being given to the Knights Templar, whose name derives from their use of the site. The vaulted areas under the southeast corner of the Temple

Mount, now the El-Marwani Mosque, were used to quarter horses and were named Solomon's Stables.

Crusader use of the temple precincts illustrates how Christian attitudes towards biblical places have shifted over time. Transcending temple worship, early Christians turned Jerusalem place names into metaphors of the Christian life. The Byzantines envisioned Constantine's Holy Sepulchre as New Jerusalem, while treating the temple ruins as negative theological space. The Crusaders had a foot in both places. They championed the tomb of Christ and used the Holy Sepulchre as a place for royal burials. While indulging legends of a Solomonic past, they appropriated Islamic buildings and Jewish foundations on the Temple Mount.

The Post-Crusader Period

In the aftermath of the Crusades, Muslim hegemony—namely, the Ayyubid (1187–1250), Mamluk (1250–1517), and Ottoman (1517–1917) dynasties— was reestablished over the Holy Land, ending only with World War I (1914– 18) and the British Mandate (1920–48). The Ayyubids were bolstered by the legendary Saladin, who retook Jerusalem from the Crusaders in 1187, though the city exchanged hands until 1244. Mamluk architecture is one of the jewels of Jerusalem, while the Ottomans, who rebuilt the walls of Jerusalem in the 1530s, ruled through a fascinating nineteenth century that witnessed the influx of Jewish and Christian interests. The first Jewish neighborhoods outside the Old City were started in 1860, while the return of Jews to Israel began in earnest with the First Jewish Aliyah (1882–1903).

With respect to the holy sites, today's pilgrim encounters relatively few contact points between the end of the Crusades and the rediscovery of the Holy Land in the 1800s. In the immediate aftermath of the Crusades, the tomb of Lazarus and the place of the ascension became Muslim possessions, and the keys of the Holy Sepulchre were entrusted to two Muslim families whose descendents still open and close the building each day. Through negotiations with various Muslim rulers, the Franciscans emerged in the thirteenth and fourteenth centuries as the dominant Christian presence in the Holy Land and were officially declared the Catholic custodians of the Holy Places in 1342 by Pope Clement VI. They presently take care of twenty-four sites. The Cenacle of the Lord's Supper is a fourteenth-century structure, and, influenced by Christian practice in Europe, the Via Dolorosa took its present-day shape in the post-Crusader period. While pilgrimage continued, the Christian Holy Land deteriorated under Ayyubid, Mamluk, and Ottoman rule.

The Status Quo

When the Ottoman Turks took Constantinople in the fifteenth century, they made the Greek Patriarch of Constantinople the religious and civil authority for all Christians residing in the Ottoman Empire, and in 1517, when the Turks gained control of Jerusalem, the balance of power began to shift from the Franciscans to the Greeks. Following clashes between the Christian groups in 1757, the Ottomans assigned the Church of the Nativity, the tomb of Mary, and most of the Holy Sepulchre to the Greeks. Following a fire in 1808, the Greeks consolidated their position in the Holy Sepulchre, and in February 1852 and again in May 1853, the Sultan issued a decree stating that "the actual status quo will be maintained and the Jerusalem shrines, whether owned in common or exclusively by the Greek, Latin and Armenian communities, will all remain forever in their present state."[28] The provisions of the Status Quo, which apply to a number of sites, were never formally set down, and *The Status Quo in the Holy Places*, prepared by L. G. A. Cust for the British Government of Palestine in 1929, is the standard text on the subject. The British, Jordanian, and Israeli governments have subsequently recognized the Status Quo, though not without incidents, and to this day, the rules regulating the Holy Sepulchre are a mixture of Islamic sharia law and Ottoman property law. Neither church law nor common law categories apply. Under sharia law, a holy place of any religion is a waqf, an inalienable religious endowment. Groups have rights of possession but no entity owns the property. According to Ottoman property law, whoever owns the covering of a structure owns the building, and paying for repairs indicates possession. Nothing, from liturgical practice to the physical arrangement of the building, can be changed without common consent, and reaching agreements on necessary repairs is extremely complicated as witnessed by the protracted response to the 1927 earthquake.[29] The iconic image of the Status Quo is the so-called immovable ladder on the upper façade of the church that has purportedly been there since 1757.

The Holy Sepulchre is shared by six denominations. Three major communities, Greek Orthodox, Roman Catholic, and Armenian Orthodox, have rights of possession and usage, namely, liturgy, and three minor communities, Coptic, Ethiopian, and Syrian Orthodox, have the right of usage without possession (the right of possession is different from the legal concept of ownership). While some view the Holy Sepulchre as a parable of

28. Quoted in Cohen, *Saving the Holy Sepulchre*, 8.

29. See Cohen, *Saving the Holy Sepulchre*. In May 2019, an agreement was announced concerning future renovations of the Holy Sepulchre, including the tomb of Christ.

the fractured church—a place where resurrection gives way to fisticuffs—
the site boasts the presence of six Christian communities co-existing under
a common roof.[30]

The Rediscovery of the Holy Land

With the weakening of the Ottoman Empire in the nineteenth century, a
foreign Christian presence, bolstered by the support of imperial powers,
renewed its interest in the Holy Land, reoccupied old sites, and acquired
new land. The French government, for instance, received the Church of St.
Anne (the nativity of Mary) from the Ottomans in 1856 for their support
in the Crimean War. The pool of Bethesda was subsequently discovered on
the site. The rediscovery of the Christian Holy Land has witnessed the rise
of biblical archaeology, the advent of Protestant pilgrims, and the building
of modern shrines.

The Rise of Biblical Archaeology

The nineteenth century gave rise to the biblical archaeologist, who, with a
Bible in one hand and a trowel in another, began unearthing the biblical
past. The history of biblical archaeology is extremely interesting: its major
digs and important excavations, who found what and when, how techniques
and theories were tried and tested, and how we came to learn what we
know.[31] While biblical archaeology continues to make the headlines, pilgrims should be familiar with some basic critiques: (1) using archaeology to
prove the Bible runs into a number of methodological problems concerning the relationship between texts and material evidence; (2) while, on one
hand, the black market in antiquities encourages the looting of archaeological sites, the field has been vulnerable to frauds and counterfeits, and (3) the
field has been prone to politicization by the Israeli–Palestinian conflict.[32]
Nonetheless, archaeology is fundamental to the pilgrim experience. First of
all, most Holy Land churches have an archaeological element. Secondly, archaeology has identified a number of lost sites from Capernaum to the pool
of Bethesda. Third, museums and archaeological sites are essential components of Holy Land pilgrimage. From the Israel Museum to the Galilee

30. Color-coded maps of the Holy Sepulchre depicting the individual and common
areas of the six Christian communities can be found on the internet.

31. See Cline, *Biblical Archaeology*.

32. Emek Shaveh (www.alt-arch.org) is an Israeli NGO working to prevent the
politicization of archaeology in the context of the Israeli–Palestinian conflict.

Boat at Ginosar to common items, such as wine and olive presses, material culture offers unprecedented insight into the biblical past.

Protestant Pilgrims

The modern period has also given rise to Protestants pilgrims. A 2011 study by Stephanie Stidham Rogers focuses upon American middle-class Protestants who began visiting the Holy Land in the second half of the nineteenth century. Unlike Catholic and Orthodox pilgrimage, which was characterized by the egalitarian participation of lower-class laity, American Protestant pilgrimage was led by clergy and scholars who had a celebrity-like status. Feeling alienated from the shrines and rejecting the piety of other Christians, they were often disappointed in what they found. Consequently, Protestant theology focused upon land and scripture, and for the biblical archaeologist E. G. Robinson, the physical landscape of the Holy Land contained the "basic, original and undeniable truths of the Gospel"—it was the "tangible, empirical counterpart to the infallible text of the Bible."[33]

The same was true for English Anglicans, who went to the Holy Land to "vivify the Bible." Seeking places that provided "a livelier imagining of various biblical scenes," they tended to withdraw from the established holy sites. Rather than commemorating the death of Jesus in the Holy Sepulchre, a nineteenth-century Anglican pilgrim wrote: "we would rather go forth, without the walls, and seek some solitary spot, and endeavour, with the page of the New Testament before us, in silence to image forth the awful scene."[34] Dismissing the dark, interior spaces of the historical churches, Protestants felt connections with the biblical landscapes, and nature itself became the Protestant shrine.[35] A preference for outdoor settings and the lack of liturgical access to the Holy Sepulchre inevitably led Protestants to look for an alternative place to commemorate the death and resurrection of Christ, and the Garden Tomb eventually became the quintessential Protestant site.

Despite the idea that the land contained the "basic, original and undeniable truths of the Gospel," nineteenth-century Protestants did not view Palestine as a land of promise. Ottoman society was regarded as primitive and benighted, and many Protestants, citing scriptural references to Jesus'

---

33. Rogers, *Inventing the Holy Land*, 32.

34. Hummel, "The Sacramentality of the Holy Land," 79, 82–83. Also see Wynn, *Faith and Place*, 139–41.

35. See Rogers, *Inventing the Holy Land*, 136. While present-day Protestants are largely appreciative of the shrine churches, they feel overwhelmed by the sheer number of them. Like their nineteenth-century predecessors, they generally prefer outdoor spaces.

death, viewed Palestine as a cursed land, an attitude that alienated them from local Christians. Protestants considered Arab society to be frozen in time with an uninterrupted link with the biblical past, and art and photography depicted the local population as biblical characters. The point still applies: how do we view the Living Stones today? Do we see Christ in the faces of the Israelis and Palestinians, or do we view them as caricatures of a biblical past?

The Recognized Churches of Jerusalem

The nineteenth-century imperial interests of Britain and Germany secured an official Protestant presence in Jerusalem, and today there are thirteen recognized churches in the Holy Land: six Catholic (Roman, Greek, Maronite, Syrian, Armenian, and Chaldean), five Orthodox and Oriental Orthodox (Greek, Armenian, Syrian, Coptic, and Ethiopian), and two Protestant denominations (Lutheran and Anglican).

The Modern Shrines

Since the rediscovery of the Holy Land, numerous modern churches, each individually unique, have been built upon the ancient sites, integrating the ruins and floor plans of their Byzantine and Crusader counterparts. Of note is the work of the Italian Franciscan Antonio Barluzzi (1884–1960), the so-called Architect of the Holy Land, who designed a significant number of the modern shrines. His legacy leaves an indelible impression upon the pilgrim imagination. His work includes:

- the Church of All Nations at Gethsemane (1924),
- the Church of the Transfiguration on Mount Tabor (1924),
- the Chapel of the Flagellation on the Via Dolorosa (1929),
- the Church of the Beatitudes overlooking the Sea of Galilee (1938),
- the Church of Lazarus in Bethany (1953),
- the Chapel of the Angels at the Shepherds' Field (1954),
- the Church of Dominus Flevit (where the Lord wept) on the Mount of Olives (1954), and
- the Church of the Visitation in Ein Kerem (1955).

Barluzzi also restored the Franciscan Chapel of Calvary (1937), the St. Jerome Cloister in Bethlehem (1947), and the church at Bethphage

(1955). His distinguished career ended on a sour note, however, as he was denied the commission for the Church of the Annunciation in Nazareth, despite having previously been awarded the project. The commission was given instead to Giovanni Muzio, a Milanese architect. The Annunciation church, the largest in the Middle East, was built throughout the 1960s and consecrated in 1969.

Modern shrines built by non-Franciscan groups include:

- the German Benedictine Dormition Abbey on Mount Sion (1900),

- the French Dominican Church of St. Stephen (1900),

- the French Carmelite Sanctuary of the Eleona (1920s, unfinished),

- the French Assumptionist Fathers Church of St. Peter in Gallicantu (1931), and

- the German Benedictine Church of the Multiplication at Tabgha (1985).

The Franciscan Church of St. Peter at Capernaum (1990) and the Greek Orthodox Church of Jacob's Well in Nablus (2007) are among the more recent editions. Other Orthodox churches include Cana (1886), Mount Tabor (1911), and Capernaum (1931). Along with recently opened parks, museums, and pilgrim centers, the modern shrines remind us that much of the Holy Land experience is a relatively new and evolving phenomenon.

The Holy Land Today

The Christian presence in Jerusalem is more global than ever with an increasing number of pilgrims coming from Africa, Asia, and South America, including countries with a Christian minority, such as Sri Lanka and Malaysia. North Americans wait in line at the tomb of Christ alongside Brazilians, Ukrainians, and Koreans. A national lottery supports a steady flow of Nigerian pilgrims. Ethiopian Christians fill the streets at Easter, and overseas foreign workers, particularly Filipinos, are visibly present at the annual Palm Sunday procession. Despite being an unfulfilled dream for many Christians, Jerusalem is the center of global Christianity, the gathering point for the nations of the world (Ezek 5:5).

While Holy Land pilgrimage is more diverse than ever, the actual number of Christian travelers ebbs and flows as the Palestinian–Israeli conflict, which shows no signs of abating, cautions people away. As the future of Palestinian Christianity weighs in the balance, there is growing concern that the Christian Holy Land will become an open-air museum void of Living

Stones, while, in recent years, the Christian presence in the Holy Land has suffered harassment, arson, and the disruption of Status Quo worship. Despite the uncertainties, Holy Land pilgrimage remains a pinnacle experience of the Christian faith.

7

Understanding the Holy Sites

While numerous guide books describe what one sees at the holy sites, little attention is given to how they actually work. How do they function, how should we think about them, and what terms and concepts can we use to describe them? What tendencies should we be aware of? Are there alternative sites? Do places ever move? The aim of the chapter is to help pilgrims engage the sites and stories of the Christian Holy Land.

Describing the Holy Sites

The Language of Commemoration

Christianity is a religion of stories, and remembering the biblical narratives is fundamental to the Holy Land experience. The Holy Land is a landscape of collective memory, a place to remember the events of the Christian faith, and the holy sites function as stations of biblical storytelling. Whereas Christians throughout the world commemorate the life of Jesus in their own churches, pilgrims go to the Holy Land to commemorate the stories at, on, or near where the events actually took place. Pilgrims travel to Bethlehem to commemorate Jesus' birth, to the Jordan River to celebrate his baptism, to the Galilee to remember his ministry, and to Jerusalem to recall the events of his death and resurrection. The fourth-century pilgrim Egeria notes with excitement the convergence of time, place, and scripture that occurs in the Holy Land: "what I admire and value most is that all the hymns, prayers, and readings are always relevant to the day and the place in which they are used. They never fail to be appropriate."[1] Evoking the spirit of Egeria, the aim of Holy Land pilgrimage is to commemorate biblical stories in appropriate places by reading scripture, listening to the

---

1. Egeria, *Egeria's Travels*, 47.5.

presentations of guides, scholars, and chaplains, by observing related art, architecture, and archaeology, and through prayer and worship, pilgrim practices, group discussions, and personal reflections.

One of the strengths of commemorative language is that it provides neutral terminology for accurately describing the sites. The language does not imply that such-and-such a site is *merely* a commemoration, as if it is not otherwise authentic; rather, it permits an accurate statement about a site and its commemorative function regardless of other considerations, namely, its locational precision. The memory of Jesus' resurrection provides a relevant example. It is an objective fact that the Holy Sepulchre commemorates the death and resurrection of Christ regardless of a person's attitude towards the building. It is likewise true that the Garden Tomb commemorates the death and resurrection of Christ regardless of its archaeological credibility. Both sites have the same commemorative function, and depending upon the group, either site can be an appropriate place to remember the events. At least one of the sites is not historically accurate, which underscores the point that commemoration is not dependent upon location. One of the advantages of approaching the holy sites as stations of biblical storytelling is that pilgrims can initially by-pass the issue of locational precision, giving themselves permission to enter the narrative space of a site. While locational accuracy is an important follow-up question, understanding the sites as venues of biblical commemoration can provide shrine-skeptic pilgrims with the latitude they need for a richer encounter with the sacred places.

The Four Components of Holy Sites

Holy sites have four basic components: commemoration, location, appearance, and sequence. What event does the site remember? Where is it located, including its vicinity to other places? What does it look like? At what point in the itinerary does the site appear, and where does it fit in the biblical timeline or the life of Christ?

Commemoration

Commemoration concerns the narrative, event, person, or idea to which a site is dedicated. It is the historical or narrative memory attached to a place. The Christian Holy Land remembers Old Testament stories while focusing upon the life of Christ. It also marks difficult narratives, such as Herod's massacre of the innocents, Jesus' passion, and the stoning of Stephen. The Holy Land commemorates Christian legends, historical events, and theological ideas, such as atonement, resurrection, and reconciliation. Christian commemoration also has an eschatological element. The sites beckon pilgrims into the biblical past, give witness to God's ongoing providence, and anticipate the fulfillment of divine promise.

While biblical memory is attached to church sites, archaeological ruins, and natural landscapes, the Holy Land experience culminates in the tomb of Christ. Tombs are a special commemorative category. Holy Land tombs recall the pioneers of the Christian faith, including Old Testament heroes, New Testament characters, and monastic figures. Tombs foster the eschatological dimension of pilgrimage and function as physical expressions of theological ideas. The tomb of Adam at the base of Calvary commemorates human redemption; the tombs of Christ and Lazarus proclaim the mystery of resurrection, while the former is associated with the center of the world.

Location

Location speaks to the spatial position of a site, including its geographical, demographical, and political context, and sites are generally described in relative terms to other landmarks. Location is ultimately interested in the question of precisional accuracy, which warrants some initial observations. First of all, each site has its own locational argument, and some traditions are stronger than others. Secondly, biblical place names seldom convey locational information. To recognize Golgotha as the place of the crucifixion is not the same as knowing where it is. Third, biblical stories seldom contain enough details to pinpoint locations. Church tradition has filled in the gaps. Fourth, as discussed below, scriptural discrepancies, such as the location of Rachel's tomb, forced pilgrim tradition to choose between conflicting accounts. Fifth, tradition has occasionally placed a commemoration in a location that seems at odds with the biblical text or at least stretches the imagination. Overall, however, the locations of the holy sites are largely credible, and it is easier to dispute the position of a given site than to offer a positive alternative.

As pilgrims travel the Holy Land, they become aware of the spatial relationships between sites. Some are impressed by the expansiveness of the land; others find it extremely compact: salvation enacted upon a small-scale stage. Jesus' boyhood village of Nazareth was only four miles, or six kilometers, from Sepphoris, the capital of the Galilee. What relationship, if any, did the Holy Family have with Sepphoris, and why do the Gospels completely ignore it? By the time Jesus established his base in Capernaum,

Herod Antipas had moved the capital to Tiberias, both sites were on the Sea of Galilee. Place informs their relationship.

Certain narratives come into focus once their locational settings are properly understood. Capernaum was on a major, regional highway near the mouth of the Jordan River—the river served as the border between the areas ruled by Antipas and Philip—contextual details that are important for understanding the Capernaum stories and the movements of Jesus' ministry. While the Gospels do not place Peter's confession of Christ precisely in Caesarea Philippi, its setting as a cultic center for Greek and Roman gods provides the backdrop for Jesus' question: who (which god) do you say that I am (Matt 16:13–28; Mark 8:27–38; Luke 9:18–27)? The visitor to Gethsemane immediately realizes that Jesus was not praying in an isolated garden; he was almost literally in the shadow of the temple. As pilgrims encounter the physical settings of scripture, they acquire insights that are missing from the text. Location frames the Gospel stories.

As we walk in the footsteps of Jesus, we are continually relocating ourselves within the scriptural narrative. When we hear Peter's confession of Christ near Caesarea Philippi or commemorate the raising of Lazarus in Bethany, we review biblical locations that we have recently encountered while reflecting upon places that lie ahead. Where are we, where have we been, and where are we going? We hear the echoes from one place at another. A site reminds us of upcoming stories. Gethsemane takes us back to the wilderness, while pointing us towards the cross. At the transfiguration, we recall God's voice at Jesus' baptism while glimpsing his resurrection glory.

Our sense of location is determined by what we know and changes as we see what is around the corner and beyond the horizon. Our perspective of place is relative, and personal location relates to our physical, spiritual, and emotional proximity to people and places. Pilgrims are constantly reflecting upon their sense of where they are. How does it feel to be at the center of the world and far from home? Does the Holy Land feel emotionally crowded, or it is a lonely landscape? How is location related to time as well as place or determined by the presence and absence of other people? Location extends beyond the placement of the holy sites to the physical, emotional, and narrative journeys of the Christian traveler.

Appearance

The question of appearance moves our focus from what happened (commemoration) and where it is remembered (location) to what is there (appearance). Despite their interest in scripture, the ancient pilgrim texts almost never describe the biblical past. Instead, they record what the pilgrims actually saw, such as churches, crosses, lamps, and columns, giving particular care to commemorative focal points. The texts are attentive to colors and materials and include numbers, sizes, and measurements. Christians approached the sites as if scriptural truths were manifest through their commemorative features. The sites were testaments to God's providential care, signs of encouragement to persevere amidst the travails of the earthly life. Pilgrims observed the holy sites in enough detail to describe them to others, and medieval Christians back in Europe valued information on the contemporary appearance of the holy sites. As sites of spiritual encouragement, the holy sites function as present-day witnesses to gospel truths.

In short, while pilgrims seek an understanding of the biblical past, the most fundamental act of Holy Land pilgrimage is the careful observation of the holy sites. What are the natural topographical features of the place? Can anything from the biblical period still be seen, such as a wall, street, tomb, or mosaic? What have pilgrims subsequently built? Is there pilgrim-era archaeology, and how has the site been developed in the modern period? How is the commemorative focal point presented? What are the physical attributes of the churches and chapels built upon the site, and what is the nature of its outdoor spaces? Notice the designs of floors, ceilings, and windows, the details of Christian symbolism and religious art, and the presence of crosses, altars, and lamps. Are their incongruities at or near the site, such as adjacent mine fields, warnings against weapons, and separation walls, or comic juxtapositions, like gift shops selling Santas and escalators taking people to the birthplace of Jesus? Toilets at the wedding church in Cana convey the divine greeting: "Ave Maria! Please wash your hands!" A "no barbecuing" sign hangs on the Mensa Christi beach where Jesus cooked a charcoal breakfast (John 21). As pilgrims envision the biblical past playing out before them, they are attentive to the contemporary details of the holy sites as they contemplate present-day interpretations of the Gospel stories.

Sequence

In the pilgrim texts, sequential order generally implies a physical relationship between sites, and the identity of a given site can be established when multiple texts describe a group of sites in the same sequence. For on-the-ground pilgrims, sequence speaks to the order in which a site appears in the itinerary as well as its corresponding placement in the life of Christ. Despite a common core of sites that most groups visit, the Holy Land experience does not consist of standardized circuits or fixed itineraries.

Every institution, operator, guide, and scholar has their own preferences for ordering the sites, which is influenced by the length of the program, the size and ability of the group, local conditions, the day of the week, and religious and national holidays.

Walking in the footsteps of Jesus is significantly enhanced when a program takes a chronological approach, which is best achieved by a three-prong program beginning and ending in the Jerusalem area: (1) Jesus' nativity, baptism, and wilderness experience in and around Jerusalem, Bethlehem, and Jericho, (2) Jesus' ministry in the Galilee, and (3) the Holy Week commemorations in Jerusalem (see appendix 3). Some New Testament narratives will be inevitably out of order. There are discrepancies in the Gospel sequencing; certain sites, like Nazareth and Jerusalem, cover multiple phases in the life of Jesus, and geographical considerations influence Holy Land itineraries. Old Testament stories should likewise be included, especially when landscapes overlap.

Nonetheless, a chronological template of Jesus' life can be followed with relative ease. In doing so, the pilgrim experience becomes greater than the sum of the individual sites. A chronological paradigm captures the Gospel drama, producing a richer harvest of biblical insights, narrative understandings, and spiritual connections. Nativity gives way to baptism. The wilderness shapes Jesus' identity and discerns the direction of his ministry. In the Galilee, pilgrims are called to be disciples, hear Jesus' teachings on the kingdom of God, and witness the wonders of his ministry. Peter's confession of Christ near Caesarea Philippi, the most northerly part of the journey, provides the narrative pivot, turning faces towards the Holy City, while the transfiguration provides a pre-resurrection vision prior to arriving in Jerusalem for the Holy Week commemorations, which conclude with Jesus' death and resurrection. Following the sequence of Jesus' life layers the experience with an added dimension of sacred time: pilgrims journey from Advent and Christmas to Epiphany and Lent before culminating with Easter, Ascension, and Pentecost. In short, sequence matters.

A chronological approach should still defer to one tradition: the ancient practice of visiting the tomb of Christ upon arrival in Jerusalem. While almost every pilgrim text begins with the site, Mark Twain observes that "one naturally goes first to the Holy Sepulchre."[2] One of the ironies of contemporary itineraries that follow the sequential movements of Jesus' life is that for the first time in the history of the Christian Holy Land many pilgrims are not visiting the Holy Sepulchre until after they have completed their Holy Week commemorations—or, the visit occurs in no particular

2. Twain, *Innocents Abroad*, chapter 53.

order. Christian tradition, however, is unequivocal: pilgrims go to the Holy Sepulchre at their earliest opportunity. An initial visit to the Holy Sepulchre honors a basic tenet of pilgrimage: pilgrims persevere on the journey, but the ultimate destination is never intentionally delayed.

As the holiest place in Christendom, the Holy Sepulchre—a site that is both complex and confused—deserves multiple visits. Towards the end of his stay in Jerusalem, Twain writes: "nothing has any fascination for us now but the Church of the Holy Sepulchre. We have been there every day and have not grown tired of it, but we are weary of everything else."[3] By visiting the Holy Sepulchre at least twice, Christians can honor both pilgrim tradition and the passion sequence. Seeing significant places a second time clarifies questions, captures details, and crystallizes memories. The point applies to Jerusalem as a whole, which likewise deserves a second look, further justifying itineraries that begin and end in the Holy City.

Religious Imagination

Religious imagination speaks to the sensory experience, religious symbolism, and theological resonance of a place. What can you see, feel, smell, hear, and even taste at a site? Simply put, what is it like to be there? Religious imagination relates most directly to the element of appearance but includes all aspects of a place: its commemorative narratives, visual images, and religious practices. How does the setting allow pilgrims to envision the biblical story? How do acts of personal piety and group worship affect the mood of a place? What theological images and biblical truths are evoked by the site? A site's disposition changes depending upon the presence of visitors, liturgical activities, the time of year, and the hour of the day.

Religious imagination relates to a site's storytelling function, or the interplay of place, narrative, and symbolism. The ancient Holy Land contained a number of remarkable examples. The Byzantine Church of the Paralytic Healing was built on top of the narrow dyke separating the twin pools of Bethesda; its buttresses were literally immersed in the waters of the biblical narrative. The round, roofless Church of the Ascension left the location of Jesus' last footprints uncovered, allowing pilgrims to gaze directly into the heavens of Jesus' ascension as they contemplated the incarnation and the return of Christ. Two columns at the church represented the men in white mentioned in the story (Acts 1:10–11).[4] The religious imagination of modern shrines is likewise expressed through their narrative associations, natural settings,

3. Twain, *Innocents Abroad*, chapter 54.
4. Adomnán, *On the Holy Places*, 1.23; Hugeburc, *The Life of Willibald*, 21.

archaeological elements, architecture, art, and imagery. Dominus Flevit is a teardrop; the Church of Peter's House purports to be a boat.

While the sites tell a story, their commemorative focal points hold special meaning. The ascension footprints were surrounded by a screen containing an aperture for pilgrims to gather samples of sacred soil.[5] A large wooden cross stood in the middle of the Jordan River at the place of Jesus' baptism.[6] Perpetually burning lamps held vigil at the tomb of Christ.[7] Since the eighteenth century, a fourteen-pointed silver star representing the three sets of generations from Abraham to Jesus has marked the place of Jesus' birth. While pilgrims are often ambivalent about the x-marks-the-spot mentality of the holy sites, they should pay attention to how commemorative focal points are presented.

The concept of religious imagination reminds us that Holy Land pilgrimage is a shared experience. Pilgrims encounter a common commemorative landscape, and a collective pilgrim imagination has been shaped by the creators of the holy sites from the early Byzantine buildings to Barluzzi's twentieth-century architecture. The Holy Land as shared experience becomes evident when pilgrims cite common impressions of the holy sites, such as the statue of the pregnant women at the Church of the Visitation.

The religious imagination of the Holy Land is enhanced by the layering of scriptural narratives. John the Baptist shares common ground with the prophet Elijah, while Jesus' baptism site shares its general setting with the Israelite's crossing of the Jordan River, evoking a number of theological parallels. Bethlehem has ties to Ruth, David, and Jesus. A Ruth Restaurant and a Field of Boaz souvenir shop remind pilgrims that the genealogical line running from David to Jesus includes a matriarch of foreign descent. Certain places have been layered by Christian tradition. As pilgrims enter the theological dark space of Jesus' trial before Caiaphas at St. Peter in Gallicantu, they pass through a doorway blessed with the words of Psalm 121:8: "the LORD will keep your going out and your coming in from this time on and forevermore." Since the early Christian period, the place of Jesus' crucifixion has been associated with two Old Testament images. Christians interpret Abraham's binding of his son, Isaac, as a prefiguration of God's sacrifice of Christ. A large wall mosaic of the Old Testament scene adorns the Franciscan Chapel of Calvary, while a Greek monastery dedicated to Abraham is a stone's throw away. The belief that Adam lies buried at the base

---

5. See Adomnán, *On the Holy Places* 1.23; Hugeburc, *The Life of Willibald*, 21.

6. See Adomnán, *On the Holy Places* 2.16; Hugeburc, *The Life of Willibald*, 16.

7. See Piacenza Pilgrim, *Travels,* 18; Adomnán, *On the Holy Places,* 1.2.12; Hugeburc, *The Life of Willibald,* 18.

of Calvary, an exegetical idea that predates the development of the Holy Sepulchre, plays upon the image of Christ as the second Adam (Rom 5; 1 Cor 15). Expressing the idea that Christ redeemed humankind by literally shedding his blood upon his bones, Adam's tomb commemorates the Christian doctrine of atonement. Calvary is a layered landscape that takes pilgrims back to the brink of creation.

The concept of layers offers a rich construct for pilgrim reflections on time, place, and journey. Layers abound in the geology, history, and archaeology of the region. Scripture is layered upon the landscape, while churches have been built upon churches. The Palestinian–Israeli conflict is inextricably layered. Layers are the legacy of growth and destruction, life and death. Layers can strengthen and reinforce, providing foundations for new life. Layers also hide and conceal. They erode away, are accidentally dug up, and are intentionally peeled back. Exposed layers reveal exciting discoveries and unwanted histories, blessings and pain. The layers of history can leave us feeling both infinitely small and humbly connected. The Holy Land experience reminds us that our lives are profoundly layered.

Commemorative Credibility
(Are the Holy Sites Authentic?)

Discussing the holy sites inevitably raises the question of authenticity. Are the holy sites authentic or less than genuine? Are they real or displaced settings of pilgrim piety? The authenticity of a holy site concerns two primary issues: the historicity of the commemoration and its locational precision. The authenticity of place is obviously contingent upon whether its associated narrative occurred in the first place and, similarly, the degree to which the Bible accurately records what happened. If Jesus' miracles are discounted, one is unlikely to view a corresponding site to be authentic, regardless of its location.

The Bible abounds in allegory and non-literal thinking and contains discrepancies of place and story. The degree of biblical criticism that one applies to the sites is ultimately a personal decision, and while the Holy Land helps us to understand the Bible better, a pilgrim's approach to scripture is independent of place. The holy sites are witnesses to biblical truths, but faith resides in the heart of the individual. It is not, however, an either/or proposition. Scripture speaks to Christians at many different levels, and holding a particular interpretation of a biblical story is not requisite to engaging a holy site in a meaningful way.

Putting the interpretation of scripture aside, the authenticity of a holy site is strictly a question of location and not of faith. The debate between

Mount Hermon and Mount Tabor is not about whether the transfiguration transpired but where it took place. The rivalry between the Holy Sepulchre and the Garden Tomb is not about whether the crucifixion and the resurrection happened but where they occurred. The early church was not immune from mistakes, nor are we compelled to accept the inerrancy of tradition. Sites were carefully identified. However, various factors, including pilgrim accessibility, influenced choices, and changes have subsequently altered the landscape. The holy sites are places of biblical witness; they have no canonical status. Pilgrims should engage locational questions as points of intellectual query not as issues of faith.

Insomuch as a holy site may be imprecisely located, one may conclude that it is not genuine, but what degree of precision is necessary for determining its authenticity? Most biblical stories do not contain precise locational details. Even when we have a place name, how sure can we be of its location? Where exactly is Cana of Galilee? The range of the terrain in question varies in each instance. Numerous biblical events took place within the temple precincts, in and around Jerusalem, and on the Mount of Olives—identifiable, largely circumscribed areas. We know the specific location of a number of places, like the pool of Bethesda, the pool of Siloam, and the Temple Mount. Occasionally, we can be certain that we are walking where Jesus walked, and even if we cannot precisely locate an event in or around the Holy City, we can generally narrow it down to a few hundred feet. Within the compact landscape of Jerusalem, what degree of precision is desired, necessary, or sufficient? The traditional sites of the Lord's Supper, Gethsemane, Calvary, the tomb of Christ, and Pentecost are all credible. None of them have been challenged by more obvious alternatives, but their exactness cannot be confirmed. Within the more spacious landscapes of the Galilee, what degree of precision is necessary to authenticate a holy site? We can identify Nazareth and Capernaum as well as the Sea of Galilee and the Jordan River, but pinpointing the individual episodes of Jesus' life and ministry is another issue. Pilgrim tradition revels in the "very spot" where something occurred, but depending upon the event, it may have taken place feet, yards, or miles away from the commemorative site.

In the end, pilgrims expect locations to be commemoratively credible, or compatible with the physical settings described in the text. Over the centuries, a few traditions, like the Lord's Prayer, have been placed in Jerusalem to allow pilgrims better access to certain scriptural memories. Some of the commemorative features of the Holy Sepulchre, such as the chapels of Derision and the Division of the Raiment, are relevant to Jesus' passion but have no connection to the place itself. When a site is out of place, whether due to pilgrim convenience, international boundaries, or military zones, it should catch our attention. Yet, despite the exceptions, the Christian Holy Land has a high degree of commemorative credibility, and the sites are largely "in place." In short, while the intersection of place and story lies at the heart of the Holy Land journey, the language of authenticity distorts a more nuanced approach to the holy sites and is more effectively replaced by the concept of commemorative credibility.

The Holy Land versus the Holy Places

While Holy Land travelers, both pilgrims and scholars, desire a degree of precision in locating the settings of biblical events, many people reject the x-marks-the-spot mentality of the sites, feeling little need to pin events to exact locations. The sacred stories can be commemorated, scriptural meanings grasped, and the spirituality of place encountered without being overly concerned about the x's and o's of the biblical text. Consequently, pilgrims often find the concept of the Holy Land—the idea of a continuous plane of holiness—to be more meaningful than the notion of holy places. Instead of focusing upon the individual dots or a spirituality dependent upon circumscribed places, pilgrims commonly prefer the image of a sacred *land* that transcends x's on a map.

The "land of the Bible," akin to the Fifth Gospel, takes a more expansive approach to the incarnation. Christ lived within a broad set of borders and walked throughout the land. He gazed upon its mountain contours and knew its horizontal vistas. He was familiar with its villages and frequented the Holy City. Christ drew inspiration from the land and performed miracles on the sea. In the Holy Land paradigm, pilgrims are constantly standing on holy ground, and spiritual encounters are not limited to the sacred sites. Holiness is in every direction rather than at the end of the queue, and authenticity becomes a mute point. At the same time, the Holy Land approach challenges how we compartmentalize the sacred and the profane. Not only are hotel rooms and gift shops part of the Holy Land, so too are the checkpoints and refugee camps, the walls and barbed wire.

A Unified Landscape

Having discussed some terms and concepts for engaging the holy sites, we turn to the character the Holy Land itself. As a commemorative landscape, the Holy Land is unified and expansive—it is unchanging (i.e., conservative); yet, extensive and expanding. We begin with its unified nature. This is not a comment on ecumenical relations but a specific point pertaining to the sites themselves: Christian tradition, both East and West, has largely recognized the same locations. Alternative sites are rare. Rather, recognized traditions weigh heavily on the ground, and the infamous fisticuffs of the Holy Sepulchre belong to monks fighting over contested space. The discussion addresses the following questions: How have pilgrims dealt with biblical discrepancies, and how does pilgrim tradition influence our scriptural encounters with the Holy Land? To what degree have commemorations moved over the centuries, what do we make of the prevalence of adjacent Franciscan and Orthodox churches, and what is the influence of modern scholarship in shaping the commemorative landscape?

Scriptural Discrepancies

Pilgrim tradition has had to tend with scriptural discrepancies. The Bible gives two locations for Rachel's tomb (Gen 35:19–20; 1 Sam 10:2). Matthew and Acts differ on the cause and location of Judas' death (Matt 27:3–6; Acts 1:16–19). Different settings are given for Jesus' teaching of the Lord's Prayer (Matt 6; Luke 11), and variations of the Beatitudes take place on a mountain (Matt 5:1–12) and a plain (Luke 6:17–28). When faced with multiple options, pilgrim tradition has consistently recognized a single, dominant tradition. Rachel was buried near Bethlehem; Judas hung himself from a tree.[8] The Beatitudes are remembered on a hillside in the Galilee, while the Lord's Prayer is commemorated on the Mount of Olives.

An Aggregate of Primary Sites

Holy Land tradition not only decided which biblical versions would be recognized, it choose which narratives would be commemorated in the first place. What is often overlooked is that pilgrim tradition largely determines our scriptural connections to the Holy Land. Few would question the importance of the Sermon on the Mount and the multiplication of the fish and loaves as centerpieces of Jesus' ministry. Yet, the choice to commemorate these particular episodes was made for us nearly seventeen hundred years ago. Certain scriptures have a stronger commemorative history than others; some have none at all. Pilgrims leave the Holy Land shaped by the sites and stories they have encountered, while those they have not commemorated assume a less dominant status in their biblical imagination.

Despite the plethora of holy places, including a number of minor traditions, the Holy Land presents the Gospel story through an aggregate of

8. See Adomnán, *On the Holy Places*, 1.17; 2.7.

primary sites, and the time-limited nature of Holy Land pilgrimage, which hits the Gospel highlights, accentuates the effect. Determining the relative value of biblical stories is not particular to the Holy Land. Christian tradition emphasizes the major events of salvation history, while lectionaries, like the Revised Common Lectionary, leave out portions of the Bible. We are not suggesting that the commemorative landscape of the Holy Land distorts the Gospel story, but the questions have not been fully considered. Are there notable distinctions between the narratives of primary sites and those of minor traditions? What can we say about the texts that have little or no commemorative history? While present-day pilgrims engage biblical landscapes independent of commemorative shrines, tradition plays a significant role in determining the scriptural stories that pilgrims encounter.

Do Sites Move?

The Holy Land is a conservative landscape, and commemorations have seldom moved. When sites have been damaged or have been rediscovered centuries later, the dominant practice has been to rebuild upon existing foundations, and as pilgrims will quickly notice, most of the modern shrines have been built upon Byzantine and Crusader ruins. The resiliency of tradition is a point made in stone. Even so, changes have occurred over the centuries. The most fluctuating tradition has been the commemoration of Jesus' trial, a series of events with multiple venues that is further complicated by the divergent nature of the Gospel texts. Collectively, the trial consists of audiences with the high priests, Annas and Caiaphas, Jesus' overnight custody, the interrogation by Pilate, a visit to Herod Antipas, and the final condemnation by Pilate when Jesus is scourged, crowned with thorns, and handed his cross.

The Church of Holy Wisdom, which was somewhere opposite the western wall of the Temple Mount, was presumed by Byzantine pilgrims to be Pilate's praetorium. When Holy Wisdom was destroyed by the Persians in the seventh century, it was never rebuilt, and its ruins have yet to be found. Pilgrims consequently shifted the Pilate commemorations to Mount Sion, placing them at or near the "house of Caiaphas," which was probably on the grounds of the present-day Armenian Monastery of St. Savior just outside the Sion Gate. Both commemorations have since moved. The house of Caiaphas has slipped down the hill to St. Peter in Gallicantu. While the grounds are full of first-century archeology, the site housed a medieval monastery that probably commemorated where Peter "went out and wept bitterly" after his threefold denial of Christ (Luke 22:62).[9] At least since the early post-Crusader period, Pilate's praetorium has been associated with the Antonia Fortress on the northern wall of the Temple Mount, which marks the first station of the Via Dolorosa. Although Christian tradition has identified Pilate's praetorium with three separate locations, it was most likely at a fourth: Herod the Great's palace near the Jaffa Gate.

After centuries of siltation, the pool of Bethesda (John 5) was moved in the Crusader period to the nearby pool of Israel, which lies against the northern wall of the Temple Mount. The Bethesda complex was rediscovered in the nineteenth century, and the commemoration of the paralytic healing was returned to its original location. We have essentially lost the importance of Jesus' teaching about the Last Days, the so-called Apocalyptic Discourse (Matt 24; Mark 13; Luke 21), which was the original dedication of the Eleona on the Mount of Olives. By the Crusader period, the commemoration had shifted to the Lord's Prayer. Jesus was still teaching, but the content had changed.[10] Modern pilgrims to Pater Noster are largely unaware of the site's history.

Finally, the 1938 Italian Church of the Beatitudes, which is up the hill from the Byzantine ruins, is a rare example of a site with no archaeological history. The convenience of vehicular travel allowed the site to be moved off the ancient pilgrim footpath to its commanding view of the Sea of Galilee, while the need for monastic buildings, pilgrim accommodations, parking lots, and gift shops reflects the practicalities of modern pilgrimage. Despite the conservative nature of the Holy Land, it has occasionally been altered due to the deterioration of sites, the loss of collective memory, and for practical convenience.

Alternative Sites

Does the Christian Holy Land consist of mutually recognized sites, or is it characterized by competing traditions? With minor exceptions, Eastern and Western Christians have recognized the same locations. It is important to understand that the prevalence of adjacent Franciscan and Orthodox churches is not a sign of competing claims. Rather, it reflects the desire of the respective churches to be near a mutually recognized location that may or may not be a part of either church property. In other words, while recognizing an authoritative tradition, churches have acquired adjacent properties for commemorative, liturgical, and monastic purposes, which they

9. See Epiphanius the Monk, *Hagiopolita*, 7–9.

10. Although Matthew sets the Lord's Prayer in the Galilee, the Crusaders conflated Luke 10:38—11:4 with Mark 11:12–25.

have dedicated to the biblical event without claiming that the property is the actual biblical location. This does not mean that Eastern and Western pilgrims always visit the recognized site; in some instances, they may simply visit their own church. In short, sacred stories are commemorated in multiple places, but competing sites are rare. Christians have contested the same space far more than they have made alternative claims.

Jesus' ascension illustrates the point. Two different towers dedicated to the ascension dominate the skyline of the Mount of Olives. On the southern summit is the tall, thin tower of the Russian Orthodox Church of the Ascension built in 1870. The German Lutheran Church of the Ascension completed in 1910 stands on the northern summit. The sites do not represent competing claims regarding the location of Jesus' ascension; they are merely dedications. Since the fourth century, Christians have associated the ascension with another site on the Mount of Olives where a round, roofless church commemorated Jesus' ascent into heaven. In 1198, the site, now known as the Chapel of the Ascension, was converted into a mosque and remains in Muslim hands; yet, every year on their respective feast days, the Orthodox and Catholic churches return to the site for their Ascension celebrations. Despite Muslim custodianship, Christians have persisted in their common recognition of the ascension setting, underscoring both the unity and conservatism of the Christian Holy Land.

Two other Muslim-held sites demonstrate the Christian practice of commemorating stories in appropriate places while recognizing an authoritative tradition. As with the place of the ascension, the tomb of Lazarus came into Muslim hands in the aftermath of the Crusades. Today, two churches, Greek and Franciscan, the latter built in 1954 within the larger ruins of the Byzantine complex, are near the tomb. On the Mount of Olives, the Franciscan site of Dominus Flevit beautifully recalls Jesus' weeping over the city of Jerusalem (Matt 23:37–39; Luke 13:34–35; 19:37–44). Yet, the Franciscans acknowledge an adjacent location as the place where the event purportedly occurred: a Crusader-era site used as a mosque during the Ottoman period which they were unable to acquire when they bought the Dominus Flevit property in 1891.

The early Christian Holy Land was a dense ecclesial landscape, and one should not assume that every ancient church marked the location of a biblical event. During the Byzantine period, some two dozen churches and monasteries were on the Mount of Olives alone. Dominus Flevit contains the ruins of a fifth-century monastery; there is no evidence that it claimed to be a biblical site, and its original dedication is unknown.[11] Although the

11. See Aist, *The Christian Topography*, 194–96.

Franciscan Shepherds' Field is located on an ancient church site, they acknowledge that the nearby Greek site of Deir er-Ra'wat was traditionally
associated with the story (Luke 2:8–15).[12]

Competing sites have existed but mostly as minor exceptions. The
pre-Crusader texts indicate that the grotto of Gethsemane served as an alternative venue for the Lord's Supper. The annunciation was located in both
Nazareth and Jerusalem. Different structures were identified as Solomon's
Portico.[13] There are divergent traditions regarding the stoning of Stephen
and multiple prisons of Christ. The Syrian Orthodox Church of St. Mark in
the Armenian Quarter purports to be the house of John Mark (Acts 12:12),
which, it argues, was the setting of the Lord's Supper and Pentecost, despite
the dominant tradition of the Cenacle on Mount Sion.

The most notable dispute concerns the location of Jesus' death and resurrection, or the debate between the Garden Tomb, a recent Protestant arrival,
and the Holy Sepulchre. The Holy Sepulchre has been recognized by Christendom since the early fourth century, plausibly based upon a local tradition
going back to the New Testament period. Even if we allow that Calvary and
the tomb of Christ are not precisely located, the argument that Jesus' crucifixion and entombment took place within the grounds of the Holy Sepulchre is
credible, and with respect to location, there is no compelling reason to search
elsewhere. While Protestants can freely visit the Holy Sepulchre, Protestant
worship is prohibited due to the Status Quo. How and where can Protestants
appropriately celebrate the resurrection?

The fact that the Holy Sepulchre was inside the city, aesthetically dis-
jointed, and in the hands of Christians whose piety ran counter to Protestant sensibilities compelled an inevitable search for a suitable alternative. It
was conducted, however, as a search for the authentic biblical location and
was ultimately led by Charles Gordon (1833–85), a British military officer
on leave from Sudan. Gordon was eccentric, to say the least, but the idea
that the places of Christian salvation could be discovered nineteen centuries
after the church's purported failure to do so reflects a colonial-era hubris
that remains unacknowledged by proponents of the site. While Gordon focused on the so-called Skull Hill as the place of Calvary, the tomb eventually
purchased in 1894 by The Garden Tomb (Jerusalem) Association was not
the first one considered.[14] It has since been dated by archaeologists to the
First Temple period, centuries before Christ.

12. The "Protestant Grotto" on the grounds of the Beit Sahour YMCA offers a third
commemorative venue for the shepherds' story.

13. See Aist, *The Christian Topography*, 182–84, 156–62.

14. Walker, *The Weekend*, 128–30.

We need to dismiss any possibility of the Garden Tomb's authenticity in order to appreciate the important function that it actually serves. Gordon's story aside, the development of an Easter venue for Protestant worship was a historical inevitability. The site does a disservice to itself, however, through its insistence that the resurrection *could* have happened there. Protestant pilgrims deserve to be treated with greater intellectual integrity when it comes to Jesus' resurrection, especially in light of the deference to Holy Land traditions exemplified by their Christian counterparts. While the Protestant experience is diminished by its lack of liturgical access to the Holy Sepulchre, the Garden Tomb functions as an appropriate, aesthetically pleasing outdoor space in Jerusalem where Protestants can commemorate the resurrection through prayer and worship.[15] That is no mean status, and the site would be better served by dropping its pretence as *possibly* the place.

While the Christian Holy Land has been a resilient, conservative landscape, pilgrims and scholars alike are constantly reassessing the locational evidence, which raises an interesting question: if we become convinced that an event occurred in a place other than the traditional site, should we forego tradition and commemorate the story in a different location? A relevant example is the Via Dolorosa, which begins at Pilate's praetorium where Jesus was condemned and received his cross. While the Via Dolorosa places the praetorium at the Antonia Fortress, east of Calvary, scholars now believe that it was located at Herod's palace on the grounds of the Armenian seminary inside the Jaffa Gate: Jesus likely approached Calvary from the southwest. Should Christians continue with the traditional route or develop new stations for the Way of the Cross? The Via Dolorosa provides a powerful spiritual experience in its current form; yet, don't be surprised to find future pilgrims carrying a cross from Herod's palace.

Another example, already alluded to, concerns the transfiguration debate between Mount Hermon (9,232 feet) and Mount Tabor (1,890 feet) that goes back to the early church. By the mid-fourth century, Christian tradition had chosen Mount Tabor, almost certainly with pilgrim convenience in mind. Today, the 1924 Church of the Transfiguration is a beloved shrine, and Mount Tabor does justice to the narrative, titillating the pilgrim imagination.[16] Mount Hermon, on the other hand, is favored by a number of scholars, and a recent pilgrim guide book omits Mount Tabor due to the

15. Other venues for celebrating the resurrection include the multiple Emmaus sites and the Sea of Galilee (John 21).

16. Due to legitimate time restraints—groups must wait in a queue to be shuttled up the mountain in mini-vans at an additional cost—Mount Tabor is not on every itinerary. Some guides commemorate the event by looking at Mount Tabor from a distance.

author's preference for Mount Hermon.[17] Probability disfavors Mount Tabor; yet, we have entered a different era of Holy Land pilgrimage when we avoid traditional sites because we do not believe the events took place there, especially when the alternatives are less than certain.

While archaeology and biblical studies have shaped the Holy Land experience, the degree to which modern scholarship will influence pilgrim sites and practices remains to be seen. As with the Via Dolorosa, we should consider innovations against the spiritual significance of walking in the footsteps of other pilgrims. When we deviate from recognized traditions, we veer off the pilgrim pathway without necessarily guaranteeing that we are any closer to the biblical past.

In sum, the Holy Land is a unified landscape. Pilgrim tradition has selected which narratives to emphasize, has culled scriptural discrepancies, and has largely avoided alternative claims. Despite the deceptive impression of dedicatory churches, the East and West recognize the same sites. Save for the Garden Tomb, the exceptions are few and far between.

An Expansive Landscape

The Christian Holy Land is unified *yet expansive*. Not every text has a commemorative history, but minor memories abound, often as monastic and local church traditions. The monastery of Theodosius to the east of Bethlehem commemorates where the magi spent their first night on their way home (Matt 2:12). The cliff monastery of St. George in Choziba purports to be where Elijah spent the night fleeing from Jezebel on his way to Horeb (1 Kgs 19). According to local tradition, Joseph and Mary spent the night in present-day Al-Bireh near Ramallah when they unknowingly left the twelve-year-old Jesus in Jerusalem (Luke 2:41–50). The Holy Land is full of minor traditions and second-tier sites, like the church at Nain (Luke 7:11–17). The less-trafficked sites aside, the expansive nature of the Holy Land is expressed in two primary ways: as extra-biblical legends and through same-story commemorations.

17. See Luker, *An Illustrated Guide*, which omits Mount Tabor as a place of contemporary visitation. His only mention of the Mount Tabor commemoration occurs in the section on "Mount Hermon and the Upper Golan," in which he refers to it as a Byzantine designation, while unequivocally stating that Mount Hermon is the site of the transfiguration. We can discount Mount Tabor more easily than we can affirm Mount Hermon. The event could have occurred in any number of locations.

Extra-Biblical Traditions

The Christian Holy Land commemorates several extra-biblical traditions, or stories not found in scripture, including a number of scenes from the second-century text entitled *The Protoevangelium of James*.[18] The text, which recounts the births of Mary and Jesus, contains many of the nativity traditions held by the church, including the names of Mary's parents, Joachim and Anne, Mary's childhood service in the temple, Joseph as an older widower with his own children, and John the Baptist's escape from Herod's soldiers. The Jerusalem-based text sets Mary's early life, including the annunciation, in the Holy City in contrast to the Nazareth setting of Luke (Luke 1:26).[19]

Pilgrim texts refer to Joseph's house in Jerusalem and note a blood-colored stone among the temple ruins purportedly associated with the death of Zechariah, the father of John the Baptist, who, according to *The Protoevangelium*, was put to death by Herod's soldiers while serving in the temple.[20] The monastery of St. George in Choziba still commemorates the flight of Joachim into the Judean wilderness, where he successfully prayed for Anne to conceive a child.[21] The birthplace of Mary, marked by the Crusader Church of St. Anne and commemorated by an adjacent Greek property, likewise reflects the traditions of the text. The ruins of the Byzantine-era Kathisma church, discovered in 1992 and visible along the Hebron Road near Ramat Rachel (Jerusalem), commemorate where Mary rested three miles before reaching Bethlehem.[22] Solving the mystery of how John the Baptist escaped Herod's massacre, *The Protoevangelium* recounts how a rock cave protectively swallowed the boy John and his mother, Elizabeth, as they fled from Herod's soldiers.[23] A large rock relic and a wall mural depicting the escape are prominent features of the Church of the Visitation in Ein Kerem.

18. Also known as *The Infancy Gospel of James*, *The Protoevangelium*, which means "before the Gospel," appears in Elliot, *The Apocryphal New Testament*, 48–67. It can also be found on the internet.

19. A Jerusalem-based commemoration of the annunciation is referenced in two seventh-century texts: Adomnán, *On the Holy Places*, 1.10 and Epiphanius the Monk, *Hagiopolita*, 4. See Aist, *From Topography to Text*, 85–86.

20. On the death of Zechariah, see *The Protoevangelium*, 23–24 and the Bordeaux Pilgrim, *Travels*, 591. The tradition of Zechariah, the father of John the Baptist, being murdered in the temple conflates 2 Chr 24:20–21 with Matt 23:35.

21. *The Protoevangelium*, 1.

22. *The Protoevangelium*, 17.

23. *The Protoevangelium*, 22.

While early Christians were keen to know the details of Mary's early life, a Jerusalem-based tradition regarding her last days also emerged.[24] According to legend, Mary died or fell asleep on Mount Sion, marked by the Dormition Abbey built in 1900 upon the Byzantine and Crusader ruins of Holy Sion. Mary was subsequently carried by the disciples to her tomb in the Jehoshaphat Valley. On the way, a group of Jews tried to steal her body before an angel of the Lord intervened. The encounter was marked in the early medieval period by a column outside the city's eastern gate and is depicted on Eastern icons of the Dormition in the form of a sword-bearing angel fending off the attack.[25] During the Byzantine period, a large, two-story round church was built over Mary's tomb; the lower level, containing her sepulchre, still remains.

Church traditions and the lives of saints have been important features of the Christian landscape, none more significant than the discovery of the Holy Cross by Helena.[26] The finding of the Holy Cross was originally associated with the apse of the basilica of Constantine, which was destroyed in 1009. Since the Crusader period, the event has been commemorated in the crypt of the Holy Sepulchre. The monastery of the Holy Cross, west of the Old City, marks where the tree, which became the Holy Cross, purportedly grew in the time of Abraham and Lot, preserving a prequel to Calvary that is as expansive as the Helena legend.

Mary the Egyptian, an enigmatic figure from the fifth or sixth century, is another saint connected to the Holy Sepulchre. A prostitute of ill repute, Mary arrived in Jerusalem for the feast of the Holy Cross, which was part of an annual, eight-day festival celebrating the dedication of the Holy Sepulchre. When Mary tried to enter the church, she was denied access by an unknown force until she repented to a icon of Mary the Mother of God (the Theotokos), which was on or near the façade of the church. Returning to the icon upon visiting Christ's tomb, Mary was told by the Theotokos to go beyond the Jordan River where she would find spiritual peace. She did as she was told, becoming a desert mother of the Christian faith. A chapel near the southern entrance of the Holy Sepulchre is dedicated to the Egyptian saint, and she is likewise remembered at the monastery of St. Gerasimus in the Jordan River Valley. Regarding more historical figures, the tombs of Sabas and Jerome have been recognized pilgrim sites since the pre-Crusader period. Supplementing

24. On the Dormition traditions of Mary, see Shoemaker, *Ancient Traditions.*

25. See Aist, *The Christian Topography,* 165–74.

26. See Borgehammar, *How the Holy Cross Was Found* and Baert, *A Heritage of Holy Wood.*

the tapestry of scriptural landscapes, the commemorative fabric of the Holy Land is interwoven with extra-biblical traditions.

Same-Story Commemorations

The expansive nature of the Holy Land is also expressed through same-story commemorations, or the marking of multiple events from a single, common narrative. The Via Dolorosa, which commemorates fourteen stations from trial to tomb, is the most salient example. Within the Nativity cave, two events are pointed out: Mary gave birth to Jesus *and* laid him in a manger. As one enters the grotto, the Star of the Nativity marks the place of Jesus' birth on the right, while the purported manger is to the left. The three temptations of Jesus have been remembered in separate locations—two on a mountain in Jericho and one among the ruins of the Temple Mount—while the three apses of the Gethsemane church have marked Jesus' threefold prayers. Peter's denial of Jesus and the place where he wept afterwards were both recognized in the pre-Crusader period.[27] Occasionally, a commemorative expansion stretches belief. The Church of the Visitation in Ein Kerem purports to be the house of Elizabeth, while a church across the valley contains a grotto commemorating the birth of her son, John the Baptist. The churches do justice to the respective elements of the story, but the events in question—Mary's visit to Elizabeth, Mary's Song of Praise (the Magnificat), the birth of John, and Zechariah's prophecy—presumably occurred in a common, circumscribed area (Luke 1).

Extra-biblical traditions have the same expansive tendency. Both events of the Holy Cross legend—Helena's discovery of the three crosses and the miraculous healing of the True Cross—have been recognized in the Holy Sepulchre at different points in its history. Likewise, the end of Mary's life on Mount Sion and her entombment in the Jehoshaphat Valley are separate episodes from a single, continuous narrative, or same-story commemorations. In short, pilgrims should recognize the expansive nature of religious commemoration, noting the difference between competing sites of the same event (rare), multiple sites dedicated to the same event (common), and distinct commemorations derived from the same story (common).

27. See Epiphanius the Monk, *Hagiopolita*, 7–9.

8

Pilgrim Practices

What are the religious practices of Holy Land pilgrims? The chapter discusses pilgrim practices at the holy sites, surveys some perception-based tenets of pilgrim spirituality, and concludes by reemphasizing the importance of pilgrim memory.

At the Holy Sites

Seeing the Holy Sites

The Holy Land experience is fundamentally about *seeing the holy places*. One occasionally finds pilgrims lost in prayer—eyes closed in supplication and oblivious to time. The Holy Land, however, is not a closed-eyed experience. Pilgrims are agents of observation, and Holy Land pilgrimage is an open-eyed encounter with the land, a dialogue of the senses. In the words of Paulinus of Nola (d. 431), "no other sentiment draws people to Jerusalem than the desire to see and touch the places where Christ was physically present, and to be able to say from their very own experience, 'We have gone into his tabernacle and have worshipped in the places where his feet have stood.'"[1] Seeing where Christ was physically present is the most basic act of Holy Land pilgrimage. Ancient pilgrims concentrated on the observable particulars of the holy places, and modern-day travelers likewise attend to the details. They carefully read the sites, noting their topographical, architectural, and archeological features. They observe religious imagery and gaze at other pilgrims. They appreciate aesthetic beauty, while noticing the unusual and unexpected. Holy Land pilgrims practice the art of awareness, attentive to the present moment.

---

1. Paulinus of Nola, *Letter,* 49.14.

Pilgrims create and cherish memories. They do so through direct, un-aided observation, while using photography, videos, and on-site journaling to record details and impressions, which, with the right intention, become forms of open-eyed prayer. While the incessant quest for photos can dimin-ish real-time experience, approaching it as a devotional act can transform a frantic exercise into a sacred practice. By taking images for later viewing, strategic photography can also maximize time at a site. Pilgrims observe, absorb, record, and remember.

Pilgrims Read Scripture

One of the most ancient practices of Holy Land pilgrimage is reading scrip-ture at the holy sites. Egeria (fl. 380) writes with enthusiasm about hearing the Bible read as she journeyed throughout the Holy Land: "what I admire and value most is that all the hymns, prayers, and readings are always relevant to . . . the place in which they are used. They never fail to be appropriate."[2] Read-ing scripture at church shrines, archaeological sites, and related locations—as well as on the bus—preferably aloud in a group setting, is fundamental to the Holy Land experience, and appropriate places can always be found. There are suitable spaces for groups to gather outside the Status Quo churches, and while Bibles cannot be taken on the Haram esh-Sharif (Temple Mount), there are appropriate settings for reading temple-related passages, including the Southern Steps excavations and various overlooks on the Mount of Olives. Since some sites are associated with multiple scriptures and a biblical narra-tive may have more than one version, consideration needs to be given to the selection and length of the readings.

Pilgrims Worship

Pilgrims worship at the holy sites. While readings, explanations, reflections, and prayer generally occur at every site, group worship is celebrated at spe-cial junctures in the journey. Pilgrims sing Christmas carols in Bethlehem, reaffirm their baptism in the Jordan River, and mark the Stations of the Cross through the streets of Jerusalem. Groups worship beside the Sea of Galilee and conclude their journey with a resurrection celebration.

Most of the shrine churches have worship spaces, indoors and outdoors, with possibilities and limitations for Protestants. Some archaeological parks and natural landscapes, including Qasr al-Yahud (the baptism site), Wadi Qelt (the Judean wilderness), Kfar Nahum (Capernaum), Bethsaida, and Caesarea

---

2. Egeria, *Egeria's Travels*, 47.5.

Philippi (Banias), are also conducive to group worship. Some settings require advance reservations. Some can be arranged on site with permission. Others are available on a first-come, first-served basis.

Whether on site or at a hotel or guest house, worship is important to the life of a short-term pilgrim community, fomenting group formation and the individual journey. Devotional gatherings and reflection time provide opportunities for debriefing experiences, addressing issues, and acknowledging joys and concerns. Pilgrims also worship with other Christians. Pilgrimage is a celebration of the universal body of Christ, and the language and liturgies of other traditions help us see Christ through a kaleidoscope of Christian diversity. Along with observing the worship of other pilgrims, Western Christians should attend an Eastern liturgy, like the Armenian vespers, and should join Arab Christians for Sunday worship, if at all possible. There are a number of English-language services in Jerusalem, including daily Catholic options and Sunday worship in the Anglican, Lutheran, and Reformed traditions, which are attended by pilgrims, short-term volunteers, peace and justice workers, international students, ex-pat residents, and their families.[3]

Pilgrims Reenact Sacred Stories

Distinct from readings, prayers, and worship, pilgrim practices include the informal, devotional ways that pilgrims reenact scriptural narratives and engage the physical settings of the holy sites. They are embodied commemorations, which are generally individual acts, though, in certain instances, a number of people can perform them at the same time. The ancient texts contain a number of examples, some of which continue today. Arculf, a pilgrim from Gaul, drank from Jacob's Well when he visited the site in the seventh century. The well, now covered by a stone crypt, is housed by a modern Orthodox church, which was dedicated in 2007. By means of a noisy crank and a simple bucket, pilgrims take turns drawing water, sharing in the refreshment of the ancient well, and reflecting upon Jesus' words to the Samaritan Woman: "everyone who drinks of this water will be thirsty again, but those who drink of the water that I will give them will never be thirsty. The water that I will give will become in them a spring of water gushing up to eternal life" (John 4:13–14).

At the church in Cana, pilgrims commemorated Jesus' wedding miracle by reenacting the story of the water-made-wine (John 2). Two of

---

3. For worship opportunities in the Holy Land, including arranging worship at a Franciscan site, see the Christian Information Center website (www.cicts.org).

the six stone jars were purportedly still there when the Piacenza Pilgrim visited in 570: "I filled one of them up with wine and lifted it up full onto my shoulders. I offered it at the altar, and we washed in the spring to gain a blessing."[4] Imagine the scene for a moment. After waiting his turn, a pilgrim from Italy takes a large stone jar associated with the Gospel miracle, fills it with wine, places it upon his shoulders, and proudly presents it on the altar. The pilgrim is playing the role of one of the servants whom Jesus told to fetch the water. Filling the jar with wine instead, the Piacenza Pilgrim places himself at the point in the story after the water had been turned to wine, thus celebrating the fulfillment of the miracle. Emulating the wedding guests, the eighth-century pilgrim Willibald explicitly mentions drinking the wine, exemplifying how pilgrimage is a sensuous encounter with place and story. Today, a cottage industry of Cana wedding wine still entices pilgrims, though those who have sampled the product are said to be waiting for another miracle.

Cana remembers weddings as well as wine, and couples go there to renew their vows. The Piacenza Pilgrim wrote his parents' names on the wedding couch, suggesting that the blessing of couples, even *in abstentia*, has been linked with Cana since the Byzantine period. Carrying stone jars, drinking wine, and celebrating marriage are pilgrim practices long associated with the Cana church.

At Jesus' baptism site on the Jordan River, pilgrims literally immerse themselves in the story. While baptism and its reaffirmation are forms of worship, pilgrims interact with the water in less formal ways as they recall the biblical images of the river and use the place as a setting for personal reflection. Arculf swam both ways across the river, while a few decades later, Willibald bathed there, reporting that "at the place where they now baptize, a rope has been stretched across the Jordan, which is fastened at each side. On the feast of the Epiphany, cripples and sick people come and, using the rope to steady themselves, go down to dip themselves in the water. Women who are barren also come there."[5] From reflective wading to full immersion, modern-day pilgrims enter both stream and story. Playing upon the baptism theme of dying and rising in Christ, Orthodox pilgrims wear white gowns into the river which will later serve as their funeral dress.

Elsewhere in the Holy Land, pilgrims kiss the silver star marking Jesus' birth. Fishing nets are thrown off boats in the Sea of Galilee. In Bethany, pilgrims call Lazarus forth from his tomb. At the Russian Hospice near the Holy

---

4. Piacenza Pilgrim, *Travels*, 4. The spring was presumably thought to have been the water source of Jesus' miracle.

5. Adomnán, *On the Holy Places*, 2.16; Hugeburc, *The Life of Willibald*, 16.

Sepulchre, some squeeze through the "eye of the needle," which purports to be a narrow slit in the ancient city wall. The faithful recall Jesus' trial and imprisonment by descending into a rock pit at St. Peter in Gallicantu, while, on Calvary, they touch the socket of the cross. Pilgrims enter the empty tomb as Easter-day disciples. They kindle candles, evoking the light of resurrection, and size up the last footprint of Jesus at the place of the ascension.

A number of practices, including measuring the sites, allowed pilgrims to take objects home as religious souvenirs. The Piacenza Pilgrim reports that pilgrims took string measurements of Jesus' column of scourging, which bore imprints of his hands, and wore them as blessings around their neck.[6] The same practice occurred at Pilate's praetorium where Jesus' footprints could be seen in the rock of judgment: "from this stone where Jesus stood come many blessings. People take 'measurements' from the footprints and wear them for their various diseases, and they are cured."[7] Pilgrims also marked distances with their bodies. Arculf measured the burial bench of Christ with his hands and found it to be seven-feet long.[8]

Today, one of the most peopled stations of Christian piety is the stone of anointing, or the stone of unction, immediately inside the Holy Sepulchre.[9] The station commemorates the anointing of Jesus' body after he was taken down from the cross and consists of a horizontal red stone measuring six meters by one meter that is framed by eight hanging lamps. Joseph of Arimathea anointed Jesus' body with a mixture of myrrh and aloes and wrapped it in linen cloths before placing him in the tomb (John 19:38–40). Modern-day pilgrims, especially Orthodox Christians, pour oil on the rock as they kneel in prayer, rubbing their fingers along the stone. Their tactile prayers are driven by the idea that they are touching a stone that has touched the body of Christ. Although the station is a Crusader addition and the current stone has only been in place since 1810, pilgrim emulation of Joseph's devotion, the emotional intimacy of preparing Jesus' body for burial, and the latency of resurrection that inhabits the station make it one of the most spiritually poignant settings in the Holy Land.

Pilgrims use the stone of anointing for more than just prayer. It is a place for blessing the physical accoutrements of the spiritual life: objects

6. Piacenza Pilgrim, *Travels*, 22.

7. Piacenza Pilgrim, *Travels*, 23.

8. Adomnán, *On the Holy Places*, 1.2.10–11.

9. The main entrance to the Holy Sepulchre was originally to the east. Pilgrims consequently passed the place of the crucifixion prior to arriving at the tomb of Christ. Following the destruction of the complex in 1009, the entrance was moved to the south between Calvary and the tomb of Christ. As a result, pilgrims walk into the middle of the story, encountering the stone of anointing as they enter the building.

acquired in the Holy Land and those brought from home. Pilgrims place objects on the rock, like crosses, icons, and rosaries, which are prayed over, dedicated, and taken home as sacred mementos. The white gowns previously seen at the Jordan River are laid upon the stone and anointed in a fashion reminiscent of Jesus' body, producing baptism-cum-burial gowns to be worn as resurrection garments.

In short, pilgrims reenact aspects of the biblical narrative by engaging the physical settings of the Holy Land. Christian travelers to Jerusalem should become familiar with pilgrim customs, observing what others are doing at the holy sites, including traditions that are not their own. Although certain practices may embrace a piety that runs counter to one's beliefs and sensibilities, the pilgrim life engages the Other. Pilgrims are encouraged to explore ways of reenacting Gospel narratives by reviving ancient traditions, adapting current customs, and developing new forms of embodied practice. Whether we imitate a tradition as it is, alter it to suit our tastes, or simply observe the actions of others, we may be surprised by the commonalities that we share with other Christians.

How can one use art, objects, and physical movement to reenact Gospel stories and to physically engage the sites in devotional ways? There are a few points to keep in mind. First of all, access to commemorative focal points, such as the tomb of Christ and the Nativity grotto, is generally limited. One often has just enough time to touch an object, take a photo, and say a short prayer. Secondly, some of the above examples, like the Cana church and Jacob's Well, do not appear on every itinerary, and schedules may be revised at the last minute resulting in sites being dropped from the program. Third, pilgrims should consider practices that can be enacted in the general vicinity of a holy place and which do not elicit the undo attention of others, especially at Status Quo sites. Finally, pilgrim practices—both traditional customs and innovative ideas—can be discussed as a group with leaders and guides. In short, pilgrims do not always have the time or opportunity to perform a specific act at a particular site, but they will have ample occasion to engage in pilgrim practices throughout the journey, especially during their free time in Jerusalem. The art of Holy Land travel is managing one's expectations while being ready to respond to spiritual opportunities.

Perceiving the World

Jesus said, "Come and see." As previously stated, observation is the most fundamental act of Holy Land pilgrimage. Nothing drew Christians to Jerusalem more "than the desire to see . . . where Christ was physically present," while the modern adage, "to see the Holy Land," expresses the same idea: the Holy Land is an open-eyed experience. Pilgrim spirituality broadens the application: to be on pilgrimage is to see the world differently. Pilgrim perception extends from places to people, from a focus on self to attending to others. Pilgrims have a heightened sense of awareness; they see possibilities, recognize opportunities, and discern situations. On pilgrimage, we perceive mysteries that are otherwise hidden to us and assume a more expansive perspective of the world. Pilgrims see God in the details of everyday life. God is present in the ordinary as well as the extraordinary, in the mundane as well as the miraculous.

The Third Eye of the Pilgrim

Over an advent dinner in her Assisi guesthouse, Sister Giovanna shared stories of her pilgrim experience:

> I worked a long time with the mentally ill, and for many years, I gave hospitality to traveling pilgrims. Then I asked God to allow me to be a pilgrim. I have been a pilgrim ever since. I used to go on pilgrimage throughout Italy, hitchhiking without any money. But now hitchhiking is illegal, so I carry enough money for a bus ticket. There are a lot of poor people in Italy, a lot of refugees. People living on the streets. By being a pilgrim, my heart learns to hear the cries of those who have no choice but to be pilgrims. As a pilgrim, I become more attentive to God and more aware of the conditions and needs of God's children. That is what I call the third eye of the pilgrim.

Sister Giovanna's use of the third eye speaks to the way that pilgrims see the world differently from others.

While the street is a metaphor for the everyday world, Sister Giovanna is referring to actual roads and alleyways, places inhabited by refugees and immigrants, the abandoned and abused, the poor, the mentally ill, and those suffering from addictions. Pilgrims are servants of the road; acute observers of the human condition. They hear the cries of the street, and with a penetrating third eye, they discern the needs of others and respond with compassion. The Christian journey calls us to recognize fellow pilgrims in the faces of those we meet along the way. For the Holy Land traveler, the third eye applies to how we perceive the Living Stones, our gazeful care of foreign pilgrims, and our attention to fellow pilgrims in our group: to the way we see strangers, new acquaintances, and old familiar faces.

God Is in the Facts

The writings of Gerard W. Hughes speak to the contemporary pilgrim life. God calls us through the facts in which we find ourselves;[10] God is in the facts.[11] Pilgrims perceive God in the details of what actually happens. God is neither theory nor a hypothetical presence. We do not encounter God in what *could* or *should* have been. God is not in the sunny day that never materialized but in the rainy day that *actually* occurred. We encounter God in the realities of lived experience and in the actualities of the unfolding day. A trip may be full of disappointments. The weather may be less than perfect; we may get sick or injured. Pilgrims experience sadness and frustrations, and while a God-is-in-the-facts spirituality may not tell us *why* something happened (nor does it condone evil or tragedy as the will of God), the risen Christ is in the ashes. Immanuel, God-with-us, inhabits a real world, and the lessons of the pilgrim journey are revealed by a God who calls us through the actual events of our lives.

The God of Mystery and Surprise

As God's presence is revealed in the unfolding details of the journey, our encounter with God is always one of mystery and surprise. As he walked from England to Rome, Hughes reflected upon the relationship between pilgrimage and the God of surprises:

> If we are to be pilgrims, then we must want this at-oneness [with God] more than anything else, and if we really want it, our lives will be characterized by openness and adaptability. If we are led by the mysterious God, our lives will be anchored in only one certainty, that we are mysteriously called beyond ourselves. . . . Our faith teaches us that God is the God of surprises, who will always be mystery for us.[12]

In contrast to the legibility of the Fifth Gospel and our legitimate efforts to understand the first-century context of Jesus' life, the Holy Land journey is clouded in mystery and surprise. We find ourselves searching less for the contours of a visible deity than for signs of divine mystery that are revealed along the way.

---

10. Hughes, *Walk to Jerusalem*, 119.

11. See Hughes, *God of Surprises*. The phrase—God is in the facts, and the facts are kind—is used throughout.

12. Hughes, *In Search of a Way*, 90.

Seeing the (Extra)ordinary

Pilgrims seek the extraordinary in the ordinary and the ordinary in the extraordinary. Pilgrimage is an extended appointment with extraordinary events. Pilgrims anticipate the holy and bask in moments of divine favor as God breaks through in moments of unpredictable surprise. The routine of everyday life has been broken, replaced by a litany of novel encounters. One traverses new scenery, meets new people, explores new thoughts, and receives new insights and inspiration. As the journey progresses, however, it is the ordinary aspects of life—common tasks, simple necessities, familiar habits, and common friendships—that become tinged with sanctity. Pilgrimage captures the miracle of ordinary experience, and upon returning home, everyday life becomes infused with a greater awareness of God's extraordinary presence in a commonplace world. Pilgrims see in double vision, perceiving God's presence in (extra)ordinary ways.

Pilgrims Remember

Reflection, memory, and commemoration are fundamental practices of Holy Land pilgrims.

Pilgrims Remember the Stories of Faith

Holy Land pilgrims remember the life of Christ and the stories of Christian salvation. Walking the land, exploring archeological sites, and visiting the holy sites are acts of Christian memory that recall the biblical past and its application to contemporary faith.

Pilgrims Remember Their Journey of Faith

Pilgrims reflect upon their own journey of faith, recognizing God's continued presence over the years and giving thanks for those who have shaped their faith along the way.

Pilgrims Remember Home

People back home are never far from the thoughts and prayers of Holy Land pilgrims.

Pilgrims Preserve Memories of their Journey

Pilgrims observe the sites, take photos, and keep journals. Debriefing with fellow pilgrims solidifies memories by clarifying confusions, remembering details, recalling highlights, and articulating meaning. Pilgrims are constantly learning from past experience.

9

The Blessings of Pilgrimage

Material objects are an integral part of the spiritual journey. They are catalysts of memory, physical extensions of our spiritual lives, expressions of meaningful experience. The Holy Land is a sensuous, physical journey, and spirituality does not rise above the land, it inhabits it. As religious experience takes place upon the ground, spiritual memory becomes attached to physical, transportable materials, like water, rocks, oil, and candles, which, along with clergy stoles and olive wood carvings, comprise the mementos bound for home, where the journey is shared with others and sacred memories are recalled for years to come.

The Blessings of Pilgrims Past

Ancient pilgrims referred to holy objects and the benefits they conveyed as blessings. The sixth-century Piacenza Pilgrim "took a blessing" by filling a small souvenir ampulla with oil from a lamp inside the tomb of Christ.[1] He likewise observed that earth was placed in the tomb for the same reason: "those who go in take some as a blessing."[2] As previously mentioned, pilgrims took string measurements of the column of scourging and wore them around their neck as blessings. At the place where Jesus was judged by Pilate "come many blessings. People take 'measurements' [of Jesus'] footprints, and wear them for their various diseases, and they are cured."[3] According to Egeria (fl. 380), at the place of the multiplication of the fish

---

1. Piacenza Pilgrim, *Travels*, 18. Pilgrim ampullae were small flagons, generally made of tin and lead, that were decorated with biblical scenes, such as the resurrection. The largest collections are in Monza and Bobbio, Italy.

2. Piacenza Pilgrim, *Travels*, 18.

3. Piacenza Pilgrim, *Travels*, 22.

and loaves, pilgrims "take away small pieces of the stone to bring them prosperity, and they are very effective."[4]

In setting sail from the Holy Land, Willibald (720s) smuggled balsam through customs at Tyre. Willibald filled a common gourd with balsam. He then took a hollow cane with a firm bottom and filled it with petroleum. He inserted the cane into the balsam-filled gourd and closed the hole. The scheme worked to perfection. When the Umayyad authorities searched his baggage, they opened the gourd, smelled the petroleum, and let Willibald proceed to the port.[5] What are present-day travelers to make of the blessings of pilgrimage and the material takeaways of the Holy Land journey? The idea that objects can be imbued with holiness speaks to a piety dismissed by most modern traditions. Even so, Christians of all backgrounds seek, at the very least, physical reminders of spiritual experience.

The Practice of Sacred Objects

The above examples present three types of Holy Land objects. Willibald's balsam shows an interest in the natural products of the promised land. Palm fronds and olive sprigs, frankincense and myrrh, spices and Dead Sea products are modern-day equivalents.

Secondly, pilgrims prized pieces of the Holy Land that were directly associated with Jesus' life. Pilgrims chipped stones away from the rock of Calvary, the tomb of Christ, and various places of Jesus' ministry, a damaging practice that diminished the sites. An acceptable substitute is water from the Jordan River or a stone from the Judean Wilderness.

Third, based on the idea that holiness can be transferred from one object to another, pilgrims desired mementos that had physically touched what Christ had touched. Ordinary items could be transformed into holy objects, manufactured at the will of the religious traveler. Strings that had measured impressions of Jesus' body and oil from the tomb of Christ were favored blessings. Today, laying items on the stone of anointing, wearing baptism robes into the Jordan River, and lighting take-home candles at the tomb of Christ play upon the same idea: physical contact with a sacred object or its use in a meaningful setting adds value to the item.

The practice is common to our religious and civic life. A baptism candle, a confirmation Bible, and items from weddings and funerals become important keepsakes. The United States Capital Flag Program flies American flags over the United States Capital, which are available for purchase by

4. Egeria, *Egeria's Travels*, V 3; see Wilkinson, *Egeria's Travels*, 98.
5. Hugeburc, *The Life of Willibald*, 28.

individuals and organizations. The flags have an increased, derivative value by virtue of their physical link with the U.S. Capital and are treasured by veterans, scout groups, and union halls across America. Likewise, a cross necklace dipped in the Jordan River or laid upon the tomb of Christ becomes a special memento. Even if we differ on what the act actually signifies, Christians share a common sentiment: an object's physical association with a special place or event enhances its value.

Christians of all backgrounds desire a tangible connection to the Holy Land, and Protestant sensibilities are more aligned with other traditions than is commonly assumed. The Orthodox have a penchant for candles, oil, and icons. Catholics like crosses and rosaries. Protestants love the Jordan River, taking water home for baptism blessings. How does Protestant water differ from Orthodox oil? The stone of anointing may be seen as the antithesis of Protestant spirituality, a station serving up do-it-yourself relics, giving spiritual life to inanimate objects. Or, it can be approached as a spiritual encounter with the crucified Christ, a surface of tactile prayer and spiritual reflection alongside Christians from around the world, a station where the acquisitions of Holy Land travel can be dedicated for the journey home. The blessings of pilgrimage are the physical representations of the biblical truths, spiritual encounters, and personal insights that we acquire on religious travel. They expand our imagination, preserve our memories, and affirm our commonalities with other Christians.

The Replication of the Holy

Sacred objects play an important role in the replication, or expansion, of the holy, a theme discussed in the final chapter. The good news of Jesus' resurrection spread from the empty tomb to the ends of the world, and the replication of the holy is central to the Christian faith. Every worship experience replicates the holy, and Holy Land objects can play an important role in translating the gospel to local settings. Holy Land water transforms sanctuaries into the Jordan River; palm branches turn worship space into the gates of Jerusalem. The use of pilgrim blessings, including candles, chalices, and clergy stoles, connects the Holy City with home.

Teaching the Stories of Jesus

Holy Land objects, such as frankincense and myrrh, are valuable resources for Christian education, bringing the Bible to life for children, youth, and adults. Gifts shops are full of teaching and storytelling aids as well as instructional resources, like maps and atlases, that contain information on the topography, history, and archaeology of the Bible, including the temple and the Judaism of Jesus' day.

Blessings for Remote Pilgrims

Christians around the world seek the blessings of Jerusalem, and tangible contact with the Holy Land is gratefully received by remote pilgrims. While living in Jerusalem, I went to Nepal to teach a two-week course at a Bible college comprised of young evangelical Christians, many of whom were serving in local churches in Kathmandu. Since the course was intended to replicate aspects of the Holy Land experience, I brought a collection of objects, including crosses and olive sprigs. At the end of our discussion on Jesus' baptism, I presented the class with a bottle of Jordan River water for immediate use in a reaffirmation of baptism service. The room was instantly filled with an audible excitement, accompanied by an acute sense of anticipation. Gathering around the handheld font, the students received water on their heads, shoulders, and foreheads—in the form of the cross and the laying on of hands—as they absorbed the physical blessing of the Jordan River into their familiar forms of prayer. What is the value of Jordan River water, and what, if any, special properties does it have—either before or after its consecrated? Is it merely sentiment and symbolic meaning, or is there something more? The students were receptive to the stirrings of the Spirit as if the river itself was present. The water was a tangible reminder of God's presence in twenty-first-century Kathmandu, which, more generally, is the point of a Holy Land blessing.

Fifth Gospel blessings are prized by Christians around the world. On a social media post, a Hawaiian parishioner expresses his profound gratitude for a reaffirmation of baptism service using Jordan River water that took place the Sunday after his priest returned from Jerusalem. A pilgrim posts a photo of her hospitalized father clutching an olive wood cross that she bought for him in the Holy Land. Bethlehem Christmas ornaments are cheerfully received by an international congregation in Italy. As instruments of celebration and supplication, Holy Land blessings remind remote pilgrims that God is in their midst.

Blessings for the Modern-Day Pilgrim

Religious Mementos

Jordan River Water

Pilgrims can take water from the Jordan River at the baptism sites of Qasr al-Yahud (near Jericho) and Yardenit (at the south end of the Sea of Galilee). Significantly clearer water may be gathered from the river's headwaters in northern Israel at Banias (Caesarea Philippi) and Dan. The sites sell empty bottles, if you do not have one. River water can also be purchased in gift shops throughout the Holy Land.

Olive Sprigs and Palm Fronds

Especially popular as Bible markers, olive sprigs and palm fronds are Holy Land favorites. Olive trees are ubiquitous, and leaves can be easily gathered. Vendors on the Mount of Olives occasionally offer sprigs for a small donation. Jerusalem pilgrims were traditionally known as palmers. While the nickname is all but lost, Holy Land travelers may consider using the palm—either real fronds or depicted images—as a way of expressing their pilgrim identity.

Rocks and Stones

Some pilgrims gather pebbles from places they visit, such as the Galilee and the Judean Wilderness. While the practice is not illegal, there is a strict prohibition against transporting archaeological items out of the country, so make sure that your stones are common rocks—or find a different souvenir.

The Jerusalem Cross

The Jerusalem cross, consisting of a central cross potent, or crutch cross, surrounded by a smaller Greek cross in each of the four quadrants, is the dominant image of the Christian Holy Land. The cross, which adorns various souvenirs, is particularly popular as a pendant necklace.

Olives Wood Products

From simple machine-made crosses to skillfully crafted nativity sets, Bethlehem olive wood is the most iconic Holy Land product. Christmas ornaments are ideal gifts for large groups, like a congregation or children's ministry. While olive wood products are sold throughout the Holy Land, pilgrims should consider buying directly from the factories in Bethlehem.

Clergy Stoles

Available in various liturgical colors, elegant hand-embroidered clergy stoles are meaningful gifts for pastors and seminarians.

Thirty-Three Candles

Souvenir shops near the Holy Sepulchre sell bundles of thirty-three candles representing the years of Jesus' life. Pilgrims light the candles at the tomb of Christ for a couple of prayerful seconds, snuff them out, and take them home as gifts and blessings.

Icons

Pilgrims like to purchase icons of biblical events they have commemorated in the Holy Land, such as Jesus' nativity, baptism, transfiguration, and resurrection. Gift shops carry mass-produced images as well as beautiful handwritten icons, some of local production. Antique collections fill the backrooms of a number of shops.

Holy Land Tattoos

As early as the sixth century, Procopius of Gaza mentions Holy Land pilgrims who bore tattooed crosses and symbols of Christ.[6] Epitomizing the embodied blessing, the practice was popular with medieval pilgrims, and a tattoo shop in the Old City claims a heritage going back to 1300. Popular once again, Holy Land tattoos allow present-day pilgrims to partake in a centuries-old

---

6. Procopius of Gaza, *Commentary on Isaiah*, 44.5, mentioned in Gustafson, "Inscripta in Fronte," 98–99.

tradition. St. George the Dragon Slayer and the Jerusalem cross are the most popular designs.

Oil, Frankincense, and Myrrh

For teaching, healing, prayer, and worship, oil, frankincense, and myrrh are popular Holy Land blessings.

The Stone of Anointing

As previously discussed, the stone of anointing and other sites, such as the tomb of Christ, may be used by pilgrims to bless religious objects that have been bought in the Holy Land or brought from home.

Ancient Traditions

Walking in the footsteps of ancient pilgrims includes replicating their traditions. The image of the medieval palmer waits to be revived. Taking measurements of certain holy sites may appeal to pilgrims willing to carry a ball of string and a pair of security-proof scissors. For the religious entrepreneur, opportunities exist for replicating historical souvenirs, like the Monza ampullae.

Photos, Albums, and Journals

While the chapter has focused on tangible, material objects, no mementos are more important than photos and personal journals. Pilgrims journal, jotting down thoughts and impressions as well as memorable quotes and conversations. Carrying a small notebook in the field allows details to be recorded in real time. Along with packing a second camera, extra memory chips, and additional chords and batteries, attention should be given to backing up photos, videos, and written notes on a daily basis. Upon returning home, pilgrims will turn photos into albums and journals into compositions. The results are dependent upon the images and impressions captured on the journey.

Local and Regional Products

Along with religious items, pilgrims purchase other Holy Land products.

Palestinian Embroidery

Palestinian embroidery, including Bedouin textiles, can be bought through local cooperatives and organizations supporting fair trade practices.

Jerusalem Pottery

Jerusalem pottery, containing traditional, local, and religious designs, comes as tiles, plates, vases, bowls, and chalices. While cheap, mass-produced items flood the markets, a number of Armenian pottery shops produce beautiful decorative art.

Hebron Glass

Known for its distinctive blue and green colors, Hebron glass goes back to the Roman period. While the glass can be found in Bethlehem, Jerusalem, and Jericho, the Hebron factories are worth a visit.

Dead Sea Products

Dead Sea products, including body creams, mud packs, and bath salts, are available throughout the Holy Land.

Eilat Stone

Eilat stone, also known as the King Solomon stone, is the national stone of Israel. Popular as jewelry, the stone contains a beautiful mixture of blue azurite and green malachite.

Dates and Olive Oil

Dates and olive oil are among the high-quality consumable products available in the Holy Land.

In sum, souvenirs are not antithetical to the pilgrim life, which does not mean that shopping is immune from critique. Pilgrims must navigate the material journey that accompanies religious travel, grappling with questions of spirituality, materialism, and economic justice.

The Pilgrim Economy

Holy Land pilgrimage has always been supported by local services supplying the needs of Christians travelers from souvenirs to food, lodging, transport, and guides. While the pilgrim economy exists for the benefit of pilgrims, the subject warrants a few observations. First of all, despite their usefulness, gift shops and souvenir vendors are prolific, contributing to the noise and irritations of the journey. Pilgrims will encounter a cacophony of voices selling anything from water, coins, and bookmarks to bags, scarves, and crosses. Vendors vie for your attention with various verbal greetings, and physical acknowledgment of any kind from eye contact to an oral response will invite the shopkeeper's persistence, making it harder to shake off unwelcomed solicitation. Politeness often does the pilgrim a disservice. In short, shop when you are ready to shop; otherwise, ignore them when you are not.

Secondly, at a number of sites, especially in East Jerusalem and the West Bank, vendors greet pilgrims as they get on and off the bus. While vendors want an opportunity to sell their goods and will respectfully leave once that is granted, groups can lose an inordinate amount of time getting on and off the bus if the situation is not carefully managed. To maximize time, groups must focus on where they are going when they disembark from the bus, and guides should tell vendors to wait until the group returns. Later, as people are loading the bus, transactions can efficiently occur. Better yet, once everyone is on board, products and prices can be announced to the entire group while vendors remain outside. A significant amount of sales can be quickly done in a couple of minutes, or it can take five seconds to determine that no one is interested in an item. While facilitating this is up to group leaders, pilgrims can help monitor effective time management practices for the benefit of everyone involved.

Third, while the vast majority of street vendors are honest people trying to make a living, there is a problem with pickpockets around certain sites in Jerusalem, particularly at the Garden Tomb and on the Mount of Olives. It is worth repeating that there are virtually no street assaults in Jerusalem; it is a very safe city to walk around. There is, however, a commonly repeated pattern for pick-pocketing pilgrims, which occurs under the guise of a street vendor. The culprit pretends to be selling a wide item, like the long horizontal photos of Jerusalem, which he cradles in his arms, leaving his hands free underneath his wares. Taking a frontal approach, the fake-vendor makes bodily contact with the pilgrim, furtively removing items, such as phones and wallets, from the victim's anterior pockets. Once the technique is understood—and it is largely limited to the Garden Tomb and the Mount of Olives—it is simple to spot and easy to stop, especially if group members are looking out for each other. Pilgrims should not allow an apparent vendor to make frontal contact with them, and if one does, shouting, turning around, and/or walking away is sufficient to thwart the attempt. If you catch a pickpocket red-handed, confronting or chasing him will often result in him dropping what he took as he wants nothing to do with the local police. As a precaution, pilgrims should avoid putting items in front external pockets of shirts and vests, including zipped pockets, and should not wear external money belts. Internal jacket pockets, pockets inside handbags, and trousers with tight front pockets are best. Pilgrims should limit the amount of cash and credit cards they have on them at any one time and are wise to distribute their valuables, placing money, phones, and documents in more than one pocket.

Fourth, the Middle East has a unique market culture. While some shops use fixed prices, bartering is the norm, which means that prices are set intentionally too high. Shopkeepers expect counteroffers and will generally lower the amount, especially as you begin to leave the store. Know that the prices are inflated and enjoy the bartering experience. Be equally aware that when tourism suffers because of the Palestinian–Israeli conflict shopkeepers struggle to make ends meet, especially in the West Bank. Pilgrims should pay what they are willing to pay, approaching transactions with a balance of wisdom, caution, and respect. When shopping, especially for big items, like rugs and icons, pilgrims will commonly be offered coffee or tea. It is a part of Middle East hospitality and provides an opportunity to converse with a local shop owner. It does not obligate you to make a purchase.

Finally, pilgrimage provides vital income to local economies. While Holy Land travel contributes to the overall Israeli economy, pilgrim groups are encouraged to patronize Christian businesses, to shop at least once in the West Bank, and to support the numerous co-ops and fair trade initiatives empowering local women and promoting quality Palestinian handicrafts. For pilgrims extending their stay in the Holy Land, there are opportunities for alternative and sustainable tourism, including the Abraham Path, which integrates culture, heritage, and hospitality while facilitating socioeconomic development in the region.

Homebound Blessings

As pilgrims prepare for home, travel supplies give way to homebound blessings. Our anxiety increases according to our investment in the physical takeaways of the journey as we worry about getting gifts and mementos back home. Pilgrims, no less than tourists, become emotionally involved in the outcome of souvenirs as if the experience is somehow preserved by the tangible evidence of the journey. However, travel is precarious; items break. There is a palpable anticipation over purchased items, and real disappointment when ideas fail to meet our expectations back home. Souvenirs gone wrong are part of the pilgrim experience, an unpleasant reminder that life is a constant journey of losing things along the way, which underscores the point of the chapter: that the material blessings of religious travel matter to us.

10

Holy Land Challenges

Not all aspects of Holy Land travel are enjoyable. For all of its rewards, it has its share of challenges. The Holy Land is full of irritants, unpleasantries, distractions, and sideshows. The profane infiltrates the sublime; context encroaches upon content. Pilgrims must navigate security situations, crowded holy sites, and challenging weather conditions. They incur accidents and illnesses and hear bad news from home. Disappointment follows when realities differ from ideals, and expectations turn to frustrations when things do not go according to plan. Religious travel comes with risks and non-guarantees.

Holy Land challenges range from minor annoyances that temporarily occupy our attention to jarring situations that leave a lasting impression. Some challenges remain more or less constant throughout the trip: the weather, the behavior of fellow pilgrims, thoughts of home. At times, the crowds, vendors, and bus chatter are relentless. The art of pilgrimage is persevering through the dull and the difficult, dealing with distractions, and turning contextual noise into meaningful content.

Pilgrim Challenges

Risks and Dangers

To follow Christ is to encounter hardships in a precarious world, and religious travel, like life itself, is a venture in vulnerability. Medieval pilgrims departed for Jerusalem not knowing if they would ever reach the Holy City, let alone return home. Upon sailing into Jaffa, the twelfth-century pilgrim Saewulf and his companions were warned of an approaching storm. They hired a boat and made it safely from ship to shore. The next morning, they heard reports of "new and unheard-of horrors" and running down to the port, they saw "innumerable human bodies of both sexes who had been drowned lying miserably on the shore."[1] According to John of Würzburg (c. 1170), more than fifty deaths a day was not unusual at the Hospital of St. John near the Holy Sepulchre.[2]

Holy Land pilgrimage no longer carries a significant risk. Air travel is reliably safe, and the on-the-ground issues for foreign pilgrims are relatively benign. Pickpockets are present near a couple of sites; young boys occasionally throw rocks in isolated areas. However, street crime is virtually non-existent, and Jerusalem is far safer than most American cities. The city can be walked, even at night, and assaults on tourists are essentially unheard of. While travelers should be prudent, the Holy Land is pilgrim-friendly.

The Israeli–Palestinian conflict does not target foreign tourists. The Christian pilgrim is easily identified and largely ignored by all but shopkeepers. The danger lies in getting caught up in an incident—being in the wrong place at the wrong time. Pilgrims should quickly distance themselves at the first signs of tension and should generally avoid the Old City during the Friday noontime prayers when incidents are more likely to occur. Although situations can quickly arise, much of the conflict is strangely predictable, and despite its enduring tension, Jerusalem has a remarkable ability to return to normalcy once an incident plays out. Perils still exist, though, which is why pilgrims seek prayers of protection. While Christian institutions, tour guides, and bus companies are experts in safely navigating the Holy Land, pilgrims should take sensible precautions, receiving news alerts, seeking on-the-ground advice, and adjusting their movements accordingly.

Physical Challenges

International plane travel and air-conditioned buses have replaced the arduous land and sea journeys endured by medieval pilgrims. Today's Holy Land experience is not overly strenuous, but there are definite physical demands. A number of sites, including Jerusalem's Old City, can be difficult for challenged walkers, and pilgrims must occasionally remain on their feet for extended periods of time. A person should have the ability to walk at least a mile at a time, to manage steep uneven terrain, and to navigate slick steps and paving stones without the help of a handrail. While walking sticks are useful, non-slip shoes are essential. Although groups generally go the second mile to assist fellow pilgrims, individuals ill-matched to navigate the physical requirements of the journey can struggle, taking time and attention away from others. Pilgrims should understand the particulars of their program, discuss their fitness with

1. Saewulf, *The Pilgrimage of Saewulf*, 7.
2. John of Würzburg, *Description of the Holy Land*, 158.

doctors and program organizers, and make an accurate assessment of their physical ability before signing up for a trip.

Climate presents its own set of challenges. While the Middle East has some wonderful weather, especially in the spring and fall, the summer is extremely hot and dry. Dehydration and heat exhaustion are real threats and can strike without warning. Proper head covering, sunscreen, and copious amounts of water are essential. In the non-summer months, seasonal dust storms sweep across the region, negatively effecting human health. The winters are uncomfortably cold and damp, and the Holy Land has its share of colds, flu, and viruses. Snow occasionally falls—thick, wet, and heavy—and when it rains, it pours, creating running water in the streets and flash floods in the valleys. Winter travel requires warm rainproof clothing and good footwear. The elevation extremes between Jerusalem and the Jordan Valley mean that pilgrims commonly experience multiple climates in a single day. Layered clothing is advised. In sum, preparation and self-care are axioms of the pilgrim life, which, with respect to the physical challenges of Holy Land travel, begin with water, diet, clothing, and footwear.[3]

Temptations

From divine encounters to devilish enticements, pilgrimage is life intensified in every respect. Almost every aspect of the human condition finds commemorative expression in the Holy Land, and temptation is no exception. The Pater Noster church on the Mount of Olives commemorates Jesus' teaching of the Lord's Prayer: lead us not into temptation. Christians remember Christ's temptations of power, pride, and possessions near a mountain in Jericho, and the aptly named Mount of Temptation Souvenir Store at the base of the hill is one of the amusing juxtapositions of the Holy Land—a temptation that most pilgrims succumb to! The temptations that pilgrims most commonly face are the indulgent distractions that threaten their focus. The Holy Land is an extravagant experience. Pilgrims feast on falafel, kanafeh, and pomegranate juice. Shopping is sacrosanct. A Dead Sea float and a camelback ride punctuate the trip. Pilgrims must balance pleasure, consumption, and materialism against the primary objectives of the journey. The challenge of pilgrimage is distinguishing between the indulgences that are personally enriching and those that impede our spiritual progress.

---

3. For the more physically inclined, the Holy Land offers an array of meaningful adventures. There are mountains, walls, and towers to climb and ancient water systems to explore. The region contains a number of long-distance walking routes, including the Jesus Trail and the Abraham Path.

One of the critiques of pilgrimage is the lack of accountability, or the moral behavior of religious travelers. In their classic 1978 work, *Image and Pilgrimage in Christian Culture*, Victor and Edith Turner explore the liminal concept of communitas, or undifferentiated community. Pilgrims transition from their everyday lives into an anonymous social context. In doing so, they are freed from former patterns of social behavior, and as former identities are dissolved, pilgrims form a new community with other pilgrims. While the shedding of former constraints offers opportunities for personal transformation, new-found freedoms expose pilgrims to a range moral choices.

The dynamic is very much in play in experiences, like the Camino de Santiago, where individuals meet other pilgrims with whom they share intense, emotional encounters in the context of a fluid, relatively anonymous community. Since the majority of Jerusalem pilgrims travel with people they already know, often as a church group with their pastor or priest, the Holy Land experience often contains a hedge of accountability that is as strong or stronger than structures back home. Even so, moral character is tested in the Holy Land like anywhere else. Pilgrims assume responsibility for their actions and behavior, recognizing, in the words of Jerome, that "what is commendable is not to have been in Jerusalem but to have lived well in Jerusalem."[4]

Faith Challenges

Despite promises of spiritual transformation, the Holy Land can challenge our faith. Encountering the Fifth Gospel may deconstruct our concept of Jesus, shredding Sunday School images and long-held views of the Bible. Historical episodes antithetical to the Christian faith, like the Crusades and the Holocaust, weigh heavily on the pilgrim mind, while violence, oppression, and human rights abuses enacted in the name of religion threaten our faith in humankind. The fanaticisms of Holy Land religion send pilgrims searching for a common center or questioning organized religion altogether. Jerusalem exposes the hopes and fears of our Christian faith.

Group Dynamics

Despite the benefits of an organized program and the blessings of short-term Christian community, group pilgrimage has its share of challenges. The irritating habits of fellow pilgrims can negatively impact the experience, and one person's pilgrimage can become another person's penance. Group pilgrims surrender significant control to others, and the daily schedule is

4. Jerome, *Letter* 58.2.

out of their hands. Time management is a particularly sensitive issue, and pilgrims often find themselves waiting for others.[5] People arrive late to meeting points; groups proceed slowly, and bathroom breaks can take an inordinate amount of time. Nonetheless, when individuals sign up for a group pilgrimage, they are agreeing to certain terms and conditions. Individuals must adhere to a set itinerary, live in covenant with fellow pilgrims, and follow the instructions of guides and leaders.

Home

Home tugs upon the Holy Land pilgrim. Family and friends are never far from the thoughts of Christian travelers, and latent homesickness can be a constant companion. Pilgrims are sad to miss events back home. Relatives want frequent updates; some pilgrims must check in with work, and time differences between home and the Holy Land limit the hours of convenient communication. Pilgrims occasionally receive bad news, and whether to return home early or continue the journey can be a difficult decision.

Mundane Moments

Certain aspects of the Holy Land journey are simply mundane: dull, boring, and nondescript. Pilgrims stand around, sit on buses, and wait in line. Pilgrim spirituality speaks to the in-between moments, to living well in the lulls, to readjusting expectations of a yellow-bricked journey. Will delays and downtimes be filled with positive, beneficial choices, such as reading, journaling, and visiting with others, or will they be spent in restless, wasteful ways? How we fill the gaps determines the tenor of the journey. Holy Land travel also includes chores and errands. Pilgrims seek out cash machines and pharmacies. They do their laundry and take their medication. The challenge of Jerusalem travel lies in the successful navigation of otherwise ordinary tasks.

---

5. There are a number of ways to maximize time throughout a program, including having people refrain from taking photos until the group portion of a site visit is over. Restricting purchases, especially as pilgrims are getting on/off the bus and walking to/from sites, is also important. Significant time is saved when groups make use of full-service toilet facilities with multiple units (the wrong set of toilets will take an inordinate amount of time, so think ahead!). While facilitating this is up to guides and leaders, pilgrims can help monitor effective time management.

Pilgrim Responses

The pilgrim experience is shaped by how we react to the challenges of the journey. Pilgrims practice perseverance, navigate emotions, manage expectations, and focus on others.

The Virtue of Perseverance

Pilgrims embrace challenges, knowing that the blessings of pilgrimage often occur because of hardships not in spite of them. There is satisfaction in completing goals and reaching destinations, all the more so when the experience has not been easy. Patience and perseverance are the quintessential virtues of the pilgrim life. Endurance produces character (Rom 5:2–5), and "the one who endures to the end will be saved" (Matt 10:22). A link between Matthew 10 and Holy Land travel is made in the eighth-century account of Willibald's travels. On his way to Jerusalem, Willibald and his companions endured the "horrible cold of the icy winter," and, at one point, "they were so straitened by the sharpness of severe hunger, that their inward parts being torn with want of food, they began to be afraid that the fatal day of death was at hand."[6] When he finally arrived in Syria, Willibald was arrested as an alleged spy and imprisoned for weeks before being allowed to travel to Jerusalem. In reflecting upon his journey decades later, Willibald viewed his hardships through the lens of Matthew 10: "the one who endures to the end will be saved."

Pilgrimage is an exercise in perseverance, physical endurance, and internal fortitude. While modern-day travel is far less demanding, perseverance remains embedded in the Holy Land experience. For many, visiting the Holy Land is the culmination of a protracted wait, and throughout the journey, pilgrims assume a posture of constant prayer, maintain their focus in the face of distractions, and persevere through fatigue. Pilgrims encounter Christ's perseverance in the Judean Wilderness, at Gethsemane, and on the Via Dolorosa and witness the perseverance of the human spirit in Palestinians and Israelis alike.

Navigating Emotions

Pilgrimage is an emotional journey. Pilgrims are moved by a holy place, enraptured by worship, and grateful for the companionship of others. They laugh, play, and celebrate. More generally, pilgrims respond to their

6. Hugeburc, *The Life of Willibald*, 11.

context, and disappointment and frustration are bedfellows of the pilgrim life. Pilgrims hope for pleasant weather, comfortable buses, short queues, and small crowds and are naturally disappointed when conditions are less than ideal. There may be incessant fog on the Sea of Galilee or heavy rain in Jerusalem; a security situation may change the program, and certain amenities may not be up to par. Pilgrims are disappointed when things are rushed, when time is wasted, and when a site doesn't "speak" to them. They become frustrated by the lack of sleep or by the misfortune of catching a cold. The Holy Land experience contains mini-disappointments that are quickly forgotten as the journey proceeds, and, for the most part, emotions are landscapes that we travel through and leave behind. At times, emotions linger, spilling over from scene to scene.

Emotions are an integral part of the pilgrim experience. First of all, our physical, emotional, and spiritual journeys are profoundly interwoven. Emotions ground us in our human condition, reminding us of the possibilities and limitations of the earthly life. Secondly, emotions personalize the journey. They place an indelible stamp on lived experience. They give texture to the journey, precisely because life is felt in the details. Third, pilgrims embrace the emotions of the journey, experiencing the sanctity of life in the rippled nature of human affections. Emotions are the lens through which we see the world, fundamental to the experience itself. Pilgrims feel the rainy day, the tension of conflict, the grief of departure. They stand pat through sadness, disappointment, frustration, and pain, seeking meaning and perspective in the broadsides of life, confident of God's guidance through pathways of darkness. Pilgrimage is predicated upon a resurrection hope that is glimpsed through tears.

Managing Expectations

Pilgrims head-off disappointment by managing expectations, which are distinct from goals and objectives. While goals provide clarity and motivation, expectations can diminish an experience. Instead of fostering expectations, which anticipate what will happen, pilgrims focus on questions, which anticipate enlightenment.[7] Above all, we should be measured in our claim that the Holy Land will change a person's life. While the Holy Land consistently delivers, spiritual encounters are often elusive, and a pilgrim can go from site to site seeking a connection that never occurs. Pilgrims should be confident of positive outcomes; they should be so by tampering expectations. Instead of striving for a life-changing experience or a spiritual

---

7. See Campbell, *Thou Art That*, 13; Abbott, *The Cambridge Introduction to Narrative*, 60.

connection at a specific site, pilgrims should focus on simpler guarantees. Holy Land pilgrimage changes the way we read the Bible. With new-gained insights into the Christian faith, one's relationship with God is strengthened, and life has changed. The Holy Land pilgrim is transformed less by life-changing moments than by the accumulative effects of the journey. Furthermore, pilgrims manage expectations by embracing a long-term perspective. The Holy Land experience is a springboard for lifelong spiritual growth, and its impact is never over. The Jerusalem pilgrim can be confident of this: that "the one who began a good work among you will bring it to completion by the day of Jesus Christ" (Phil 1:6).

Focusing on Others

While discomfort, hardships, and frustrations can isolate us, community has a curative effect. Difficulties remind us of our dependency on God and our interdependence on one another. Pilgrims respond to Holy Land challenges by focusing on others.

Fellow Travelers

Pilgrims journey as a short-term Christian community, attending to fellow travelers, offering encouragement, sharing vulnerabilities, and listening to one another's stories. Pilgrims find strength in numbers, and giving ear to fellow voices resources our journey with additional perspectives, helping us respond more faithfully to the challenges of Holy Land travel.

People in the Holy Land

The historical tendency of religious travelers to Jerusalem has been to view the Holy City in terms of one's own faith: "Jewish sources mention Jews, Christians mention Christians, and Muslims mention Muslims, but 'the other' is treated as if he [or she] did not exist."[8] One of the challenges of Holy Land pilgrimage is to break loose of old ways of being religious. Pilgrims see God in the hopes and fears of Christians, Jews, and Muslims alike and pray for peace between Israelis and Palestinians.

---

8. Murphy-O'Connor, *Keys of Jerusalem*, 225; also see Aist, *The Christian Topography*, 245.

People Back Home

Pilgrims are in constant prayer for people back home, making Jerusalem travel a journey of intercessory prayer. Likewise, they receive encouragement from home, strengthening their resolve to persevere.

The Noise of Holy Land Travel

The Holy Land experience is full of noise and static—peripheral sounds, minor irritants, and bewildering sideshows—from the chatter of fellow pilgrims to the carts and tractors of the Old City. The journey includes in-harmonious images and jarring juxtapositions: minefields line the road to the Jordan River, military exercises echo in the Judean Wilderness, garbage collection interferes with the Way of the Cross, the solemnity of a sacred site is interrupted by a monk yelling for silence, and signs prohibiting weapons welcome pilgrims to the holy shrines. How does one distinguish between noise and substance? What is the difference between content and context? What lessons can be found in the extraneous details of the pilgrim life? The art of pilgrimage is learning to hear the cacophony of religious travel as meaningful notes.

The Judean Wilderness

Upon Jesus' baptism, "the Spirit immediately drove him out into the wilderness. He was in the wilderness forty days, tempted by Satan; and he was with the wild beasts; and the angels waited on him" (Mark 1:12–13). The Judean Wilderness is an area of land that stretches east from Jerusalem to the Jordan Valley. High plateaus offer breath-taking panoramas of undulating hills and barren desert landscapes. Down below, the Wadi Qelt, a steep mountain valley containing springs, a Roman aqueduct, and the cliff monastery of St. George in Choziba, cuts through the hills on its way to the Jordan River. As the general setting of Jesus' wilderness experience, pilgrims spend time immersed in the biblical landscape, reflecting upon the story, spellbound by the scenery, seduced by the desert silence. There are pathways for exploration and places for personal solitude. The Judean wilderness is a land of longing and fulfillment, a place of paradox and contradictions, a place of retreat and intrusion.

As the bus pulls up to the panorama, four generations of Bedouin vendors suddenly appear. The Holy Land's ubiquitous gift shop hangs from their arms—scarves and keffiyehs, necklaces and bracelets, belts and bags. Pilgrims are greeted by the entrepreneurial persistence of their desert hosts:

weathered elders, young men, and an array of waist-high kids hawking their wares. Keffiyehs are placed on unsuspecting heads. Disheveled boys peddle dollar bracelets. They are honest and trustworthy but utterly determined. No means no, but it needs to be said a number of times. Pilgrim space is repeatedly prodded, and solitude proves elusive. But the flurried scene soon settles down. Pilgrims walk and sit in silence, meditating on wilderness themes. Visual prayers are cast upon vast horizons. A few pilgrims push prayer aside to engage the kids, and, in the end, bracelets are bought, keffiyehs acquired, and perspectives gained. For some, the Bedouins are a frustrating distraction; for others, they give life to the wilderness encounter. According to Mark, Jesus was with the beasts, and the angels attended him. So, who's who in the story? The wilderness teaches us that we sometimes find ourselves unexpectedly in the presence of angels.

The wilderness solitude can also be interrupted by the sound of distant gunfire from a firing range of the Israeli army. The occasional fighter plane streaks down the Jordan Valley. It can be quite disconcerting to pilgrims still adjusting to the realities of the promised land. The noise stirs up disquiet and awakens anxiety. Gunfire in the wilderness begs questions of safety and security, and the militarization of the Holy Land weighs heavily on pilgrim hearts. Intrusions find a home in the wilderness. After all, isn't wilderness precisely what jars us, experiences that rest uneasily with us, leaving us longing for the presence of angels? Wilderness is where our thoughts are disturbed, places of provocation, the settings that threaten to undo our goals and objectives. Jesus' wilderness experience was a time of discernment; it was not a blissful retreat. It was full of challenges and confrontations, threats and temptations. Yet, in the end, the diabolical moments gave way to the ministry of angels. From bracelets to bullets, the noise of the wilderness takes us deeper into the Gospel story.

The Via Dolorosa

No experience is more conducive to the vagaries of pilgrimage than walking Jerusalem's Via Dolorosa. The Way of the Cross is a fourteen-station devotional walk from the traditional site of Jesus' condemnation by Pilate to his crucifixion and entombment at the Holy Sepulchre. Groups generally carry a large cross and offer scriptures, hymns, and prayers at each station. Tracing the final steps of Jesus' life can be deeply moving; pilgrims are lost in prayer, sometimes in tears, and for many, the Via Dolorosa is the spiritual climax of the journey. The journey takes place on the everyday streets of Jerusalem, past souvenir shops and lemonade stands. Children are on their way to school. Soldiers are positioned on corners. Tractors collecting rubbish shake the streets with a thunderous roar; push carts loaded with merchandise dart through the crowds. A local Christian stops to pray; someone spits on the cross. Most ignore the familiar scene of foreign pilgrims, but the crowds beg the question: should groups walk the Via Dolorosa in the early morning when the streets are more empty, when the conditions are more conducive to prayer and reflection? Or, remembering that Jesus encountered people along the way, should pilgrims mark the stations when the streets are full of life? Whenever one does it, the contextual noise is part of the journey.

My first experience of the Via Dolorosa was participating in the Franciscan's Friday procession, which was led by four priests with a portable speaker. After the first station in the courtyard of the Al-Omaria School, the former site of the Antonia Fortress, the pilgrim throng filed out into the busy street. Kids were hawking pamphlets with the readings, and I was glad that I bought one as I soon became lost in the crowd. Stuck in the back, I reached most of the stations long after the priests had left. I had a strange feeling—like I was queuing for a hot dog at the Super Bowl. Something significant was happening, but I was missing the action. The processional tail pressed on without a head. A man lit a cigarette. Someone burped. Others were laughing. I reminded myself that Jesus died for the end of the line. We passed shops and restaurants, tempting pilgrims with alluring sights and exotic smells. A few would-be followers dropped out along the way. It's overcrowded; some of the stations commemorate things that are not mentioned in scripture, and scholars now think that Jesus approached Golgotha from a different direction. Still, it's the Via Dolorosa—on a Friday—in Jerusalem; this is sacred stuff. People are deep in prayer, walking with Christ, navigating obstacles on the way to Calvary.

Pilgrim noises are not the impediments that threaten to unravel a trip. They are the irritants, sideshows, and distractions that accompany the journey. The chatter should often be ignored, but, here and there, attending to the noise of pilgrimage can turn peripheral context into meaningful content.

Pilgrim Fatigue

Holy Land pilgrimage begins and ends with fatigue. Jet lag takes a couple of days to sort out. As pilgrims adjust to time and place, the heart of the journey is exhilarating. But the days are packed, and rest is limited. The bus journeys and site visits take a toll, and the evening buffets eventually get old. Navigating foreign cultures, the tensions of Jerusalem, and the militarization of the region is wearisome, especially for first-time pilgrims. Pilgrims commonly reach a saturation point, and they are ready to go home.

The educational component of Holy Land pilgrimage is overwhelming. The sheer number of sites, each with its own biblical, historical, and archaeological context, leaves pilgrims gasping for reprieve, and as pilgrims encounter ideas that differ from long-held views of the Bible, the Holy Land journey effects a rethink about the life of Jesus, his Nazarene roots, his Galilean ministry, and his relationship to Jerusalem and the Jewish faith. Who was he? What was his self-identity? What were his major influences and motivations? How did Jesus express his Judaism? What did he mean by the kingdom of heaven, and what were his eschatological views? Why was he crucified, and how did his followers experience his resurrection? The questions beckon pilgrims homeward, where, rested, the insights of the journey can be prayerfully engaged.

Given the eventuality of fatigue, should pilgrims slow down and omit certain sites? There are certainly ways to manage the pace. For guides and leaders, it starts with a carefully planned itinerary that factors in the minimum time desired at each site, a knowledge of driving times, and an awareness of the speed and limitations of the group. It likewise requires an efficient approach to the sites, one that balances group presentations with personal time for prayer and exploration. The days are full, but they should not be rushed. Attention should also be given to the evening program. Despite the importance of debriefing the day, informational lectures, and evening devotions, groups should generally limit—or carefully manage—the after-dinner program, giving participants options for early evenings, personal free time, and informal fellowship.

The pace of Holy Land programs warrants three additional points. First of all, every biblical story commemorated in the Holy Land becomes indelibly marked in one's imagination, permanently resourcing one's faith. Since most pilgrims only visit the Holy Land once in their lifetime, it is worth the effort to take in as many sites as reasonably possible. Secondly, nothing wears out a pilgrim more than free time! Pilgrims routinely expend more energy during their free time in Jerusalem than they do on the programmed parts of their course. Pilgrims desire freedom more than rest. Third, during my time at St. George's College, we occasionally offered a slow-paced pilgrimage, a retreat at the sites, led by a colleague, in which individuals spent a significant amount of time at a selection of sites and concluded most days by mid-afternoon. Despite the reduced nature of the program, dinnertime conversations were no different from those of other courses: pilgrims acknowledging their sense of fatigue. Holy Land travel is tiring, and adjusting the length, contents, and pace of a pilgrim itinerary does little to mitigate fatigue.

Once weariness sets in, pilgrims should take additional precautions to avoid accidents. Otherwise, tired pilgrims persevere by absorbing content that can be processed back home, observing, as before, the physical appearance of the sites, taking photos, and making notes of presentations, conversations, and personal reflections. Fatigued travelers place a premium on debriefing each other for the sake of solidifying memories. What did people like or dislike about a site? What details did they notice, and what impressed them? What may have escaped their attention? What were the highlights and surprises of the day? Tired pilgrims safeguard their journey through conversations with others.

Mark Twain, who visited the Holy Land in 1867, adeptly conveys the overwhelming nature of Jerusalem. While his account of the city begins with descriptive prose, background stories, personal reactions, and humorous anecdotes, by the end of his sojourn, his journal entries are reduced to a mere list of places. His parting words on Jerusalem vividly capture his fatigue:

> The sights are too many. They swarm about you at every step; no single foot of ground in all Jerusalem . . . seems to be without a stirring and important history of its own. . . . I did not think such things could be so crowded together as to diminish their interest. . . .We have been drifting about for several days, using our eyes and our ears more from a sense of duty than any higher and worthier reason.[9]

In leaving Jerusalem, Mark Twain was tired but grateful: "We are satisfied. We can wait. Our reward will come. To us Jerusalem and today's experience will be an enchanted memory a year hence—a memory which money could not buy from us." Twain knew that his Holy Land journey was not over; in many ways, it had only begun:

> We do not think, in the holy place; we think in bed, afterwards, when the glare and the noise and the confusion are gone, and in fancy we revisit alone the solemn monuments of the past and summon the phantom pageants of an age that has passed away.[10]

Many factors contribute to pilgrim fatigue: the physical demands of the journey, the dynamics of group travel, the tension of foreign cultures in conflict, being away from home, the sheer number of sites, and the dissonance that arises from unexpected surprises, new perspectives, and challenging insights. The tired pilgrim eventually yearns for home where spiritual growth takes root in the aftermath of the journey.

9. Twain, *Innocents Abroad*, chapter 54.
10. Twain, *Innocents Abroad*, chapter 55.

11

Preparations

Taking pilgrims from home to the Holy Land, the chapter covers pre-departure planning, the act of departure, the outbound journey, and Jerusalem arrival.

Pre-Departure Planning

How do you prepare for the Holy Land? How do you lay the ground for a successful journey, and what should you know before you go? Preparation begins in informal ways by considering the image of Jerusalem, noting place names in scripture, and following news about the Middle East. It consists more intentionally of prayer, study, and strategic thinking: practical details and symbolic acts. Pilgrimage is a personal journey that escapes generic templates and formulaic checklists. While Jerusalem-bound readers should selectively choose from the following ideas, the entire book is a pre-departure manual for Holy Land pilgrims.

Spiritual Resources

Pre-trip planning is the time to address Fosdick's observation that many Holy Land travelers have "not known how to make the trip or [have] been inwardly unfitted to make it."[1] Pre-departure pilgrims equip themselves with the spiritual resources needed to grasp the lessons of religious travel. This begins with a pre-trip prayer list that focuses upon personal health, practical guidance, and God's will for the journey. Prayers are offered for fellow pilgrims, stay-at-home support groups, and the peace of Jerusalem.

Jerusalem-bound travelers posture themselves by reflecting upon the pilgrim life, meditating on God, self, and the Other, and pondering the

1. Fosdick, *A Pilgrimage to Palestine*, 23.

categories of time, place, journey, and people. Pilgrims are encouraged to keep a pre-departure journal, practicing the art of observation, attending to the spirituality of everyday life, and recording pre-trip reflections. Tasked with describing the indescribable and putting words to thoughts, feelings, and experiences, pre-trip pilgrims reflect upon the use of language to describe God and the spiritual life, familiarizing themselves with concepts discussed in the book, and testing terms for personal use, like commemoration, religious imagination, and the Fifth Gospel.

Calling

Pilgrims are called to "come and see" (John 1:39, 46). Reflect upon the events, conversations, and influences that have led to your decision to go to the Holy Land. Are you approaching the journey as a calling? What responsibilities and obligations come with being called to the Holy Land? How does a calling reduce the pressure of a perfect trip?

Pilgrim Identity

Pilgrims should review the definitions, concepts, and motives discussed in chapters 2–5, making a list of favored themes to reflect upon throughout the journey.

The Third Eye of the Pilgrim

To be on pilgrimage is to see the world differently. Jerusalem pilgrims observe the holy sites, perceive the workings of God around them, and are attentive to the needs of others. Pilgrims practice the art of observation, intentionality, and awareness.

God Is in the Facts

Pilgrims encounter God in the details of lived experience, perceiving God in the actualities of life, embracing the physicality of spiritual experience, and reflecting upon the incarnational nature of God. God calls us through the actual events of our lives.

Pilgrimage as a Microcosm of Life

The pilgrim life consists of the miraculous and the mundane, beatitudes and boredom, hardships and the holy, enlightenment and temptation. Pilgrimage is life intensified, a concentrated exercise in self-care, decision-making, and personal management. Regardless of the circumstance, pilgrims assume responsibility for their actions.

Life as Change

Change is a two-sided coin. Life is a journey of losing things along the way. Life is tenuous and temporary; God is our only permanence. On the other hand, pilgrimage reminds us that change is always possible. The Christian life is one of continuous transformation into the likeness of Christ.

Theological Tensions

Pilgrims engage paradox and ponder juxtapositions, investigating old ideas with new eyes. Pilgrims embrace the tensions of the Christian life. God is intimate and mysterious, immanent and transcendent. Christ is human and divine; pilgrims are strangers and citizens. God is everywhere; there are holy places. Life is already and not yet. The Holy Land is instantly familiar and forever foreign.

Goals and Objectives

Pre-departure pilgrims reflect upon their goals and objectives, recognizing that a calling may not reveal the purpose of a journey. Goals and objectives give focus and clarity but may limit one's faculty to follow where the journey may lead. Pilgrimage is measured by its long-term outcomes, and the immediate aim of Jerusalem travels is to live faithfully in the Holy Land.

Educational Preparation

While pilgrims learn in the field, they absorb the details in far greater depth if they have a working knowledge of the biblical, post-biblical, and contemporary contexts of the Holy Land. For many, the educational preparations are invigorating; yet, the material should be approached strategically, especially by time-strapped pilgrims. Focusing on reference materials, such as maps and timelines, and concentrated internet searches on places, dates, events, and people can be more time efficient than reading full-length sources (see appendix 2).

Biblical Landscapes and Narratives

Holy Land pilgrimage is an exercise in place and story, or connecting biblical narratives to physical locations. Pilgrims should begin by reading the Gospels, paying attention to place names, narrative details, and the sequencing of stories, noting differences in the various accounts. They should concentrate on books and websites that focus on landscapes and narratives, such as the works by Bargil Pixner and Peter Walker.

Holy Land Topography

Pilgrims should be familiar with the natural topography of the Holy Land, noting the physical characteristics of the Galilee, the Jordan Valley, the coastal plains, and the biblical hill country of Judea and Samaria. Special consideration should be given to Jerusalem, paying particular attention to its hills and valleys. Note that while Mount Sion was originally associated with the Eastern Hill (the City of David, Mount Moriah, and the temple), since at least the Byzantine period it has been identified with the Western Hill (Holy Sion).

Time Periods

Pilgrims should be familiar with the region's commonly used time periods, noting that time periods often overlap or have multiple designations. The Second Temple period (530 BCE–70 CE) is a long sweeping era that spans numerous concurrent periods, while the time of Jesus—the first century CE—can be referred to as the Second Temple, Herodian, Early Roman, or New Testament period. To understand New Testament context, one needs a working outline of the Intertestamental era, which consists of the Hellenistic (Greek), Hasmonean, Roman, and Herodian periods. For post-biblical history, including the Christian Holy Land, pilgrims should have a basic grasp of the Byzantine and Crusader periods. As for the Islamic dynasties, one should be aware that the Umayyads built the Dome of the Rock, that the Mamluks left a rich architectural legacy in Jerusalem, and that the Ottomans rebuilt the city walls and governed the Holy Land into the modern period.

To understand the contemporary complexities of the Holy Land—distinguishing, for instance, between Israel, the West Bank, East Jerusalem, West Jerusalem, and the Old City—pilgrims should consult various maps, including those that show (1) the 1949 Armistice Line, or the Green Line, (2) the A, B, and C zones of the Oslo Accords, and (3) the Israel–Palestine Separation Barrier. Terms, dates, and readings related to the Israeli–Palestinian conflict appear in appendix 2.

Narrative histories of the Holy City are presented in Karen Armstrong's *Jerusalem: One City, Three Faiths* (1996) and Simon Sebag Montefiore's *Jerusalem: The Biography* (2011).

Archaeology and Material Culture

For archaeological sources begin with Jodi Magness, *The Archaeology of the Holy Land* (2012). Jerome Murphy-O'Connor, *The Holy Land: An Oxford Archaeological Guide*, 5th ed. (2008), remains the best hands-on guide. *The Carta Jerusalem Atlas* by Dan Bahat (2011) is an indispensable resource on the Holy City. Note the history of the city walls.

Additional Questions

Pilgrims are encouraged to explore areas of personal interest, such as flora and fauna and local cuisine. What questions emerge as you imagine yourself walking through the Old City of Jerusalem or riding on a bus through the Galilee or the Jordan River Valley? Pilgrims commonly ask questions about agriculture, water and natural resources, Bedouin culture, Jewish and Muslim practices, and other Christian traditions.

Ideas and Strategies

The pre-trip period provides pilgrims with an opportunity to organize ideas for the journey. While one can overplan what is already a content-rich program, the simplest of ideas can enhance the journey, producing cherish memories and treasured mementos of the Holy Land. Pilgrims may want to create an intercessory prayer bag containing physical representations of prayer requests, including small personal possessions of others, such as photos, small crosses, and written notes, to be prayed for in the Holy Land. How can pilgrim identity, like the image of the palmer, be reinforced by what you take, wear, or carry? Certain pilgrim practices require planning, like packing a spool of string for taking measurements of the holy sites. You may want to write letters to yourself or gather short prayers and blessings to be read at particular junctures in the journey. How will you structure your personal devotions? I reflected upon a daily psalm as I walked the Camino de Santiago. Afterwards, I turned my devotional template into a photo exhibit, using a verse from the respective psalm and a single photo to represent each day of my journey. The pre-trip period is the time to arrange meaningful practices and symbolic acts for the journey ahead.

Pre-Trip Gatherings

Church groups traveling together to the Holy Land generally hold pre-trip gatherings to cover logistics and practicalities, to discuss educational and spiritual resources, and to focus on community formation.

Logistics and Practicalities

Group travel involves a significant amount of information gathering, organizational details, and intra-group communication. Face-to-face meetings are effective for distributing information, answering questions, and sharing ideas. Day of departure details, including gathering points and packing instructions, are particularly important.

The Itinerary

Pre-trip gatherings are useful for discussing the itinerary (see appendix 3). What decisions have already been made, and what can still be decided upon, changed, or reconsidered? How close does the trip follow the general chronology of Jesus' life? Where are the overnight accommodations in Jerusalem? Will you be staying in the Galilee for couple of nights? Besides Bethlehem, will you visit sites in the West Bank, like the tomb of Lazarus (Bethany) and Jacob's Well (Nablus)? To what extent will the program engage local Christians, and will the tour guide be a Palestinian Christian? Will Muslim and Jewish voices be heard, and is there time to visit an Orthodox liturgy? How will the respective holy days of Friday, Saturday, and Sunday impact your program? How much personal time will there be, such as a free day in Jerusalem? Are there options for an extended stay?

Calendars

Groups should look at personal, secular, and liturgical calendars. What events and celebrations will be missed in families, churches, and local communities while the group is away, including birthdays, anniversaries, and one-off occasions? Will you be gone over a national or cultural holiday or miss a favorite sporting event? Will someone in the group celebrate a birthday or a special occasion in the Holy Land or mourn the anniversary of a difficult event? During what liturgical season are you traveling, and what Christian holy days will you observe while you are there? Have a look at the Jewish, Muslim, and Orthodox calendars as well as the calendars of Israel and Palestine. While local events and religious holidays can add special context to the trip, they impact crowds, traffic, and opening hours.

Community Formation

Pre-departure gatherings begin the process of community formation. What does it mean to be a sacred people on a journey? What is the nature of short-term Christian community? Groups should discuss how to live well together in the Holy Land, the expectations and responsibilities of group pilgrimage, and the virtues of patience, respect, and mutual cooperation. Pilgrim communities should be comfortable with group silence, give voice to individual participants, value large and small group discussions, and treasure times of informal fellowship. Christian community should be formed in natural and unforced ways, creating personal and theological space that allows individuals to comfortably engage the group process on their own terms. For groups joining others in the Holy Land, the importance of large group formation should also be discussed.

Sharing Resources

Strategic group packing helps to secure a well-prepared trip. What items can be shared? What extra supplies can be packed that would be difficult for someone to replace? Common-use items include guide books, first aid supplies, adapters, cords, and extra cameras. Not everyone needs a laptop, but a couple can serve a common use. Strategies for backing up photos may also be discussed.

Program Sessions

Pre-trip gatherings often include program sessions, and groups are encouraged to use *Jerusalem Bound* as a discussion guide. Along with the pilgrim material, Holy Land topography, biblical and post-biblical time periods, and the Israeli–Palestinian conflict are good topics for pre-departure gatherings.

Field Trips

A local field trip can foster group formation while previewing Holy Land content. A visit to a mosque or synagogue turns thoughts towards the religious diversity of the Holy Land. A tour of an Orthodox church provides a useful introduction to the Eastern churches. The life of Christ icons adorning an Orthodox sanctuary provides a virtual overview of the journey ahead. Bible parks contain Jerusalem themes, while a trip to a civic monument allows pilgrims to explore concepts of commemoration, place, and memory similar to those encountered in the Holy Land. Pre-trip excursions can also be done on an individual basis.

Returning Home

Thinking ahead, pre-departure gatherings prepare pilgrims for the far side of the journey by discussing post-trip presentations and the long-term objectives of Holy Land travel.

Leaving One's House in Order

Uncertain of safe return, pilgrims have traditionally put their assets in order before leaving home. While Holy Land travel is reliably safe, pilgrimage reminds us that life comes with few guarantees. The spirituality of departure is both practical and symbolic. Focusing on reconciliation, material assets, and personal mortality, pilgrims put their house in order prior to departure. This may include:

- reconciling broken and strained relationships,
- paying off outstanding debts or a symbolic portion of them,

- making or updating an advance healthcare directive (a living will), and

- making or updating a last will and testament.

The pre-departure period is about laying "aside every weight and the sin that clings so closely [in order to] run with perseverance the race that is set before us" (Heb 12:1). By reconciling relationships, pilgrims are travel-ready: "straining forward to what lies ahead" (Phil 3:13).

Pilgrim Baggage

Luggage or baggage? Luggage denotes something that is lugged or carried, while baggage has the connotation of an impediment: something that encumbers one's progress or development. Baggage speaks to spiritual and emotional issues; it includes everything that we take with us: our histories, hurts, and heartaches as well as our health and happiness. In terms of concrete objects, what are the tools and resources of religious travel? What, on the other hand, distracts us from our purpose? What is the difference between necessities and preferences? How do we distinguish between needs, wants, and desires? These questions are at the heart of a Holy Land journey.

The spirituality of packing is an exercise in personal, practical decision-making. While Holy Land programs provide packing lists, pilgrims should be mindful of their head, skin, and feet, focusing on hats, scarves, sunscreen, and, above all, good footwear. The Holy Land's natural landscapes and urban terrain are steep and uneven, and pilgrims must navigate rough rocks and slick stones. Walking sticks are useful. Clothing depends upon the season, and dramatic differences in elevation create multiple climates within a matter of miles. The winters are cold and damp requiring coats, sweaters, and warm socks, while light breathable clothing is best for the hot dry summers. In choosing clothing and travel bags, consideration should be given to securing money, phones, and passports.

Pilgrims are wise to think ahead about their homebound journey. What will you collect along the way, and how will you get it home? Pilgrims can make room in their luggage by donating supplies, such as shoes and clothing, to local charities and refugee camps, which leaders should confirm before leaving home. Gift shops will often ship items, and you can post packages on your own; however, post offices can take an enormous amount of time. In the end, paying for an extra airline bag may be the easiest and most reliable measure, and luggage can be purchased in gifts shops and markets throughout the Holy Land.

Packing includes final checks and last minute errands. Along with the arrangements of house and home, passports should be copied, phone plans confirmed, and banks and credit card companies notified of one's impending travel. It is helpful to have a small amount of Israeli shekels before arriving in the Holy Land, which can be acquired through a local bank or at airports along the way. Pilgrims should discuss communication expectations with loved ones to avoid unnecessary anxiety. Internet access in the Holy Land is ubiquitous but not always reliable. The Tel Aviv airport has free internet service, and pilgrims may want to contact home before exiting the airport.

Departure

Leaving nothing to chance, pilgrims should make arrangements for a travel blessing, which may occur in the context of congregational worship, as a special liturgical occasion, or less formally with family and friends and should be led by a clergy or lay person representing the remain-at-home support group. The blessing may consist of formal readings, specially written prayers, or extemporaneous petitions. Themes should include thanksgiving, safety and protection, perseverance, faithfulness, God's guidance, fellow pilgrims, the peace of Jerusalem, and those staying home. Relevant scriptures should be read, sprinkled perhaps with pilgrim quotes. The blessing may include the laying on of hands, the use of anointing oil, and the presentation of small gifts, such as a cross for the journey, and pilgrims can use the occasion to dedicate their journey to a particular person or cause. The accoutrements of pilgrimage, such as shoes, walking sticks, journals, and prayer objects, may also be blessed.

As pilgrims take their first step towards the Holy Land, they enter a new dimension of sacred time, and the image of a spiritual threshold invites pilgrims to consciously mark their departure as they physically exit the door of their house, if only for a few prayerful moments. With the act of departure, the journey finally begins, but one does not walk alone. While traveling in Japan a number of years ago, I was told about a monk who wanted to spend a year alone in prayer. Although the hermitage experience was not a normal practice of his order, the chapter decided to accompany him to his place of retreat. There, they worshipped together, offering special prayers for the monk, before leaving him in solitude. A year later, the chapter returned to the site, where they worshipped again, before accompanying the hermit back home. The community's gesture of solidarity was a symbolic reminder that the monk was never alone. Community is an integral part of pilgrimage, playing a special role in the act of departure. Rather than saying goodbye at home, family and friends are encouraged to journey with departing pilgrims as far as they reasonable can—to churches, gathering points, and airports—as a physical act of prayerful support.

The Outbound Journey

Medieval travel to Jerusalem consisted of long, arduous journeys over land and sea, and it was not unusual for pilgrims to winter along the way. Today, outbound travel is a relatively short and straightforward affair with even the longest journeys, as uncomfortable as they may be, measured in hours. Holy Land pilgrimage focuses upon being "in place" rather than the journey to get there.

So, what can we say about the outbound journey? How should pilgrims act now that the journey has begun? Should they prepare for their course with Bible and guide book in hand? Should they be deep in prayer, rejecting the indulgences of international travel? Or, should they sit back, relax, and enjoy the flight? Should the journey be a contemplative exercise or a celebratory venture? There is no one way for pilgrims to travel. Rather, situational discernment defines religious travel as pilgrims engage their surroundings and learn along the way. A travel indulgence may be a celebration or a distraction. Study, restraint, and self-denial may foster a calm, anticipatory focus or come at the expense of other enriching options. The point is not to calculate regret but to incubate intentionality, awareness, and self-reflection.

The outbound journey introduces religious travelers to the supplemental material of pilgrimage—or the content that completes the whole—the isolated scenes, random snapshots, and extraneous matter that add to the content, themes, and connective tissue of the journey: encounters at the airport, newsstand images, conversations with strangers, scenes from a film. In a number of perceptible ways, the outbound traveler experiences important aspects of the pilgrim life: the virtues of patience and perseverance, the unfolding of the journey, and God's presence in the details of time and space.

Every phase of pilgrimage offers its own perspectives, emotions, and meanings, and throughout the outbound journey, pilgrims are "in flight" and "on the way." As pilgrims look at flight maps and note the passing of the hours, they transition from the immediacy of home towards the gates of Jerusalem. Feeling the journey as they close their eyes, pilgrims are wise to get as much rest as they can, saving their energy for the sojourn ahead.

Holy Land Arrival

Mark Twain recalls his first glimpse of the Holy City. Approaching the city from the north, he and his fellow pilgrims "spurred up hill after hill" stretching their necks minutes before they reached the top only to be disappointed by "more stupid hills. . . . still no Jerusalem came in sight." At last, "perched on its eternal hills . . . the venerable city gleaned in the sun [and] every sinner swung his hat on high! . . . There was no individual in the party whose brain was not teeming with . . . images . . . invoked by the grand history of the venerable city that lay before us. . . . The thoughts Jerusalem suggest are full of poetry, sublimity, and, more than all, dignity."[2]

Holy Land arrival produces sighs of relief, tears of joy, and thoughts of veneration. Marking arrival can be as spontaneous as throwing hats in the air, as traditional as kissing the ground, or as automatic as checking phones and internet signals. Arrival moments include landing on the runway, passing through passport control, and locating your bags. It is marked by the hospitable welcome of guides, institutional staff, and travel operators. Reaching the guest house, seeing the walls of Jerusalem, and visiting the Holy Sepulchre are the serial moments of sacred arrival. Just as exiting one's house commenced the journey, entering the Holy Land evokes the symbolism of doors and thresholds: as immediate as walking off the plane and as hallowed as entering the gates of the Holy City.

Laced with anticipation, Holy Land arrival glimpses the journey ahead. The Holy Land is a series of Gospel arrivals. Pilgrims arrive with Mary at the house of Elizabeth, with the shepherds for the birth of the Christ Child, and with Jesus for his Jordan River baptism. They arrive with the crowds for the teachings and miracles of his Galilean ministry and ascend Mount Tabor in time for the transfiguration. Pilgrims enter Jerusalem with Jesus, accompany him to Calvary, and follow the women to the empty tomb. But Holy Land arrival should not get ahead of itself; it is a station to be savored. There are times to tarry on the journey, moments to relish, and few are more sacred than Holy Land arrival. Programs should include an opening worship service that celebrates arrival—not simply as the start of things to come but as a sacred moment in and of itself—offering thanksgiving for safe travels and prayers for people back home. Holy Land arrival gives pause for reflecting upon one's overall life journey. It elicits gratitude for mentors, peers, and role models and invites reflection upon the string of events, years in the making, that have led to the present moment. Who has shaped and nurtured your faith? What events, decisions, and influences have led you to the Holy Land? While worship speaks to the individual experience, the sacred act of gathered arrival constitutes a newly created Christian community. Summonsed on a sacred journey, the Holy Land sojourn has now begun.

---

2. Twain, *Innocents Abroad*, chapter 52.

12

The Aftermath: Returning Home

"We do not think in the holy places;

We think in bed, afterwards, when the glare
and the noise and the confusion are gone."

—MARK TWAIN[1]

F ew things are more satisfying than concluding a Holy Land pilgrimage. Having relished the journey, returning home is the ultimate goal
and final destination. Reflections take place "in bed, afterwards," and back
home, we seek the lessons of the journey, the meaning of religious experience. On the far side of pilgrimage, Christians possess a deeper understanding of scripture, a renewed commitment to Christ, and a new capacity for
Christian service. The chapter begins by exploring biblical reactions to the
resurrection: the lessons from Emmaus and the assertion that what happens
in Jerusalem can't stay in Jerusalem. It then surveys the pilgrim's final days
in the Holy Land, the journey home, and the celebration of return, before
exploring the aftermath of pilgrimage: the replication of the holy, the local-
ization of the gospel, and post-trip reflections.

Lessons from Emmaus

Luke tells the story of Cleopas and an unnamed companion walking to Emmaus on the day of Jesus' resurrection (Luke 24:13–35). Along the way, Jesus appears as a stranger on the road, feigning ignorance concerning recent
events in Jerusalem. Cleopas tells the stranger about a crucified prophet and
the confusing accounts of his resurrection. In visiting his tomb, some women

---

1. Twain, *Innocents Abroad*, chapter 55.

discovered that his body was gone, and rumors were circulating that he had risen from the dead. It is late in the day as they approach Emmaus, and Cleopas invites the stranger to stay the night. When the guest breaks bread for the evening meal, Cleopas and his companion's eyes are opened, and they recognize Jesus, who immediately disappears. Having seen the risen Christ, they depart for Jerusalem, returning from whence they had come.

Pilgrims encounter three special tables on a Holy Land journey, each ideally set for Holy Communion. Upon arrival, pilgrims gather around a table of anticipation. The Galilean lakeside evokes a table of multiplication: just as Jesus miraculously multiplied the loaves and fishes, the table represents the multiplication of faith, friends, and spiritual insights that occurs throughout the journey. Emmaus concludes the circuit with a table of recognition that invites us to review recent events. A lot has happened on the journey, and the risen Christ has been walking beside us along the way. Holy Land pilgrimage has opened our eyes.

Cleopas' response to the risen Christ was not to linger but to return to Jerusalem—his point of departure—to celebrate what had happened with his community of faith. Emmaus is not a story about Jerusalem per se; it is a story about returning to where we started, sharing our resurrection experience with friends and family back home. The mysterious identity of Cleopas' companion invites us to play the part. We have walked with Jesus in the Holy Land, talked about him with burning hearts, and recognized him in the breaking of the bread. Like Cleopas, we haste back home to those we know, to our churches, families, and communities of faith. The Emmaus story exhorts us not to linger in the Holy Land but urges us homeward to be reunited with those we have left behind, to celebrate our experience of the risen Christ, and to discern, on familiar ground, God's calling to Christian service.

Emmaus teaches us a final lesson about the pilgrim life. In returning home to share our stories of the road, we are greeted with reports that the risen Christ has appeared in our absence. Life has happened while we were away, and people back home have their own resurrection encounters that occurred while we were in the Holy Land. The remote pilgrim has experienced Jerusalem without ever leaving home, and, ironically, religious travelers, like Cleopas, can find themselves on the outside looking in. The Holy Land journey is not complete until we return to the Upper Rooms of house and home where our first task is to listen to the stories of others. In the end, the risen Christ is found not so much in the places we have been but through the communities we are in.

What Happens in Jerusalem Can't Stay in Jerusalem

Jerusalem and Las Vegas are the tale of two cities. They are cities of great imagination and international gathering. They each claim a king—David and Elvis—and have their own syndrome. The Jerusalem Syndrome is an intense religious psychosis, sometimes accompanied by a messianic complex. The Las Vegas Syndrome is a physical state brought on by too little sleep, too much heat, and other dehydrating factors. The condition is fostered by too many shows and casinos—too much to do in too little time. The Las Vegas Syndrome is similar to pilgrim fatigue, which is brought on by too many sites and churches—too much to do in too little time—and exacerbated by too little sleep, too much heat, and other dehydrating factors.

Leaving aside additional comparisons between Sin City and the City of God, Vegas' famous tag line—what happens in Vegas stays in Vegas—provides the perfect foil for Jerusalem pilgrims. What happens in Vegas stays in Vegas plays off the idea that nobody needs to know what you are up to in Vegas. From bachelor parties and gambling sprees to more compromising situations, the desert city presents itself as an oasis of secrets. Vegas is a moral black hole that has no reach beyond its own borders, surrounded by a firewall of collusion that sequesters information and detains rumors. We are led to believe that what happens in Vegas is inconsequential to the rest of our life, immaterial to the rest of the world.

By contrast, what happens in Jerusalem *can't* stay in Jerusalem. The secret of the resurrection was broken by dawn. The risen Christ could not be sequestered, and rumors of the empty tomb could not be contained. Like concentric waves emanating from a dropped stone, Acts records the rippling effect of the resurrection as news expanded in every direction from Jerusalem to the ends of the earth. As pilgrims leave the Holy Land, they are replicating the movement of Acts, proclaiming the good news of Christ's resurrection to the corners of the world. The gospel cannot be contained: what happens in Jerusalem can't stay in Jerusalem.

The Final Days in Jerusalem

As previously discussed, pilgrims become physically, mentally, and emotionally fatigued towards the conclusion of their journey. By the end of his visit, Mark Twain admits that the sights "swarm about you at every step. . . . I did not think such things could be so crowded together as to diminish their interest. . . . We have been drifting about for several days, using our eyes and our ears more from a sense of duty than any higher and worthier reason."[2] Fatigue leaves one more susceptible to harm and injury, and the goal now is to complete the trip in a safe and meaningful manner, giving special attention to self-care.

As the trip winds down, it is not uncommon for people to begin disengaging from the program as they increasingly think about home. While readiness for home can leave pilgrims with a sense of unease—that they are somehow short-changing the experience—transitioning towards departure is a normal process of Holy Land travel. Discussing the issue as a group gives individuals permission to approach the final days with a range of emotions and behaviors and is appreciated by tired pilgrims who feel a nudge towards home. Persevering to the end does not preclude homebound thoughts and preparations.

While the conclusion of a program can be somewhat hectic with final photos, last-minute shopping, and packing for the airport, one's final moments in the Holy Land are something to be savored. Most programs culminate with worship, group reflections, and a final meal, and winding down with fellow pilgrims, sharing humorous stories and meaningful highlights, celebrates the lasting treasures of the journey.

Departing the Holy Land

Years ago, as I was departing Africa University in Zimbabwe after a two-week visit, Hilary, a young student from Kenya, told me: "Goodbyes are like death. We know they're inevitable; yet, they're always a surprise." Some cultures have an art for departure, combining wisdom, faith, and blessing in the act of separation. Still, as a whole, we struggle with goodbyes. Even if we are ready for home, leaving a holy place is not always easy, especially if we are unlikely to return. Grief is the fear and actuality of separation, and pilgrims grieve as the Holy Land sojourn and its short-term community come to an end.

Even so, pilgrims give importance to the act of departure, acknowledging it with words, prayers, and appropriate gestures. For courses consisting of people who have gathered in the Holy Land from around the world, formal goodbyes occur at the end of the program. Saying goodbye to fellow pilgrims can be supplemented with written notes and tokens of appreciation, and gifts may be offered to pilgrim guides, bus drivers, and institutional staff. There is wisdom in gradual closure—sharing words of gratitude with people prior to the ultimate act of separation—which allows sentiments to be expressed in less emotional settings. Seeking people out

2. Twain, *Innocents Abroad*, chapter 54.

prior to departure avoids the risk of missing them altogether, which can happen as staff and fellow participants disperse at the end of a program. Participating in a pilgrim course as a single individual often leads to significant friendships, and departure is tinged with a corresponding degree of emotion as the traveler transitions from a community of shared experience back to the status of a solitary pilgrim. For church groups traveling home together, departing the Holy Land is largely about the separation of place. Since everyone checks out of the hotel, rides to the airport, and flies home together, it can be somewhat difficult to determine what actually constitutes the moment of departure.

However defined, pilgrims are encouraged to mark the end of their Holy Land sojourn and the beginning of their homebound journey. For many, visiting the Holy Sepulchre during their last twenty-four hours in Jerusalem is a departure ritual marking the end of their stay and invoking travel mercies for the journey ahead. Being cognizant of when the sojourn returns to journey allows pilgrims to reflect upon the shifting perspectives of religious travel as they move outwards from the center of the world. As the plane takes off from Tel Aviv, flight maps will show the aircraft heading home with a clock counting down the hours to touchdown. As soon as westbound flights take-off, land gives way to water. Departure takes most homebound pilgrims over the Mediterranean Sea, offering yet another point of reflection: just as limitless horizons represent the possibilities of an unknown future, primeval waters remind us that we are new creations in Christ.

The Journey Home

Walking a labyrinth reminds us that the journey home is an essential element of Holy Land travel. The parallels are worth considering, particularly since Christian tradition associates the center of a labyrinth with New Jerusalem. A labyrinth invites spiritual pilgrims to prayerfully follow the straights, bends, and turns of its path before arriving at its destinational center. After spending time in the middle, pilgrims retrace their steps until they exit the circle, covering as much distance going out and as they did going in. The labyrinth emphasizes the act of returning: the liminal state between Jerusalem and home, between the already left and the not-quite arrived.

Just as the labyrinth does not conclude in the center, Holy Land travel does not finish in Jerusalem. Cutting across the maze after praying in the middle—a possible but nonsensical act—short-changes the experience. Likewise, pilgrims lose perspective when they become inattentive to the journey home. The trappings of international travel—security, luggage, and layovers as well as airline food and in-flight entertainment—are the straights, bends, and turns that must be navigated before exiting the circle at the original point of entry: the threshold of home. The homebound journey may not be as meaningful as time spent in the center; yet, every phase of pilgrim travel has its singular perspectives and opportunities for spiritual encounter. Ignoring the homebound journey distorts, even in subtle ways, the Holy Land experience.

While the journey home is an opportune time for sustained reflection, like the outbound journey, there is no prescription to pilgrim travel. Intentional awareness, being immersed in the moment, and sensing physical, mental, and emotional transitions are more important than a directed set of behaviors. There is an indulgence to international air travel, exciting in its rarity, that is worth enjoying. Pilgrims read, wander about airports, and peruse the duty free shops; in the air, they sleep, watch films, and talk to others. Whatever they do, pilgrims live out the journey, relishing the venture until they physically return to their point of departure or arrive at their next station.

The Celebration of Return

As with other aspects of religious travel, the celebration of return is a combination of intention, spontaneity, and surprise. Homebound arrival is a serial process that includes landing, luggage, and border controls, reuniting with family, ground transportation, and the front door of house and home. Individuals should mark their return in some way, such as touching the ground, offering a simple prayer, or reading a self-addressed message prepared prior to leaving home. Church groups should gather, if possible, for a final prayer—at the airport or an appropriate location and ideally with those who have welcomed them home—gratefully acknowledging their safe arrival. Pilgrims celebrate their return with friends and family in restaurants and over home-cooked meals, while group celebrations extend to congregational worship, reunions, and presentations in the immediate wake of the journey.

Replicating the Holy

Replicating the holy is a fundamental practice of the Christian faith. Every time a new church is consecrated, it becomes a meeting point between heaven and earth, assuming various characteristics of the temple, Christ's tomb, and New Jerusalem. To cross the threshold of a medieval church was to enter the gates of heaven, and while the imagery is less noticeable in Protestant sanctuaries, it is, nonetheless, present. Christians replicate the holy, and they do so using the template of Jerusalem.

Over the centuries, Christians have replicated the city of Jerusalem.[3] The attention that pilgrims gave to measuring the holy sites facilitated their re-creation on European soil. The medieval complex of Santo Stefano in Bologna, Italy recreates the sites of Jesus' passion. Eichstätt, Germany boasts a twelfth-century model of Jesus' tomb, and round churches throughout Europe are inspired by the Anastasis, the circular building that houses the tomb of Christ. In northern Italy, the sacred mountain of Varallo, initiated in the late fifteenth century by a Franciscan monk returning from the Holy Land and recognized by UNESCO as a world heritage site, depicts over forty scenes in the life of Christ with some eight hundred life-sized wood and terracotta statues.

The 1904 St. Louis World's Fair contained an exhibit of Jerusalem covering eleven acres, twenty-two streets, and three hundred buildings and stalls. The exhibition included a full-sized model of the Dome of the Rock and replicas of the Western Wall, the Tower of David, and the Holy Sepulchre. Instead of sculptures, one thousand Holy Land residents—Muslims, Christians, and Jews—traveled from Jerusalem to work as guides and merchants. The exhibit was described by its designers as "gigantic in its conception" and "gigantic in its execution."

While the European examples are monuments of Catholic faith, the impetus behind the St. Louis exhibit was a growing Protestant interest in the Holy Land. Earlier, in 1874, Palestine Park, a 1.75 feet-to-the-mile scale model of the Holy Land, was created at Chautauqua, New York, a training ground for the Methodist church. Since the late nineteenth century, visitors arriving by ferryboat have taken their first steps on Chautauquan soil as if they were Holy Land pilgrims on their way to Jerusalem. The reproduction of the Holy Land is a passion of Protestant America; examples include The Fields of the Wood Bible Park in Murphy, North Carolina, which boasts the world's largest Ten Commandments, the Passion Play in Eureka Springs, Arkansas, the Holy Land Experience Theme Park in Orlando, Florida, and the Ark Encounter in Kentucky, a life-sized replica of Noah's Ark. While biblical theme parks are prone to punch lines, when we remember why people go to Jerusalem in the first place—to know the Bible better and to connect with God—we can appreciate how the replication of the holy impacts the lives of remote pilgrims around the world.

3. See Warton, *Selling Jerusalem.*

When the early church shifted from a temple religion to a table religion, it experienced the risen Christ in the gathered church. All that was needed was a loaf of bread, a cup of wine, and the presence of the Holy Spirit. Just as the early church sought holiness in people rather than places, the replication of the holy ultimately takes place within the life of the individual pilgrim, who, in returning home, embodies the gospel's movement from Jerusalem to the ends of the world. Called to create more compassionate communities and to serve a world in need, the Jerusalem pilgrim returns with a clearer vision of the Christ-filled life. Jerusalem pilgrimage is less about what one experiences in the Holy Land and more about the person one becomes in the aftermath of the journey.

Localizing the Gospel

Despite inspirational efforts to replicate the Holy Land, our task is to move beyond literal reconstructions of the holy places. We do not live in the biblical past; rather, we use the Bible to inform a contemporary faith. The power of scripture is its ability to transcend time and place, and the task of theology is to translate first-century gospel truths into forms that speak to our modern world. Just as the crowds at Pentecost heard the word of God in their own language, the gospel speaks to our local context.

Artists are renown for adapting biblical stories to local, contemporary settings, and one of my favorite examples is *The Census at Bethlehem* (1566) by Pieter Bruegel the Elder. The painting depicts a snow-covered Flemish village on a late winter's afternoon. On the left, a number of people are gathered around a building, waiting to be registered. Others are making their way, including Joseph and Mary, who is sitting on a donkey. The painting is peopled with winter activity. Men and women are working in the cold, sweeping the snow, building a house. A few are gathered around a fire; a man is slaughtering a pig. Children are playing on the ice, skating, and throwing snowballs. The painting is the biblical story of Bethlehem depicted as a contemporary, common-day scene in sixteenth-century Flanders.

The replication of the holy is less about historical reproduction than it is about contemporary application. Pilgrims investigate scripture to discern how its message applies to everyday life. How are biblical stories embodied in the world in which we live? What is the spiritual meaning of Bethlehem, the Jordan River, and Jerusalem? How do Mary and Joseph appear in our midst? Who are the shepherds and magi among us? Who are the fishermen and tax collectors being called into mission? Challenged by the example of the Good

Samaritan, which of our enemies acts more like God than we do? The object of Holy Land travel is to translate the gospel back home.

The God of Reflection

The Holy Land experience is never over. As John, a young Dutch doctor, reflected during a week at Taizé: "I am still learning from a year I spent eight years ago in a leprosy colony in India." What pilgrims discover in the wake of religious travel is that the God of the journey is also the God of reflection. Pilgrimage provides us with experience to sift through for ages: spiritual transformation is a life-long process.

Pilgrimage seldom provides us with final answers; rather, it facilitates a faith response that acknowledges God's long-term activity in our lives. Paul famously writes: "for now we see in a mirror, dimly, but then we will see face to face. Now I know only in part; then I will know fully, even as I have been fully known" (1 Cor 13:12). Pilgrimage reminds us to keep looking in the mirror. At times, the glass is less smudged, and we glimpse a divine reflection. Together with Paul, we can be "confident of this, that the one who began a good work among [us] will bring it to completion by the day of Jesus Christ" (Phil 1:6).

While people go on pilgrimage to discern specific issues, the experience is more often about resources than answers, more about seeing than knowing. We reach the future by living in the moment. I concluded my around-the-world pilgrimage with a forty-day retreat, camping alone in the Ozark Mountains of northern Arkansas. An abstract from my wilderness journal reflects upon the question of how God leads us from here to there, from the present to the future:

> While God's presence illuminates my immediate path with peace and contentment, the future remains undisclosed, shrouded in a veil. And so we wait upon God. We wait for answers to our petty problems, for help to our cries of desperation, and for the ultimate consummation of our lives. As we journey into the unknown, we discover, much to our surprise, that crumbs appear upon the pathway, and we are nourished by the bread of life along the way.

As we reflect upon the past, God is preparing our future. Pilgrimage is what we practice in the meantime.

Appendix 1

Terms and Concepts

Accountability: Pilgrims face temptations and moral choices removed from everyday structures of accountability. Since the majority of Jerusalem pilgrims travel with people they already know, often as a church group, the Holy Land experience may contain a hedge of accountability that is as strong or stronger than those back home. Even so, moral character is tested in the Holy Land like anywhere else, and pilgrims are responsible for their actions and behavior.

Adages and Aphorisms: Adages and aphorisms are the quotable quotes and shareable sayings concerning life and faith that emerge throughout a pilgrimage and give shape and focus to rest of the journey. Forged from experience or borrowed from others, they are concentrated verbal tools for perceiving, exploring, and interpreting the pilgrim life. They encapsulate pilgrim wisdom and provide subjective definitions of pilgrimage.

The Agendaless Pilgrim: Some people find themselves in the Holy Land without a clear idea of why they are there. It can be a blessing, though, to arrive in Jerusalem without preconceived ideas, pressing expectations, or a fixed agenda, shorn of specific goals yet open to the stirrings of the Spirit. The agendaless pilgrim follows where the journey leads, perceiving the Divine as the trip unfolds.

Alternative Sites and Traditions: The Holy Land has relatively few alternatives sites and competing traditions. With minor exceptions, Eastern and Western Christians have recognized the same locations. The common pairing of Franciscan and Orthodox churches near a holy site is not a sign of competing claims. Rather, it reflects the desire of the respective churches to be near a mutually recognized location that may or may not be a part of either church property. Contested space is more common than alternative claims.

Anticipation: Anticipation is a function of hope, optimism, patience, and perseverance. Pilgrims reflect upon the difference between anticipation and expectations. Whereas expectations can diminish an experience, anticipation fosters questions, which lead to enlightenment.

Appearance: Appearance is one of the four components of a holy site. What does a site look like? What are its topographical, commemorative, archaeological, and architectural features? What is noteworthy or otherwise incongruous about a place?

Arrival: Few moments are more sacred than Holy Land arrival, which is as immediate as walking off the plane and as hallowed as entering the gates of Jerusalem. The Holy Land journey is a series of gospel arrivals.

Ascetic Pilgrimage: Matthew 10:9–10 tells Christian pilgrims to travel lightly: "take no gold, or silver, or copper in your belts, no bag for your journey, or two tunics, or sandals, or a staff." What should pilgrims take on the journey? What supplies are needful, and which ones should be left at home? Ascetic pilgrimage speaks to acts of simplicity and self-denial. Should the Holy Land experience be one of celebration or fasting? An Easter experience or a Lenten journey?

Authenticity: Authenticity concerns both pilgrims and places. The language of authenticity seeks to define, legitimate, and, subsequently, exclude; it limits and distorts. Pilgrim identity is self-determined, and pilgrims seek intentionality over authenticity. The language of authenticity distorts a more nuanced approach to the holy sites, which is more effectively replaced by the concept of commemorative credibility.

Autobiography: Pilgrimage is autobiographical, and every person's journey is unique, personal, and irreplicable. Pilgrimage is first-person experience, viewed through a first-person perspective.

Awareness: Pilgrims are self-aware, mindful of God, and attentive to the Other. Pilgrims practice the art of awareness.

Baggage: What are the tools and resources of religious travel? What is the difference between necessities and preferences? Baggage consists of everything that we take with us, including our histories, health, hurts, and heartaches.

Barluzzi, Antonio: Perhaps no single figure influences the religious imagination of pilgrims more than the Franciscan Antonio Barluzzi (1884–1960), the so-called Architect of the Holy Land, who designed a number of the modern shrines.

The Blessings of Pilgrimage: Ancient pilgrims referred to holy objects and the benefits they conveyed as blessings. Blessings are holy souvenirs, the material takeaways of religious travel. Seeking physical reminders of spiritual experience, Christians of all backgrounds desire a tangible connection to the Holy Land.

Calling: People are called to go to places that God will show them. Receiving a calling to go on pilgrimage comes with certain responsibilities: to journey faithfully, to live holy in the Holy Land, and to attend carefully to what God reveals along the way. A calling lowers the pressures of a perfect journey: it becomes God's business and that makes all the difference.

The Center of the World: Christian imagination recognizes Jerusalem—in particular, the Holy Sepulchre—as the center of the world. The idea of the center of the world introduces a spirituality of power and proximity. The existence of centers implies edges, the elsewhere, and everything in-between. Centers speak to physical and social location, to our accessibility to the holy, and to the imbalance of power that characterizes our world.

The Challenges of Pilgrimage: Not every aspect of Holy Land pilgrimage is enjoyable. The experience is full of irritants, unpleasantries, distractions, and sideshows. There is satisfaction in completing goals and reaching destinations, all the more so when the experience has not been easy. Pilgrims embrace the challenges of the journey knowing that the blessings of pilgrimage often occur *because* of the hardships, not in spite of them. Pilgrims navigate emotions, tamper expectations, and focus on others. The art of pilgrimage is persevering through the dull and the difficult, dealing with distractions, and turning contextual noise into meaningful content.

The Character of Pilgrimage: Pilgrimage is incarnational, metaphorical, autobiographical, and corporate. It is a comprehensive expression of the Christian life.

The Christian Life: Our understanding of pilgrimage must move beyond limited perceptions of personal spirituality to a holistic approach to the Christian life.

Christological Images: Christological images contain pilgrim-related themes that fuel the pilgrim journey in significant ways, including Christ as the alpha and the omega, the way, the light, and the gate. Christ as the bread and water of life nourishes the pilgrim experience.

Commemoration: One of the four components of a holy site, commemoration concerns the narrative, event, person, or idea to which a place is dedicated. The Holy Land commemorates biblical stories, theological ideas, saints, legends, and historical events.

Commemorative Credibility: The concept of commemorative credibility states that the location of a biblical site should be compatible with the physical settings of the scriptural narrative. Overall, the Christian holy places have a high degree of commemorative credibility.

Connections: The desire for a connection with God is a common motive of Holy Land travel. While God is profoundly present in the Holy Land, having a discernible spiritual moment in the Holy Land is far more elusive. The spiritual access points of the Holy Land are often surprising and ever changing. Spiritual moments happen when we least expect them.

Cultural Amenities: Cultural amenities are the familiar comforts and conveniences associated with one's cultural background. Although a number of things can be brought from home or found in the Holy Land, foreign travel is characterized by the absence of certain cultural amenities. To what extent do cultural amenities, such as food, music, news, and sports, help us maintain a sense of balance, and to what extent do they distract or hinder the pilgrim experience? How, on the other hand, can the absence of cultural dependencies shape the pilgrim journey in positive ways?

Decision-Making: Pilgrimage is an exercise in intentional decision-making, a litany of never-ending choices, a concentrated study in self-management.

Departure: The spirituality of departure is both practical and symbolic. Pilgrims put their house in order and receive a travel blessing before leaving home. Pilgrims mark their departure as they exit the door of their house and make a similar act as they leave the Holy Land.

The Dimensions of Pilgrimage: Time, place, journey, and people are the fourfold dimensions of pilgrimage.

Disappointment: Disappointments are caused by on-the-ground conditions and heightened by pilgrim expectations. The Holy Land experience commonly includes mini-disappointments that quickly dissipate. Occasionally, a pilgrim will incur a disappointment that fundamentally impacts the experience.

Discernment: A Holy Land sojourn often provides a time and place for important decisions. Whether a personal crossroads was a conscious reason for making the journey in the first place or only surfaced upon arrival, pilgrims use the Holy Land experience as a period of discernment, often related to vocational or relational issues. The Holy Land is a platform for thought and reflection. While pilgrims seek answers to specific questions, the fruit of discernment is often the faith to move forward.

The Earthly Life as Pilgrimage: The life-as-journey metaphor probes our life from the cradle to the grave with particular attention given to the struggles of our earthly existence. As strangers who are "in the world but not of the world," Christians are in pursuit of a spiritual homeland envisioned as New Jerusalem. Holy Land pilgrimage is a reenactment of the salvific journey to the City of God.

Elements: Elements are the various parts of pilgrimage that, on their own, do not comprise a complete expression.

Emmaus: Emmaus is a story about returning to our point of departure. Emmaus exhorts us not to linger in the Holy Land but urges us homeward to be reunited with those we have left behind, to celebrate our experience of the risen Christ, and to discern God's calling to Christian service on familiar ground. In returning home to share our stories of the road, we are greeted with reports that the risen Christ has appeared in our absence. The Holy Land journey is not complete until we return to the Upper Rooms of house and home.

Emotions: Pilgrims embrace the emotions of the journey, experiencing the sanctity of life in the rippled nature of human affections. Emotions are the lens through which we see the world, fundamental to the experience itself. Pilgrims feel the rainy day, the tension of conflict, and the grief of departure. They stand pat through sadness, disappointment, frustration, and pain, seeking meaning and perspective in the broadsides of life, confident of God's guidance through pathways of darkness.

Exile: The Babylonian exile is the principal motif of Hebrew Scripture. An expression of forced pilgrimage, the exile is a testament to remaining faithful in trying circumstances and highlights how one can be strengthened through difficult experiences. Its culminating theme is returning home as transformed people.

An Expansive Landscape: The Christian Holy Land is an expansive landscape containing minor traditions, extra-biblical legends, and same-story commemorations that stem from a common narrative.

Expectations: Expectations are less useful than goals and objectives and are less spiritually grounded than anticipation. Expectations can diminish experience and lead to disappointment and frustration. Pilgrims should be confident of positive outcomes; yet, they should be so by tampering expectations. The Holy Land pilgrim is transformed less by life-changing moments than by the accumulative effects of the journey.

Extra-Biblical Traditions: The Christian Holy Land commemorates a number of extra-biblical traditions, including the beginning and end of Mary's life and the legend of Helena and the Holy Cross.

The (Extra)ordinary: The Christian life is a journey of discovering the extraordinary in the ordinary and the ordinary in the extraordinary. Pilgrimage is an extended appointment with extraordinary events. As the journey progresses, it is the ordinary aspects of life that become tinged with sanctity. Pilgrimage captures the miracle of ordinary experience, and upon returning home, everyday life becomes infused with a greater awareness of God's extraordinary presence in a commonplace world. Pilgrims see in double vision, perceiving God's presence in (extra)ordinary ways.

Family Resemblance Theory: Wittgenstein's family resemblance theory informs our understanding of pilgrimage, which is connected by a series of overlapping similarities where no one feature is common to all of its expressions. The major themes of pilgrimage include time, place, journey, and people and the stranger, the foreign, and the Other.

Fatigue: Pilgrim fatigue is an inevitable part of the Holy Land experience. Contributing factors include the physical demands of the journey, the dynamics of group travel, the tension of foreign cultures in conflict, being away from home, the sheer number of sites, and the dissonance that arises from unexpected surprises, new perspectives, and challenging insights. The tired pilgrim eventually yearns for home, where spiritual growth takes root in the aftermath of the journey.

The Fifth Gospel: The concept of the Fifth Gospel provides modern-day pilgrims with a useful term for describing their encounter with the land and the clarity that it provides for understanding Scripture and the life of Jesus. It first appears in the nineteenth-century classic *The Life of Jesus*, by Ernest Renan, who describes how his familiarity with the places of the Gospels brought Jesus to life: "the striking agreement of the texts with the places, the marvelous harmony of the Gospel ideal . . . were like a revelation to me. I had before my eyes a fifth Gospel, torn but still legible, and . . . in place of an abstract being . . . I saw living and moving an admirable human figure."

The Foreign: Like Abraham, pilgrims seek God in foreign places far from home. The Christian traveler navigates between the familiar and the unknown, and being out of place exposes our cultural dependencies and personal affinities, our dislikes and vulnerabilities, making us more aware of our human condition.

God Is in the Facts: Pilgrims encounter God in the realities of lived experience. The lessons of the pilgrim journey are revealed by a God who calls us through the actual events of our lives.

The God of Mystery and Surprise: Holy Land pilgrims are on a journey clouded in mystery and surprise. Pilgrims live on the cusp of constant revelation, seeking glimpses of divine mystery that are revealed along the way.

The God of Reflection: What pilgrims discover in the aftermath of religious travel is that the God of the journey is also the God of reflection. The aftermath of the journey is full of connections, clarifications, and insights that warrant reflection over an extended period of time. As we reflect upon the past, God prepares the future. Pilgrimage is what we practice in the meantime.

Group Pilgrimage: When individuals sign up for a group pilgrimage, they are agreeing to certain terms and conditions. Individuals must adhere to a set itinerary, live in covenant with fellow pilgrims, and follow the instructions of guides and leaders. Despite the blessings of short-term community, group pilgrimage has its share of challenges and frustrations, from the lack of control over the daily schedule to the habits of fellow pilgrims.

Healing: Pilgrimage offers a time and place for spiritual, emotional, and physical healing.

The Holy Land versus the Holy Places: Many people reject the x-marks-the-spot mentality of the sites, feeling little need to pin events to exact locations. Consequently, pilgrims often find the concept of the Holy Land—the idea of a continuous plane of holiness—to be more meaningful than the notion of holy places, preferring the image of a sacred land that transcends x's on a map. In the Holy Land paradigm, pilgrims are constantly standing on holy ground, and spiritual encounters are not limited to the sacred sites. Holiness is in every direction rather than merely at the end of the queue. At the same time, the Holy Land approach challenges how we compartmentalize the sacred and the profane. Not only are hotel rooms and gift shops part of the Holy Land, so too are checkpoints and refugee camps.

Home: Home is never far from the thoughts and prayers of Holy Land pilgrims. People back home are a source of encouragement for persevering on the journey, while returning home is the ultimate destination of Holy Land travels.

Horizons: Horizons tantalize the imagination. Our sense of location is determined by what we know, changing once we see what is around the corner and beyond the horizon.

Hospitality: Hospitality is the constant companion of pilgrimage. Pilgrims are dependent upon the hospitality of others.

The Imitation of Christ: To be a Holy Land pilgrim is to walk in the footsteps of Jesus. Just as Christians imitate Christ in their everyday lives, the Jerusalem pilgrim lives holy in the Holy Land.

The Incarnational Character of Pilgrimage: Christian pilgrimage is patterned upon the incarnation. God inhabited the materiality of human flesh in time and place. Word became flesh; the immaterial took physical shape. Pilgrimage is an embodied spirituality, engaging the senses and embracing the physicality of religious experience.

Intentionality: Pilgrims practice the art of observation, self-awareness, and focused reflection. They navigate between intentionality and spontaneity, between purposeful decisions and the stirrings of the Spirit.

The Investigation of Scripture: Christians go to the Holy Land to understand the Bible better. Holy Land travel renders a life-long familiarity with the places in the Gospels, and upon returning home, Christians read the Bible with a newfound attention to detail while grasping its central truths in clearer ways. Jerome famously remarked: "Holy Scripture is studied with greater clarity by the [one] who has contemplated Judaea with his eyes." Holy Land pilgrimage changes the way we read the Bible.

Jesus as Jerusalem Pilgrim: Jesus was a Jerusalem pilgrim, who followed Jewish customs and frequented the temple festivals. Notwithstanding Jesus' critique of temple practice and his prediction of its impending destruction, Jerusalem pilgrimage was fundamental to Jesus' life and ministry, and his relationship to the temple escapes easy characterization.

Jesus as Wayfaring Messiah: Jesus led a peripatetic life as an itinerant prophet with no place to lay his head. He was a wayfaring messiah, constantly on the road, always on the go, at home in other people's houses. Walking in the footsteps of Jesus is a peripatetic journey which causes us to reconsider our attachments to the earthly life.

Labyrinth (the Homebound Journey): Emphasizing the act of returning from the center outwards, a labyrinth reminds us that the homebound journey is an essential aspect of Holy Land travel. Suspended between Jerusalem and home, between the already left and the not-quite arrived, the trappings of international travel are the straights, bends, and turns that must be navigated before exiting the circle at the original point of entry. Pilgrims live out the journey until they physically return to their place of departure.

Layers: The concept of layers offers a rich construct for pilgrim reflections on time, place, and journey. Layers abound in the geology, history, and archaeology of the region. Scripture is layered upon the landscape, and churches have been built upon churches. The Holy Land experience reminds us that our lives are profoundly layered.

Leaving One's House in Order: Focusing on reconciliation, material assets, and personal mortality, pilgrims put their house in order before leaving home, which may include reconciling broken and strained relationships, paying off outstanding debts or a symbolic portion of them, making or updating a living will, and making or updating a last will and testament.

Living Stones: Living Stones refer to the local residents of the Holy Land, which include Israelis, Palestinians, Bedouins, Jews, Christians, Muslims, and Druze.

Localizing the Gospel: We do not live in the biblical past; rather, we use the Bible to inform a contemporary faith. The power of Scripture is its ability to transcend time and place, and the task of theology is to translate first-century gospel truths into forms that speak to our modern world. The object of Holy Land travels is to translate the gospel back home.

Location: Location speaks to the spatial position of a site, including its geographical, demographical, and political context. Each site has its own locational argument, and some traditions are stronger than others. Location extends beyond the placement of the holy sites to the physical, emotional, and narrative journey of the Christian traveler. As we walk in the footsteps of Jesus, we are continually relocating ourselves within the gospel story.

Memorials and Monuments: The Bible records numerous occasions on which altars, stones, and monuments were erected to remember important events. Holy places are stations of religious memory, monuments to our spiritual past. Pilgrimage is an expression of collective memory and public commemoration.

Metaphor: The function of metaphors is neither to explain difficult concepts in simpler terms nor to tell us what we already know. Rather, metaphors allow us to discover things that we would not otherwise be aware of. They are tools for exploration and discovery. A metaphor takes something we know (a source) to explore a less familiar target. The interaction between source and target creates a new perspective whose meaning cannot be conveyed in any other way. The concept of journey, for instance, renders insights into the earthly life that we cannot otherwise obtain. Our pursuit of metaphorically produced insights calls us to engage physical expressions of pilgrimage in greater detail. Metaphor is an unexamined aspect of the Holy Land experience.

Mission (Pilgrimage as Mission): Pilgrims are missionaries—just as missionaries are pilgrims—actively engaged in Christian service, witnessing to the love of God. Pilgrimage is a proclamation of the kingdom of God.

Motives: The earliest Christian travelers went to the Holy Land for two primary reasons: the investigation of Scripture and prayer and religious practice. The motives of present-day pilgrims remain the same: to know the Bible better and to deepen one's commitment to God. Additional motives include healing, discernment, intercessory prayer, and the Living Stones.

The Mundane: Portions of the Holy Land journey are simply mundane: dull, boring, and nondescript. Pilgrim spirituality speaks to in-between moments, living well in the lulls, and adjusting expectations of yellow-bricked journeys. How we fill the gaps determines the tenor of the journey. Pilgrimage also consists of chores and errands. The challenge of Jerusalem travel lies in the successful navigation of otherwise ordinary tasks.

Narrative: Pilgrimage is first-person experience, viewed through a first-person perspective. Pilgrimage is personal narrative, and each Holy Land venture is a unique, irreplicable experience.

New Jerusalem: Christian pilgrimage is implicitly governed by a biblical prototype that envisions the Christian life as a journey to New Jerusalem, the heavenly city of Christ where God lives among the gathered nations of the world (Rev 21). Holy Land travel symbolically patterns the Christian prototype.

The Noise of Pilgrimage: The Holy Land experience is full of noise and static—peripheral sounds, minor irritants, and bewildering sideshows. It contains inharmonious images and jarring juxtapositions. How does one distinguish between noise and substance? What is the difference between content and context? What lessons can be found in the extraneous details of the pilgrim life? Attending to the noise of pilgrimage can turn peripheral context into pertinent content. The art of pilgrimage is learning to hear the cacophony of religious travel as meaningful notes.

The Object of the Pilgrim Life: The union of God, self, and the Other is the ultimate object of the pilgrim life. Pilgrimage, more generally, is about life itself. Life experience, particularly travel, teaches us about ourselves, and self-identity is shaped by moving beyond our familiarities. Pilgrimage takes us beyond ourselves: God inhabits the Other, and social relations are at the heart of the pilgrim life.

Observation: The most fundamental act of Holy Land pilgrimage is the careful observation of the holy sites. Pilgrims are agents of observation, and Holy Land pilgrimage is an open-eyed encounter with the land. Pilgrim perception extends from places to people, from a focus on self to attention to others. Pilgrims have a heightened sense of awareness; they see possibilities, recognize opportunities, and discern situations. Pilgrimage is less about movement and more about the way we see the world.

The Other: Engaging the Other is a primary object of the pilgrim life. Pilgrimage inhabits the foreign, embraces difference, and celebrates diversity.

The Outbound Journey: The Jerusalem-bound traveler senses elements of pilgrimage on the outbound flight: the virtues of patience and perseverance, the unfolding of the journey, and God's presence in the details of time and space.

Peace and Reconciliation: Listening to the stories of the Living Stones and encountering physical manifestations of the conflict, like the Israel–Palestine Separation Barrier, turn a biblical journey into a gospel response to our present-day world. While Holy Land programs differ widely on how to address contemporary issues, a balanced approach engages the Palestinian church, listens to Muslim and Jewish voices, and looks at the Israeli–Palestinian conflict from multiple perspectives. Pilgrims support initiatives of peace and reconciliation.

Perseverance: Pilgrimage is an exercise in patience, perseverance, physical endurance, and internal fortitude.

Physical Challenges: Holy Land pilgrimage is not overly strenuous, but there are definite physical demands. Pilgrims should understand the particulars of their program, discuss their fitness with doctors and program organizers, and make an accurate assessment of their physical ability before signing up for a trip. Coping with the physical challenges of the Holy Land begins with attention to water, diet, clothing, and footwear.

Pilgrim Practices: Distinct from readings, prayers, and worship, pilgrim practices are the informal, devotional ways that pilgrims reenact scriptural narratives and engage the physical settings of the holy sites. They are embodied commemorations.

Pilgrimage: Pilgrimage is the experience of God, self, and the Other through the dimensions of time, place, journey, and people and the thoughts, images, and reflections thereof.

Pre-Departure Preparations: Pre-departure preparations consist of prayer and study, practical details, and symbolic acts. Focusing on reconciliation, material assets, and personal mortality, pilgrims put their house in order before leaving home. The pre-departure period is about laying "aside every weight and the sin that clings so closely [in order to] run with perseverance the race that is set before us" (Heb 12:1).

The Rediscovery of the Holy Land: With the weakening of the Ottoman Empire in the nineteenth century, an international Christian presence, bolstered by the support of imperial powers, renewed its interest in the Holy Land. The rediscovery of the Christian Holy Land was characterized by the rise of biblical archaeology, the advent of Protestant pilgrims, and the building of modern shrines.

Reenacting Sacred Stories: Pilgrims reenact the sacred stories of the Christian faith by reading Scripture and engaging in various forms of embodied practice.

Reflection: Pilgrimage includes the thoughts and reflections of Christian experience. Pilgrims explore, examine, probe, and question. Reflection occurs in real-time and continues back home long after the journey is over.

Religious Imagination: Religious imagination speaks to the sensory experience, religious symbolism, and theological resonance of a place and relates to a site's storytelling function, or the interplay of place, narrative, and symbolism. What can you see, feel, smell, hear, and even taste at a site? Simply put, what is it like to be there? What gospel truths and spiritual parables are evoked by the site? We can also speak about the religious imagination of an individual pilgrim or the collective imagination of a group.

The Reluctant Pilgrim: The reluctant pilgrim is the less-than-eager traveler whose ambivalence may stem from a number of reasons, including obligations back home, safety and security, and the dynamics of international group travel. Hesitations generally dissipate as pilgrims become familiar with their surroundings. As reluctant pilgrims become immersed in the Holy Land experience, they embrace the blessings of pilgrimage alongside their fellow travelers.

Replicating the Holy: Just as the early church sought holiness in people rather than places, the replication of the holy takes place within the life of the individual pilgrim, who, in returning home, embodies the gospel's movement from Jerusalem to the ends of the world. Jerusalem pilgrimage is less about what one experiences in the Holy Land and more about the person one becomes in the aftermath of the journey.

Responsibility: Regardless of the situation, pilgrims assume responsibility for their actions.

Risks and Dangers: To follow Christ is to encounter hardships in a precarious world. Religious travel, like life itself, is a venture in vulnerability.

Sacred People: To be a sacred people on pilgrimage is to engage the holy as a corporate experience. The Holy Land experience fosters a particular expression of corporate holiness: the short-term Christian community. Pilgrims participate in a common life, sharing together in worship, meals, travel, site visits, and presentations. Jerusalem pilgrimage examines our Christian identity while exploring our commonalities with the religious Other.

Sacred Places: Pilgrimage takes a broad approach to sacred places, which includes the following ideas: a place is holy because one has been called by God to go there; a holy place is a dwelling place of God; a holy place is where something significant took place; a place was created holy. Holy Land pilgrimage is not reliant upon a particular concept of sacred place.

Sacred Time: Holy Land pilgrimage is a divinely-appointed event. Pilgrims travel in God's time. To embark on a Holy Land journey is to enter sacred time, leaving ordinary time behind. Pilgrimage is time set aside for a particular purpose; it is a time-based endeavor. Pilgrimage embraces the past, present, and future, often simultaneously. It is also layered by liturgical time. How should Sundays be celebrated in the Holy Land? How does the Christian season inform the journey? How do the holy sites evoke a sense of seasonal or liturgical time? Should the Holy Land sojourn to be reckoned as an Easter-like celebration or as a journey integrating both feasting and fasting, both sacred and common time?

Seeing the World Differently: To be on pilgrimage is to see the world differently. Pilgrims have a heightened sense of awareness; they see possibilities and detect opportunities. On pilgrimage, we perceive mysteries that are otherwise hidden to us and assume a more expansive perspective of the spiritual life. Pilgrims are acute observers of the human condition. They discern the needs of others and respond with compassion.

Sequence: Sequence speaks to the order in which a site appears in a Holy Land itinerary as well as its placement within the biblical narrative or the life of Christ. On a Holy Land journey, we are constantly relocating ourselves within the Gospel narrative based upon the sequence of place and story.

Short-Term Christian Community: Short-term Christian community describes the temporary, common life of group pilgrimage, which includes the shared experience of worship, meals, travel, presentations, site visits, and informal fellowship. Every short-term community, including those comprised of people who already know each other, is a one-off, irreplicable entity. Pilgrims commonly grieve the termination of short-term community.

Souvenirs: Mementos are an integral part of the spiritual journey. They are catalysts of memory, physical extensions of our spiritual lives, expressions of meaningful experience. Pilgrims must navigate the material journey that accompanies religious travel, grappling with questions of spirituality, materialism, and economic justice.

Spontaneity: Pilgrims navigate between intentionality and spontaneity, between constancy and the stirrings of the Spirit.

The Status Quo: The Status Quo is the authoritative arrangement, stemming from the Ottoman period, concerning the use and occupancy of certain Christian holy sites. In February 1852 and again in May 1853, the sultan issued a decree stating that "the actual status quo will be maintained and the Jerusalem shrines, whether owned in common or exclusively by the Greek, Latin and Armenian communities, will all remain forever in their present state." To this day, the rules regulating the Holy Sepulchre are a mixture of Islamic sacred law (sharia) and Ottoman property law. Under sharia law, a holy place of any religion is a waqf, an inalienable religious endowment. The British, Jordanian, and Israeli governments have subsequently recognized the Status Quo, though not without incidents. Color-coded maps of the Holy Sepulchre depicting the individual and common areas of the six Christian communities with rights to the site can be found on the internet.

The Street: Pilgrimage is occasionally a pathway to a sacred place but is always the streets of everyday life where we hear the cries of others and attend to those in need.

Supplemental Material: The supplemental material of pilgrimage—or content that completes the whole—are the isolated scenes, random snapshots, and extraneous matter that contributes to the content, themes, and connective tissue of the journey.

Templates: Templates are the common types or patterns of pilgrim expressions, which are defined by various criteria and degrees of specificity. Pilgrim templates are neither fixed nor finite but are logically and flexibly construed. There are one-way journeys and round-trip templates. A journey to a holy place is a particular pattern, while liturgical processions and prayer walks are another. Some templates focus on people rather than places—some on personal issues, others on the Other. There are local pilgrimages, global travels, secular adventures, and physical challenges. Short-term mission trips and pilgrimage as "the street" embrace evangelism, compassion ministry, and social justice as forms of the pilgrim life. The modern popularity of pilgrimage has focused upon a few specific templates, such as long-distance walking and alternative tourism, while other expressions have received less attention.

Temptation: Pilgrimage is life intensified in every respect, including enticements and temptations. The Holy Land experience is full of desires, distractions, choices, and decisions, and moral character is tested in the Holy Land like anywhere else. The temptations that pilgrims most commonly face are the indulgent distractions that threaten their focus. The challenge of pilgrimage is distinguishing between the indulgences that are personally enriching and those that impede the spiritual journey.

Themes: Themes are unifying ideas, prominent motifs, and reoccurring subjects. Along with the quest for God, pilgrimage coalesces around two primary sets of themes—(a) time, place, and journey and (b) the stranger, the unknown, and the Other. While every journey has its incidental themes, Holy Land experiences are variously focused on biblical landscapes and narratives, history and archaeology, ecumenical and interfaith issues, and the contemporary context of Israel–Palestine.

Theological Tensions. Pilgrims engage paradox and ponder juxtapositions, investigating old ideas with new eyes. Pilgrims embrace the tensions of the Christian life.

The Third Eye of the Pilgrim: The third eye refers to how pilgrims see the world differently. They are attentive to God's workings in the world and are acute observers of the human condition. Pilgrims discern the needs of others and respond with compassion.

Thresholds: The concept of liminality describes a transitional phase in a spiritual or social process. From front door departure to entering the gates of Jerusalem to returning home, the threshold (limen) is an important image of Holy Land travel.

Tombs: Tombs are special types of commemorations. They recall the life of a particular person, foster the eschatological dimension of pilgrimage, and function as physical expressions of theological ideas.

Topography: Topography refers to the detailed features of a landscape. It is the meaning ascribed to place and location. Pilgrimage is the exploration of sacred, profane, personal, and shared topography.

Tourists and Pilgrims: There is a time to be a tourist and a time to be a pilgrim. The task is to discern the difference. On vacation, one goes to get away from life; on pilgrimage, one confronts life's most important questions. Tourists change their environment; pilgrims let the environment change them. A pilgrimage has goals, risks, and challenges that we generally would not accept on holiday.

Transitions: Pilgrimage provides time and space to reflect upon life transitions. Pilgrims consider where they have been, where they are, and where they are going. They address the past, accept the present, and seek inspiration for the journey ahead.

The Unfinished Journey: Pilgrims are accustomed to living in the meantime of an unfinished journey.

A Unified Landscape: The Christian Holy Land is a unified commemorative landscape. Christian tradition, both East and West, has largely recognized the same locations, and the Holy Land has not been characterized by alternative or competing sites. Recognized traditions weigh heavily on the ground.

Virtues and Values: Virtues are the principles that guide and determine pilgrim behavior. They are the "what" that pilgrims always do. Pilgrimage has particular associations with hope, patience, and perseverance; hospitality is its constant companion. Pilgrim theology embraces the virtues of compassion, respect, self-awareness, and personal responsibility. Pilgrimage espouses a number of secondary, or relative, values that are not operative in every situation. Pilgrims navigate between intentionality and spontaneity, austerity and extravagance, confidence and humility, boldness and caution, which underscores the importance of context, discernment, and decision-making in pilgrim spirituality.

The Virtual Pilgrim: Those who are not able to make the trip themselves—perhaps due to age or illness, family responsibilities, work obligations, or financial reasons—often desire to be virtual pilgrims. Christians around the world seek the blessings of Jerusalem, and tangible contact with the Holy Land is gratefully received by remote pilgrims.

Walls and Barriers: The Holy Land is full of checkpoints, walls, and fences, borders, boundaries, and barriers. Walls are both spiritual metaphors and physical realities.

What Happens in Jerusalem Can't Stay in Jerusalem: The risen Christ could not be sequestered, and rumors of the empty tomb could not be contained. The secret of the resurrection was broken by dawn. Acts records the rippling effect of the resurrection as news expanded in every direction from Jerusalem to the ends of the earth. As pilgrims leave the Holy Land, they are replicating the movement of Acts, proclaiming the good news of Christ's resurrection to the corners of the world. The gospel cannot be contained: what happens in Jerusalem can't stay in Jerusalem.

Appendix 2

Educational Resources

E ducational preparations allow pilgrims to maximize their in-the-field learning. Along with relevant Bible readings, pilgrims should focus on maps, timelines, and contemporary context, including internet searches on places, dates, people, and events.

1. Reading List

Narratives and Landscapes

Pixner, Bargil. *With Jesus in Jerusalem: His First and Last Days in Judea*. Corazin, Israel: Corazin, 1992.
———. *With Jesus through Galilee: According to the Fifth Gospel*. Corazin, Israel: Corazin, 1992.
Walker, Peter. *In the Steps of Jesus: An Illustrated Guide to the Places of the Holy Land*. Oxford: Lion Hudson, 2007.

A number of websites detail the holy sites, including photos, maps, and biblical texts.

See www.biblewalks.com and www.seetheholyland.net.

Holy Land Archaeology

Cline, Eric H. *Biblical Archaeology: A Very Short Introduction*. Oxford: Oxford University Press, 2009.
Magness, Jodi. *The Archaeology of the Holy Land: From the Destruction of Solomon's Temple to the Muslim Conquest*. Cambridge: Cambridge University Press, 2012.
Murphy-O'Connor, Jerome. *The Holy Land: An Oxford Archaeological Guide*. 5th ed. Oxford: Oxford University Press, 2008.

Jerusalem (History, Archaeology, and Topography)

Armstrong, Karen. *Jerusalem: One City, Three Faiths*. New York: Ballantine, 1997.
Bahat, Dan, and Chaim T. Rubenstein. *The Carta Jerusalem Atlas*. 3rd ed. Jerusalem: Carta, 2011.
Galor, Katharina, and Hanswulf Bloedhorn. *The Archaeology of Jerusalem: From the Origins to the Ottomans*. New Haven, CT: Yale University Press, 2013.
Montefiore, Simon Sebag. *Jerusalem: The Biography*. New York: Knopf, 2011.
———. *Jerusalem: The Making of a Holy City*. BBC documentary, 2011.
Ritmeyer, Leen, and Kathleen Ritmeyer. *Jerusalem: The Temple Mount*. Jerusalem: Carta, 2015.

The Palestinian–Israeli Conflict

Cohn-Sherbok, Dan, and Dawoud El-Alami. *The Palestine-Israeli Conflict: A Beginner's Guide*. 4th ed. London: Oneworld, 2015.
Buntin, Martin. *The Palestinian-Israeli Conflict: A Very Short Introduction*. Oxford: Oxford University Press, 2013.

Palestinian Christian Perspectives

Chacour, Elias. *Blood Brothers: The Dramatic Story of a Palestinian Christian Working for Peace in Israel*. Expanded ed. Grand Rapids: Chosen, 2003.
See various titles by Naim Ateek and Mitri Raheb.

Also see the Kairos Palestine Document, available on the internet ("Kairos Palestine: A Moment of Truth. A Word of Faith, Hope and Love from the Heart of Palestinian Suffering," December 11, 2009).

News Sources

The Israeli news source, *Haaretz* (www.haaretz.com), is a reliable source for breaking news.
The Washington Report on Middle East Affairs (www.wrmea.org) focuses on "news and analysis from and about the Middle East and U.S. policy in that region."

2. Timelines

Pilgrims should be familiar with the historical periods of the Holy Land, noting alternative names and overlapping eras for respective dates. Pilgrims encounter a significant amount of post-biblical history and archeology, and it is important to differentiate between biblical and post-biblical layers.

A. The Biblical Period

The Bronze Age (3200–1200 BCE) / The Old Testament Period

c. 2000 BCE   The estimated setting of the Abraham narratives

The Iron Age (1200–539 BCE) / The Old Testament Period

1000 BCE   David captures Jerusalem from the Jebusites.

960 BCE   Solomon builds the First Temple.

586 BCE   Nebuchadnezzar destroys Jerusalem and the First Temple. The Babylonian exile begins.

The Persian Age (539–322 BCE) / The Old Testament Period

The Second Temple Period (c. 530 BCE–70 CE)

537 BCE   The Babylonian exile ends. Jews are allowed to return to Jerusalem.

516 BCE   The Second Temple is built.

420 BCE   The ministry of Malachi concludes the Old Testament.

The Intertestamental Period (420 BCE–4 BCE)

The Hellenistic Period (332–141 BCE)

Upon the death of Alexander the Great in 323 BCE, the Middle East was divided between two Greek entities—the Seleucids, based in Syria, and the Ptolemaic dynasty, based in Egypt.

332 BCE   Alexander the Great takes Jerusalem.

320 BCE   Ptolemy I captures Jerusalem. Egyptian rule of Jerusalem begins.

198 BCE   The Seleucids take Jerusalem. Syrian rule of Jerusalem begins.

167 BCE   Antiochus IV Epiphanes desecrates the temple. The Maccabean Revolt begins.

164 BCE   Judas Maccabeus recaptures Jerusalem.

The Hasmonean Period (141–37 BCE)

141 BCE	Simon Maccabeus establishes Judea as an independent state.
	Maccabean rule of Jerusalem begins.

The Early Roman Period (63 BCE–70 CE)

From Pompey to the destruction of the temple.

63 BCE	Pompey captures Jerusalem. Roman rule begins.

The Herodian Period (40 BCE–70 CE)

From Herod the Great's ascendency to the destruction of the temple.

The Herodian period includes the rule of various descendents.

40 BCE	Herod the Great is appointed king by Rome.
19 BCE	Herod begins work on the temple.
10 BCE	The temple is dedicated. Temple construction continues until 63 CE.
4 BCE	The death of Herod the Great

The New Testament Period (c. 4 BCE)

c. 4 BCE	The birth of Christ
c. 30–3 CE	The crucifixion of Christ
66 CE	The First Jewish Revolt begins.
70 CE	Jerusalem falls to the Romans. The temple is destroyed.

B. The Post-Biblical Period

The Late Roman Period (70–324)

132	The Second Jewish Revolt. The Bar Kochba Revolt
135	Hadrian establishes Jerusalem as a Roman city named, Aelia Capitolina.

The Byzantine Period (324–638)

324	Constantine takes control of the eastern part of the Roman Empire.
325	The Council of Nicea
326	Helena visits Jerusalem.
335	The Church of the Holy Sepulchre is dedicated.
380s	Egeria visits the Holy Land.
570	The Piacenza Pilgrim visits the Holy Land.
c. 600	The Madaba Map
614	The Persians conquer Jerusalem.
629	Byzantine Emperor Heraclius recaptures Jerusalem and restores the Holy Cross.

The Early Islamic Period (638–1099)

The Caliphs (638–61)

638	Jerusalem is peacefully taken by the Arabs. The end of the Byzantine period in the region.

The Umayyads (661–750)

c. 680	Arculf visits the Holy Land.
691	The Dome of the Rock is completed by Caliph Abd al-Malilk.
705	The Al-Aqsa Mosque is completed by Caliph al-Walid.
720s	Willibald visits the Holy Land.

The Abassids (750–969)

836	The Jerusalem Synod cites the story of the Persian's sparing the Nativity church.

The Fatimids (969–1099)

| 1009 | The Holy Sepulchre is destroyed by Caliph al-Hakim. |
| 1042 | The Holy Sepulchre is re-dedicated by Emperor Constantine IX Monomachos. |

The Crusader Period (1099–1187)

| 1099 | Godfrey of Bouillon captures Jerusalem. Baldwin I is named king of Jerusalem. |
| 1149 | The Holy Sepulchre is re-consecrated. |

The Muslim Period (1187–1917)

The Ayyubid Period (1187–1250)

1187	Saladin takes Jerusalem from the Crusaders.
1229	The Crusaders briefly recapture Jerusalem.
1244	The Crusader era ends when Khawarizmian Turks capture Jerusalem.

The Mamluk Period (1250–1517)

| 1250 | The Muslim caliph dismantles the walls of Jerusalem. |
| 1260 | The Egyptian Mamluks capture Jerusalem. |

The Ottoman Period (1517–1917)

1517	The Ottomans peacefully takeover Jerusalem.
1537	Suleiman the Magnificent rebuilds the city walls.
1757	The initial pronouncement of the Status Quo
1808	Fire in the Holy Sepulchre
1852	The Status Quo is reaffirmed in February 1852.
1853	The Status Quo is reaffirmed in May 1853.
1867	Mark Twain visits the Holy Land.

C. The Modern Period (1917–present)

1917	The British take Jerusalem from the Ottomans.
1920	The British Mandate begins.
	Various incidents between the Arabs, Jews, and British.
1947	A United Nations Resolution recommends the partitioning of Israel–Palestine.
	War breaks out between the Arabs and Jews.
1948	The Israeli War of Independence / The Nakba
	The State of Israel is declared on May 14, 1948.
	The British Mandate ends.
1949	The Israel–Transjordan Armistice Agreement
	The Green Line divides Jerusalem between Israel and Jordan.
1967	The Six Day War
	Israel captures the West Bank of the Jordan River, the Golan Heights, and Gaza.
	Jerusalem is a "reunified" city. Israeli occupies East Jerusalem and the Old City.
1973	The Yom Kippur War
1978	The Camp David Accords
1987	The First Intifada lasts until 1993.
1993	The Oslo Accords (Part II signed in 1995)
2000	The Second Intifada lasts until 2005.
	Construction on the Israeli West Bank Separation Barrier begins.
2006	Hamas wins the Palestinian Elections.
	Various conflicts between Israel and Gaza, including 2008–9, 2012, and 2014.
2018	The American embassy moves to Jerusalem.

3. The Biblical Herods

Having a basic understanding of the six biblical Herods will alleviate a lot of confusion. The following information can be supplemented with maps, available on the internet, that indicate the territories ruled by the respective figures.

Herod the Great (The Christmas Story)

Lived: c. 73–4 BCE

Scriptures: Matthew 2

- The Visit of the Magi and the Massacre of the Innocent
- The Holy Family flees to Egypt.

Ruled: 37–4 BCE

Notes: • A powerful client king, royal title granted by the Romans

- A violent, paranoid figure who executed members of his own family

- A colossal builder, Herod built cities, palaces, and fortresses throughout the region, including Masada and Caesarea Maritima. The reconstruction of the Jerusalem temple began in 19 BCE.

- His rule was divided between three sons: Archelaus, Antipas, and Philip.

Herod Archelaus (The Holy Family settles in Nazareth)

Lived: 23 BCE–18 CE

Archelaus was a son of Herod the Great.

Scriptures: Matthew 2:22–23

After the death of Herod the Great, the Holy Family returned from Egypt. Since Archelaus was reigning in Judea in place of his father, Joseph was warned in a dream to move the family to Nazareth in the Galilee.

Ruled: 4 BCE–6 CE

Archelaus was the ethnarch (the ruler of a people) of Judea and Samaria, which included Jerusalem. The area comprised half of Herod the Great's former territories.

Notes: Archelaus was a violent, incompetent ruler. After ruling for ten years, he was deposed by Rome and exiled to southern France. Following Archelaus' removal, the Romans began using their own governors, or procurators, based in Caesarea Maritima, to rule Judea. This is why Pilate, who was not a member of the Herodian family, was in charge of Jerusalem at the time of Jesus' crucifixion.

Herod Antipas (The so-called Herod of the New Testament)

Lived: 20 BCE–39 CE.

Antipas was a son of Herod the Great.

Scriptures:
- Luke 13:32: Jesus calls Antipas "that fox."
- Matthew 14:1–12, Mark 6:14–29, and Luke 9:7–9: Antipas puts John the Baptist to death. Antipas divorced his first wife and married Herodias, the former wife of his brother, Philip. John the Baptist spoke out against the marriage.
- Luke 23:7–12: Jesus is tried before Antipas in Jerusalem.

Ruled: 4 BCE–39 CE

Antipas ruled as tetrarch (the ruler of a fourth of his father's land), which included the Galilee and Perea. While Antipas wanted to be a king, Rome did not grant the title to any of Herod the Great's sons.

Notes: During Jesus' childhood, Antipas was based in Sepphoris, just four miles from Nazareth. Around 20 CE, he moved his capital to Tiberias on the Sea of Galilee.

Herod Philip (The "other side" of the Sea of Galilee)

Lived: 27 BCE–34 CE.

Philip was a son of Herod the Great.

Scriptures: Matthew 14:3–4, Mark 6:17–18, and Luke 3:1

Antipas marries Philip's former wife, Herodias.

Ruled: 4 BCE–34 CE

Philip was the tetrarch of Iturea and Traconitis.

Notes: Philip's region included the land to the north and east of
            the Sea of Galilee. The area was less Jewish, more pagan,
            and more peaceful than the Galilee. Bethsaida and Caesarea
            Philippi were in Philip's territory.

Herod Agrippa I (Eaten by Worms)

Lived: 11 BCE–44 CE

            Agrippa I was the grandson of Herod the Great
            and the son of Aristobulus IV.

Scriptures: Acts 12

            Agrippa I put Peter in prison and was dramatically struck
            dead in Caesarea Maritima for not glorifying God.

Ruled: 41–44 CE

            Agrippa I ruled as the king of Judea over most of the former
            territories of his grandfather, Herod the Great.

Notes: Agrippa I expanded the walls of Jerusalem, incorporating the
            traditional location of the tomb of Christ.

Herod Agrippa II (Paul's Trial in Caesarea Maritima)

Lived: 27–c. 93 CE

            Agrippa II was the great grandson of Herod the Great and
            son of Agrippa I.

Scriptures: Acts 25:13—26:32

            Agrippa II interviewed Paul when he was imprisoned in
            Caesarea Maritima.

Ruled: 50–66 CE

            He ruled over various territories.

Notes: Agrippa II was the last of the Herodian dynasty. He was ex-
            pelled from Jerusalem by Jewish subjects in 66 CE and sided
            with the Romans during the First Jewish Revolt (66–73 CE).

4. The Israeli–Palestinian Conflict

Be familiar with the following terms and designations. Consult relevant maps, which can be found on the internet.

Keys Terms and Events

The War of 1948 / The War of Independence / The Nakbar

The Green Line / The 1949 Armistice Line

The 1967 Six Day War

The First and Second Intifadas

The Oslo Accords

The Israel West Bank Separation Barrier

Territorial Designations

The West Bank / Palestine / The Occupied Territories

West Jerusalem / East Jerusalem / the Old City

Biblical Judea and Samaria

1948 Israel / pre-1967 Israel / Israel Proper

Maps

The 1947 United Nations Partition Plan

The Green Line / The 1949 Armistice Line

Post-1967 Israel, including the Occupied Territories

Zones A, B, and C of the Oslo Accords

The line of the Israel West Bank Separation Barrier

Note: (1) the distinction between annexed East Jerusalem and the occupied West Bank, (2) where the Green Line passes through present-day Jerusalem, and (3) how the Separation Barrier deviates from the Green Line.

Demographic Designations

Note definitions, identities, numbers, and percentages in both Israel and Palestine for the following religious and ethnic groups: Israeli, Palestinian, Arab, Israeli-Arab (Arab-Israeli), Bedouin, Druze, Christian, Ashkenazi Jew, Sephardic Jew, and Sunni Muslim.

Appendix 3

Holy Land Itineraries

While Holy Land institutions and advertised pilgrimages have pre-set programs, groups working with travel operators can negotiate their itinerary. In planning or booking a trip, individuals and group leaders should consider the following points.

1. The Length of Stay

Bear in mind that visiting the Christian holy sites, Old Testament locations, and related archeological parks, nature reserves, and museums requires at least a few weeks. This is without considering the ecumenical and interreligious opportunities that are unique to Jerusalem. While the Holy Land is an optimum place for an extended sojourn, short-term programs (two weeks or less) have to make a number of selective choices. Time is limited, and for every site that is included, another site must be left off the program. The major Christian sites can be visited in a reasonably-paced, chronologically-based order in about ten days. A two-week itinerary is ideal, while a one-week program still covers a lot of material. If at all possible, spend at least ten nights in the Holy Land and no less than eight.

2. A Chronological Template

Site-focused programs fall into a couple of implicit categories. Some are "the best of the Holy Land" experiences, which include a collection of great sites, like Caesarea Maritima, Megiddo, Masada, Beit Shean, and Dan. Other programs are more specifically focused on the footsteps of Jesus, though they vary considerably in how closely they follow the general chronology of Jesus' life. Before we consider the specific dynamics of a chronological template, a few points are worth noting. First of all, some New Testament narratives will be inevitably out of order. There are discrepancies in the Gospels' sequencing, and certain sites, like Nazareth and Jerusalem, cover multiple phases in the life of Jesus. Secondly, itineraries based upon the footsteps of Jesus should not ignore Old Testament stories. Old Testament landscapes are constantly traversed and occasionally undergird New Testament sites. Returning pilgrims are especially encouraged to engage Old Testament material. Third, geographical considerations influence the when and what of Holy Land pilgrimage. Even so, given the restraints of Holy Land pilgrimage—too little time for too many sites—groups should not visit a site merely because it is in the area. Creating a Holy Land itinerary requires a degree of discretion, and good sites have to be left off the schedule in order to refine thematic priorities.

In short, following the general chronology of Jesus' life renders an experience that is greater than the sum of the individual sites and is relatively easy to execute, provided the itinerary integrates a three-fold sequence that begins and ends in the Jerusalem area: (a) Jesus' nativity, baptism, and wilderness experience (the Jerusalem area), (b) Jesus' Galilean ministry, and (c) the Holy Week commemorations (Jerusalem). The Jerusalem area provides a convenient base for day trips prior to the Galilee excursion, like the tomb of the Patriarchs in Hebron and Jacob's Well in Nablus (John 4). A day in the Holy City allows for an introduction to the temple and a visit to the pool of Bethesda (John 5).

Placing the Galilee component, which is often the highlight of the trip, in the middle of the program implicitly frames it as a spiritual retreat within the overall context of the journey.[1] While three to four days is an ideal length, shorter programs face at least one critical decision: whether to include Caesarea Philippi (Banias), the northern apex of the journey, which takes half a day from the Sea of Galilee. As pilgrim movement follows the biblical narrative, Caesarea Philippi provides a pivotal turning point: upon hearing Peter's confession of Christ followed by Jesus' proclamation of his impending death, pilgrims literally turn their faces towards Jerusalem where the Holy Week commemorations loom ahead.

A chronological template not only tells the story better through a powerful convergence of place, narrative, and sequence, it fosters an added dimension of sacred time. Holy Land travel becomes a liturgical journey. Holy Land arrival commences with Advent and Christmas. Jesus' baptism and

---

1. Many pilgrim groups begin their itinerary in the Galilee, arriving in Jerusalem for the first and only time after they have commemorated Jesus' Galilean ministry. They consequently celebrate Jesus' nativity in Bethlehem half-way through the journey. By putting the Galilee portion in the middle rather than at the beginning of the program, the spiritual, emotional, and narrative rhythms of the trip are more effectively arranged.

ministry place pilgrims in the season of Epiphany. In the Revised Common Lectionary, the transfiguration is celebrated on the final Sunday in Epiphany, preparing Christians for Lent by foreshadowing Christ's resurrected glory. By commemorating the transfiguration as their final station in the Galilee— on their way to Jerusalem—pilgrims embody the same liturgical movement, transitioning from Epiphany to Lent as they enter Jerusalem for Holy Week. Following visits to Bethany, the Mount of Olives, and Mount Sion, pilgrims walk the Via Dolorosa, celebrate the Easter resurrection, and return home reflecting upon the promises of Pentecost. A chronological template merges physical movement, narrative sequence, and sacred time.

3. Holy Sepulchre

According to Mark Twain, "one naturally goes first to the Holy Sepulchre." Adding towards the end of his sojourn: "we have been there every day and have not grown tired of it, but we are weary of everything else."[2] Christian tradition is unequivocal: pilgrims visit the Holy Sepulchre upon arriving in Jerusalem and return there more than once. Groups should begin their time in Jerusalem with an introductory visit of the complex that will encourage individuals to return on their own. Later, the group can revisit the site, commemorating the death and resurrection of Jesus in its proper sequence.

To make sense of the complex, people should concentrate on its architectural history, familiarizing themselves with its original Constantinian layout. Besides extant walls and foundations of the fourth-century complex, the Holy Sepulchre is full of nooks and crannies that are worth exploring: chapels, tombs, cisterns, and rooftops. Attentive should also be given to the commemorative fabric of the building, which, along with Jesus' passion and resurrection, includes the tomb of Adam, the sacrifice of Isaac, the center of the world, and the legends of the Holy Cross and Mary the Egyptian. The building is a hive of liturgies and traditional practices, and to make sense of it all, pilgrims should familiarize themselves with the Status Quo that regulates the six Christian communities who have rights to building.

4. Attention to Acts

Following the movement of the resurrection, Acts provides a powerful climax to a Holy Land experience. Acts witnesses the spread of the gospel from the empty tomb towards the center of the empire and outwards towards the ends of the earth. In leaving the Holy Land, pilgrims embody the movement

2. Twain, *Innocents Abroad*, chapters 53–54.

of Acts, taking the good news of Christ's resurrection to the corners of the world. Along with the importance of the Jerusalem-based commemorations of the ascension and Pentecost, pilgrims should consider visiting Caesarea Maritima—the setting of Peter's conversion of Cornelius, the first gentile convert, and Paul's custody prior to his appeal to Caesar—on their final day. By culminating their journey on the shore of the Mediterranean, pilgrims stand on the physical brink of the gospel's departure from the Holy Land. Looking out at sea, pilgrims reflect upon Rome and home.

5. A Sample Template

Below is a ten-to-sixteen-day template for a Jerusalem-based program with a three-night sojourn in the Galilee. The template is merely conceptual and does not include a full list of sites. Ideas for additional days are indicated (+). Local context—Jewish, Muslim, and Palestinian Christian voices— must still be added, and itineraries must be reconciled with a real calendar, giving attention to the holy days of Friday, Saturday, and Sunday and to religious and national holidays.

Arrive in Jerusalem.

Opening worship on the theme of arrival.

Day 1. A Topographical Orientation of Jerusalem including the Holy Sepulchre

+ A day-trip to Hebron picking up themes of Abraham and
  the Old Testament covenants prior to the birth of Christ.

Day 2. Nativity Narratives: Ein Kerem and Bethlehem

Commemorations include Mary's visit to Elizabeth, the Magnificat, the birth of John the Baptist, Zechariah's song of praise, the Shepherds' field, and the birth of Jesus. The missing narrative is the annunciation story in Nazareth, which occurs later in the program. I have taken pilgrims to Nazareth and Sepphoris as a separate day-trip prior to Day 2, which has the advantage of setting up the visitation and nativity stories and allowing the Galilee excursion to proceed directly to the Sea of Galilee.

Day 3. Baptism and Wilderness: The Jordan River, Jericho, and the Judean Wilderness

Limiting the day to the Jordan River, Jericho, and the Judean Wilderness makes for a relaxing, well-paced day. Masada, Qumran, and the Dead Sea works better as a separate day.

+ A day-trip to Jacob's Well and the Nablus area (John 4).

+ A day in Jerusalem focusing on the temple and the pool of Bethesda (John 5).

Day 4. Nazareth (possibly Sepphoris) and the Sea of Galilee (overnight in the Galilee)

Some groups will want to visit Caesarea Maritima on their way to Nazareth. Caesarea Maritima fits at the beginning of a program as an introduction to Herod the Great, and a Caesarea Maritima–Sepphoris–Nazareth segment offers a nice introduction to New Testament context. The optimum place for Caesarea Maritima is at the end of the program with attention given to the post-resurrection narratives of Acts.

Day 5. Sea of Galilee Sites with Galilee Worship (overnight in the Galilee)

Day 6. Sea of Galilee Sites with Caesarea Philippi (overnight in the Galilee)

Shorter trips may have to skip Caesarea Philippi.

Day 7. The Transfiguration and Return to Jerusalem

The journey shifts from Epiphany to Lent.

Day 8. The Temple Mount and Bethany

+ A day-trip to Masada, Dead Sea, and Qumran (a break from the narrative sequence).

+ A free-day in Jerusalem. Pilgrims should have an opportunity to visit the Israel Museum and the Holocaust Museum, either as part of the program or as built-in free time.

Day 9. Mount of Olives and Mount Sion

Mount of Olives: Jesus' entry into Jerusalem, Gethsemane, and the ascension. The Chapel of the Ascension is out of sequence but worth the visit.

Mount Sion: the Lord's Supper, Pentecost, and the trial of Jesus

Day 10. The Via Dolorosa and the Holy Sepulchre

Resurrection celebration, Emmaus themes, and final worship

+ An added day-trip to Caesarea Maritima with a focus on Acts, Rome, and home.

Bibliography

Ancient Sources

Adomnán. *On the Holy Places.* In *Adamnan's De Locis Sanctis*, translated by Denis Meehan. Dublin: Dublin Institute for Advanced Studies, 1958. Also in *Jerusalem Pilgrims before the Crusades*, translated by John Wilkinson, 167–206. Warminster, UK: Aris & Phillips, 2002.

Bordeaux Pilgrim. *Travels.* In *Egeria's Travels*, translated by John Wilkinson, 26–34. Warminster, UK: Aris & Phillips, 1999.

Cyril of Jerusalem. *Catechesis.* In *The Works of Saint Cyril of Jerusalem*, translated by Leo P. McCauley and Anthony A. Stephenson, 2 vols. Washington, DC: The Catholic University of America Press, 1969–70.

Egeria. *Egeria's Travels.* Translated by John Wilkinson. Warminster, UK: Aris & Phillips, 1999. Also see Anne McGowan and Paul F. Bradshaw, *The Pilgrimage of Egeria: A New Translation of the Itinerarium Egeriae with Introduction and Commentary.* Collegeville, MN: Liturgical, 2018.

Epiphanius the Monk. *Hagiopolita.* In *Jerusalem Pilgrims before the Crusades*, translated by John Wilkinson, 207–15. Warminster, UK: Aris & Phillips, 2002.

Epiphanius of Salamis. *Panarion.* In *The Panarion of Epiphanius of Salamis, Book I (Sects 1–46)*, translated by Frank Williams. Leiden: Brill, 1987.

Eusebius. *Church History.* In *Eusebius: The Church History*, translated by Paul L. Maier. Grand Rapids: Kregel, 1999.

———. *In Praise of Constantine.* In *In Praise of Constantine: A Historical Study and New Translation of Eusebius' Tricennial Orations*, translated by H. A. Drake. Berkeley: University of California Press, 1976.

———. *Life of Constantine.* Translated by Averil Cameron and Stuart G. Hall. Oxford: Clarendon, 1999. Also in *Egeria's Travels*, translated by John Wilkinson, 16–22. Warminster, UK: Aris & Phillips, 1999.

———. *Onomasticon.* In *Palestine in the Fourth Century A.D.: The Onomasticon by Eusebius of Caesarea*, translated by G. S. P. Freeman-Grenville. Jerusalem: Carta, 2003.

Gregory of Nyssa. *On Pilgrimages.* Translated by William Moore and Henry Austin Wilson. *NPNF*, 2:5. Grand Rapids: Eerdmans, 1972.

Hugeburc. *The Life of Willibald*. In *Jerusalem Pilgrims before the Crusades*, translated by John Wilkinson, 233–51. Warminster, UK: Aris & Phillips, 2002. Also in *The Hodœporicon of Saint Willibald*, translated by W. R. Brownlow, 1–36. *PPTS* 3. London: Palestine Pilgrims' Text Society, 1895.

Jerome. *The Book of Places*. In *Palestine in the Fourth Century A.D.: The Onomasticon by Eusebius of Caesarea*, translated by G. S. P. Freeman-Grenville. Jerusalem: Carta, 2003.

———. *Letters*. In *St Jerome: Letters and Selected Works*, translated by W. H. Freemantle. *NPNF* 2:6. Grand Rapids: Eerdmans, 1995.

John of Würzburg. *Description of the Holy Land*. In *Jerusalem Pilgrimage, 1099–1185*, translated by John Wilkinson, 244–73. London: Hakluyt Society, 1988.

Justin Martyr. *Dialogue with Trypho*. In *Writings of Saint Justin Martyr*, translated by Thomas B. Falls, 139–366. The Fathers of Church 6. Washington, DC: Catholic University of America Press, 1948.

Melito of Sardis. *Paschal Homily*. In *On Pascha and Fragments*, translated by Stuart George Hall. Oxford: Clarendon, 1979.

Nikulás of þverá. *Extract from Nikulás of þverá*. In *Jerusalem Pilgrimage, 1099–1185*, translated by John Wilkinson, 215–18. London: Hakluyt Society, 1988.

Origen. *Against Celsus*. In *Origen: Contra Celsum*, translated by Henry Chadwick. Cambridge: Cambridge University Press, 1980.

———. *Commentary on St John*. In *Origen: Commentary on the Gospel according to John, Books 1–10*, translated by Ronald E. Heine. Washington, DC: Catholic University of America Press, 1989.

Paulinus of Nola. *Letters*. In *Letters of St Paulinus of Nola*, vol. 2, translated by P. G. Walsh. Westminster, MD: Newman, 1967.

Piacenza Pilgrim. *Travels*. In *Jerusalem Pilgrims before the Crusades*, translated by John Wilkinson, 129–51. Warminster, UK: Aris & Phillips, 2002. Also in *Of the Holy Places Visited by Antonius Martyr*, translated by Aubrey Stewart, 1–37. *PPTS* 2. London: Palestine Pilgrims' Text Society, 1896.

The Protoevangelium of James. In *The Apocryphal New Testament*, translated by J. K. Elliot, 48–67. Oxford: The Oxford University Press, 1993.

Saewulf. *The Pilgrimage of Saewulf*. In *Jerusalem Pilgrimage, 1099–1185*, translated by John Wilkinson, 94–116. London: Hakluyt Society, 1988. Also in *The Pilgrimage of Saewulf*, translated by A. Rogers, 31–52. *PPTS* 4. London: Palestine Pilgrims' Text Society, 1896.

Modern Sources

Abbott, H. Porter. *The Cambridge Introduction to Narrative*. 2nd ed. Cambridge: Cambridge University Press, 2008.

Aist, Rodney. *The Christian Topography of Early Islamic Jerusalem: The Evidence of Willibald of Eichstätt (700–787 CE)*. Turnhout: Brepols, 2009.

———. *From Topography to Text: The Image of Jerusalem in the Writings of Eucherius, Adomnán and Bede*. Turnhout: Brepols, 2018.

———. *Journey of Faith*. Fayetteville, AR: Self-Published, 1997.

―――. "The Monument of the Miraculous Healing in Post-Byzantine Jerusalem: A Reassessment of the North Gate Column of the Madaba Map." *Bulletin of the Anglo-Israel Archaeological Society* 26 (2008) 37–56.

―――. "Pilgrim Traditions in Celtic Christian Practice." *Perichoresis* 15.1 (2017) 3–19.

―――. *Voices in the Wind: Stories, Thoughts and Reflections along a Contemporary Christian Pilgrimage*. South Bend, IN: Cross Cultural, 2002.

Appleton, George, ed. *The Oxford Book of Prayer*. 2nd ed. Oxford: Oxford University Press, 2009.

Armstrong, Karen. *Jerusalem: One City, Three Faiths*. New York: Ballantine, 1997.

Baert, Barbara. *A Heritage of Holy Wood: The Legend of the True Cross in Text and Image*. Leiden: Brill, 2004.

Bahat, Dan, and Chaim T. Rubenstein. *The Carta Jerusalem Atlas*. 3rd ed. Jerusalem: Carta, 2011.

Baldovin, John F. *Liturgy in Ancient Jerusalem*. Nottingham, UK: Grove, 1989.

Beck, John A. *The Holy Land for Christian Travelers: An Illustrated Guide to Israel*. Grand Rapids: Baker, 2017.

Biddle, Martin. *The Tomb of Christ*. Gloucester, UK: Sutton, 1999.

Borgehammar, Stephan. *How the Holy Cross Was Found*. Stockholm: Almqvist & Wiksell, 1991.

Brookmyre, Christopher. *One Fine Day in the Middle of the Night*. London: Little, Brown and Company, 1999.

Brown, David. *God and Enchantment of Place*. Oxford: Oxford University Press, 2004.

Brownlow, W. R. *The Hodœporicon of Saint Willibald*. In *PPTS* 3, 1–36. London: Palestine Pilgrims' Text Society, 1895.

Buntin, Martin. *The Palestinian–Israeli Conflict: A Very Short Introduction*. Oxford: Oxford University Press, 2013.

Cameron, Averil, and Stuart G. Hall, trans. *Life of Constantine*. Oxford: Clarendon, 1999.

Campbell, Joseph. *Thou Art That: Transforming Religious Metaphor*. Novato, CA: New World Library, 2001.

Chacour, Elias. *Blood Brothers: The Dramatic Story of a Palestinian Christian Working for Peace in Israel*. Expanded ed. Grand Rapids: Chosen, 2003.

Chadwick, Henry. *Origen: Contra Celsum*. Rev. ed. Cambridge: Cambridge University Press, 1980.

Chitty, Derwas J. *The Desert a City: An Introduction to the Study of Egyptian and Palestinian Monasticism under the Christian Empire*. Oxford: Blackwell, 1966.

Cline, Eric H. *Biblical Archaeology: A Very Short Introduction*. Oxford: Oxford University Press, 2009.

Cohen, Raymond. *Saving the Holy Sepulchre: How Rival Christians Came Together to Rescue Their Holiest Shrine*. Oxford: Oxford University Press, 2008.

Cohn-Sherbok, Dan, and Dawoud El-Alami. *The Palestine–Israeli Conflict: A Beginner's Guide*. 4th ed. London: Oneworld, 2015.

Cousineau, Phil. *The Art of Pilgrimage: The Seeker's Guide to Making Travel Sacred*. New ed. San Francisco: Red Wheel Weiser Conari, 2012.

Cust, L. G. A. *The Status Quo in the Holy Places*. Jerusalem: Printed for the Government of Palestine by His Majesty's Stationary Office, 1929.

Davies, J. G. *Pilgrimage Yesterday and Today*. London: SCM, 1988.

Drake, H. A. *In Praise of Constantine: A Historical Study and New Translation of Eusebius' Tricennial Orations*. Berkeley: University of California Press, 1976.

Drijvers, Jan Willem. *Helena Augusta: The Mother of Constantine and the Legend of Her Finding the True Cross*. Leiden: Brill, 1992.

Elliot, J. K. *The Apocryphal New Testament*. Oxford: Oxford University Press, 1993.

Falls, Thomas B. *Writings of Saint Justin Martyr*. Washington, DC: Catholic University of America Press, 1948.

Fosdick, Harry Emerson. *A Pilgrimage to Palestine*. New York: Macmillan, 1927.

Freeman-Grenville, G. S. P. *Palestine in the Fourth Century A.D.: The Onomasticon by Eusebius of Caesarea*. Indexed by Rupert L. Chapman III and edited and introduced by Joan E. Taylor. Jerusalem: Carta, 2003.

Galor, Katharina, and Hanswulf Bloedhorn. *The Archaeology of Jerusalem: From the Origins to the Ottomans*. New Haven, CT: Yale University Press, 2013.

Geary, James. *I Is an Other: The Secret Life of Metaphor and How It Shapes the Way We See the World*. New York: HarperCollins, 2011.

———. *The World in a Phrase: A Brief History of the Aphorism*. New York: Bloomsbury, 2011.

Gibson, Shimon, and Joan E. Taylor. *Beneath the Church of the Holy Sepulchre, Jerusalem: The Archaeology and Early History of Traditional Golgotha*. London: Palestine Exploration Fund, 1994.

Grabar, Oleg. *The Dome of the Rock*. Cambridge, MA: Belknap, 2006.

———. *The Shape of the Holy: Early Islamic Jerusalem*. Princeton: Princeton University Press, 1996.

Gustafson, W. Mark. "Inscripta in Fronte: Penal Tattooing in Late Antiquity." *Classical Antiquity* 16.1 (1997) 79–105.

Hall, Stuart George. *On Pascha and Fragments*. Oxford: Clarendon, 1979.

Hartley, L. P. *The Go-Between*. London: Hamish Hamilton, 1953.

Hawari, Mahmoud, et al. *Pilgrimage, Sciences and Sufism: Islamic Art in the West Bank and Gaza: 1*. 2nd ed. Vienna: Museum with No Frontiers, 2010.

Heine, Ronald E. *Origen: Commentary on the Gospel according to John, Books 1–10*. Washington, DC: Catholic University of America Press, 1989.

Heschel, Susannah. *The Aryan Jesus: Christian Theologians and the Bible in Nazi Germany*. Princeton: Princeton University Press, 2008.

Hughes, Gerard W. *God of Surprises*. 3rd rev. ed. London: Darton, Longman & Todd, 2008.

———. *In Search of a Way: Two Journeys of Spiritual Discovery*. London: Darton, Longman & Todd, 1986.

———. *Walk to Jerusalem: In Search of Peace*. London: Darton, Longman & Todd, 1991.

Hummel, Thomas. "The Sacramentality of the Holy Land, Two Contrasting Approaches." In *The Sense of the Sacramental: Movement and Measure in Art and Music, Place and Time*, edited by David Brown and Ann Loades, 78–100. London: SPCK, 1995.

Hunt, E. D. *Holy Land Pilgrimage in the Later Roman Empire, AD 312–460*. Oxford: Oxford University Press, 1984.

Inge, John. *A Christian Theology of Place*. Aldershot, UK: Ashgate, 2003.

Joyce, Rachel. *The Unlikely Pilgrimage of Harold Fry*. New York: Random House, 2012.

Kristensen, Troels Myrup, and Wiebke Friese, eds. *Excavating Pilgrimage: Archaeological Approaches to Sacred Travel and Movement in the Ancient World*. London: Routledge, 2017.

LeSueur, Richard. "Pilgrimage: A Distinctive Practice." In *Pilgrimage in Practice: Narration, Reclamation and Healing*, edited by Ian S. McIntosh et al., 16–25. Wallingford, UK: CABI, 2018.

Levenson, Jon D. *Inheriting Abraham: The Legacy of the Patriarch in Judaism, Christianity, and Islam*. Princeton: Princeton University Press, 2012.

Liebeschuetz, J. H. W. G. *Ambrose of Milan: Political Letters and Speeches*. Liverpool: Liverpool University Press, 2005.

Luker, Lamontte M. *An Illustrated Guide to the Holy Land for Tour Groups, Students, and Pilgrims*. Nashville: Abingdon, 2013.

Lynch, Kevin. *The Image of the City*. Cambridge: MIT Press, 1960.

Magness, Jodi. *The Archaeology of the Holy Land: From the Destruction of Solomon's Temple to the Muslim Conquest*. Cambridge: Cambridge University Press, 2012.

McFague, Sallie. *Metaphorical Theology: Models of God in Religious Language*. Philadelphia: Fortress, 1982.

———. *Speaking in Parables: A Study in Metaphor and Theology*. Philadelphia: Fortress, 1975.

McGowan, Anne, and Paul F. Bradshaw. *The Pilgrimage of Egeria: A New Translation of the Itinerarium Egeriae with Introduction and Commentary*. Collegeville, MN: Liturgical, 2018.

Meehan, Denis, ed. *Adamnan's De Locis Sanctis*. Dublin: Dublin Institute for Advanced Studies, 1958.

Montefiore, Simon Sebag. *Jerusalem: The Biography*. New York: Knopf, 2011.

Murphy-O'Connor, Jerome. *The Holy Land: An Oxford Archaeological Guide*. 5th ed. Oxford: Oxford University Press, 2008.

———. *Keys of Jerusalem: Collected Essays*. Oxford: Oxford University Press, 2012.

Niebuhr, Richard R. "Pilgrims and Pioneers: Theme of Spiritual Pilgrimage." *Parabola* 9.3 (1984) 6–13.

O'Loughlin, Thomas. *Adomnán and the Holy Places: Perceptions of an Insular Monk on the Location of the Biblical Drama*. London: T. & T. Clark, 2007.

Ousterhout, Robert. *The Blessings of Pilgrimage*. Urbana, IL: University of Illinois Press, 1990.

———. "Rebuilding the Temple: Constantine Monomachus and the Holy Sepulchre." *Journal of the Society of Architectural Historians* 48.1 (1989) 66–78.

Peters, F. E. *Jerusalem: The Holy City in the Eyes of Chroniclers, Visitors, Pilgrims, and Prophets from the Days of Abraham to the Beginnings of Modern Times*. Princeton: Princeton University Press, 1985.

Piccirillo, Michele, and Eugenio Alliata, eds. *The Madaba Map Centenary, 1897–1997*. Jerusalem: Studium Biblicum Franciscanum, 1999.

Pixner, Bargil. *With Jesus in Jerusalem: His First and Last Days in Judea*. Corazin, Israel: Corazin, 1992.

———. *With Jesus through Galilee: According to the Fifth Gospel*. Corazin, Israel: Corazin, 1992.

Price, R. N. *Cyril of Scythopolis: The Lives of the Monks of Palestine*. Kalamazoo, MI: Cistercian, 1991.

Reader, Ian. *Pilgrimage: A Very Short Introduction.* Oxford: Oxford University Press, 2015.

Renan, Ernest. *The Life of Jesus.* London: Trübner, 1864.

Ritmeyer, Leen, and Kathleen Ritmeyer. *Jerusalem: The Temple Mount.* Jerusalem: Carta, 2015.

Rogers, Stephanie Stidham. *Inventing the Holy Land: American Protestant Pilgrimage to Palestine, 1865–1941.* Lanham, MD: Lexington, 2011.

Shoemaker, Stephen J. *Ancient Traditions of the Virgin Mary's Dormition and Assumption.* Oxford: Oxford University Press, 2002.

Smith, Jonathan Z. *To Take Place: Towards Theory in Ritual.* Chicago: University of Chicago Press, 1987.

Soskice, Janet Martin. *Metaphor and Religious Language.* Oxford: Clarendon, 1985.

Stopford, J., ed. *Pilgrimage Explored.* Woodbridge, UK: York Medieval Press, 1999.

Sumption, Jonathan. *Pilgrimage: An Image of Mediaeval Religion.* London: Faber & Faber, 1975.

Sussman, Steve. *Substance and Behavioral Addictions: Concepts, Causes, and Cures.* Cambridge: Cambridge University Press, 2017.

Taylor, Joan E. *Christians and the Holy Places: The Myth of Jewish-Christian Origins.* Oxford: Clarendon, 1993.

Thoreau, Henry David. *"Walking."* In *The Atlantic Monthly* 9 (June 1862) 657–74.

Todd, Richard. *The Thing Itself: On the Search for Authenticity.* New York: Riverhead, 2008.

Trout, Dennis E. *Paulinus of Nola: Life, Letters, and Poetry.* Berkeley: University of California Press, 1999.

Turner, Victor, and Edith Turner. *Image and Pilgrimage in Christian Culture.* New York: Columbia University Press, 1978.

Twain, Mark. *Innocents Abroad.* Hartford, CT: American, 1869.

Walker, Peter. *In the Steps of Jesus: An Illustrated Guide to the Places of the Holy Land.* Oxford: Lion Hudson, 2007.

———. *The Weekend That Changed the World: The Mystery of Jerusalem's Empty Tomb.* Louisville, KY: Westminster John Knox, 2000.

Warton, Annabel Jane. *Selling Jerusalem: Relics, Replicas, Theme Parks.* Chicago: University of Chicago Press, 2006.

Webb, Diana. *Medieval European Pilgrimage.* Basingstoke, UK: Palgrave, 2002.

———. *Pilgrims and Pilgrimage in the Medieval West.* London: I. B. Tauris, 1999.

Wilken, Robert L. *The Land Called Holy.* New Haven, CT: Yale University Press, 1992.

Wilkinson, John. *Egeria's Travels.* 3rd ed. Warminster, UK: Aris & Phillips, 1999.

———. *Jerusalem Pilgrimage, 1099–1185.* With Joyce Hill and W. F. Ryan. London: Hakluyt Society, 1988.

———. *Jerusalem Pilgrims before the Crusades.* 2nd ed. Warminster, UK: Aris & Phillips, 2002.

Wittgenstein, Ludwig. *Philosophical Investigations.* Translated by G. E. M. Anscombe. Oxford: Blackwell, 1963.

Wynn, Mark R. *Faith and Place: An Essay in Embodied Religious Epistemology.* Oxford: Oxford University Press, 2009.